THE VIRGIN MARY IN LATE MEDIEVAL AND EARLY MODERN ENGLISH LITERATURE AND POPULAR CULTURE

The Virgin Mary was one of the most powerful images of the Middle Ages, central to people's experience of Christianity. During the Reformation, however, many images of the Virgin were destroyed, as Protestantism rejected the way the medieval Church over-valued and sexualized Mary. Although increasingly marginalized in Protestant thought and practice, her traces and surprising transformations continued to haunt early modern England. Combining historical analysis and contemporary theory, including issues raised by psychoanalysis and feminist theology, Gary Waller examines the literature, theology, and popular culture associated with Mary in the transition between late medieval and early modern England. He contrasts a variety of pre-Reformation texts and events, including popular Mariology, poetry, tales, drama, pilgrimage, and the emerging "New Learning," with later sixteenth-century ruins, songs, ballads, Petrarchan poetry, the works of Shakespeare, and other texts where the Virgin's presence or influence, sometimes surprisingly, can be found.

GARY WALLER is Professor of Literature and Cultural Studies and Theatre at Purchase College, State University of New York. His books include *The Strong Necessity of Time*; *Mary Sidney, Countess of Pembroke*; *The Sidney Family Romance: Mary Wroth, William Herbert and the Early Modern Construction of Gender*; *Edmund Spenser: a Literary Life*; *Reading Texts* (with Kathleen McCormick); and *English Poetry of the Sixteenth Century*.

THE VIRGIN MARY IN LATE MEDIEVAL AND EARLY MODERN ENGLISH LITERATURE AND POPULAR CULTURE

GARY WALLER

Purchase College, State University of New York

CAMBRIDGE
UNIVERSITY PRESS

CAMBRIDGE UNIVERSITY PRESS
Cambridge, New York, Melbourne, Madrid, Cape Town,
Singapore, São Paulo, Delhi, Mexico City

Cambridge University Press
The Edinburgh Building, Cambridge CB2 8RU, UK

Published in the United States of America by
Cambridge University Press, New York

www.cambridge.org
Information on this title: www.cambridge.org/9781107407664

© Gary Waller 2011

First published 2011
First paperback edition 2012

A catalogue record for this publication is available from the British Library

ISBN 978-0-521-76296-0 Hardback
ISBN 978-1-107-40766-4 Paperback

Contents

Preface

Julia Kristeva calls the Virgin a "combination of power and sorrow, sovereignty and the unnameable," making up "one of the most powerful imaginary constructs known in the history of civilization." This book explores aspects of the poetry, drama, tales, ballads, and something of the theological and polemical religious writings that expressed and explored, in complex and contradictory ways, that "powerful construct" immediately before and during the Reformation period in England. Rather ambiguously we have come to term this period "early modern," but it might as easily be called "late medieval," since what I term the Virgin's "fades" and "traces," felt long after the so-called Middle Ages were supposedly over, nonetheless had their origins in the medieval period and their transformations often loop back to earlier, only gradually emergent, social practices there. I tie these aspects of the period's ideological history together with what I hope is a lightly worn but distinctive presentism that arises from an ongoing dialogue with certain aspects of contemporary thought, especially psychoanalytic cultural criticism, the sociology of popular religion, and recent Catholic feminist theology, some of which is influenced by Kristeva herself.

The year 1538 when, as part of the dissolution of religious houses in the late 1530s, a number of "images" of the Virgin were taken to London in the late summer or autumn and burned, is the fulcrum of my study. I move back and forward in time from that date, which was just one incident in a whole process by which the religious and broader cultural life of England was re-directed, but which is of great symbolic significance when we consider the Virgin Mary in England. In what sense, I ask, does that event, and similar ones across the country, mark the end of an era – not just in the material terms but also in the history of ideologies, in men's and women's emotional allegiances and their deeply rooted, even unconscious, patterns of behavior? Why (as my opening chapter shows) was the Virgin a target of unusual violence in England for the next century? Why did the reformers become so insistent on removing the presence of the Virgin from people's minds? To what extent were they successful? And what happened to the memory of Marian centers such as Ipswich, Penrhys, Walsingham, and Woolpit, and (in a sense) to the Virgin herself, after the Dissolution?

These are some of the questions around which my study is written. Both before and significantly long after the events of 1538, and throughout the following century of iconoclasm, the Virgin Mary inspired a rich tradition of poems, fiction, songs, ballads, musical compositions and folk legends, solemn devotional writings and hostile satire. Although significantly downgraded, marginalized, re-negotiated, or all-but-eradicated (all terms used by modern historians) in the dominant Protestant theology, liturgy, devotion, and the very gradually (and often reluctantly) changing recesses of popular culture, the continuities and transformations of the Virgin, I argue, continue to haunt early modern England.

This book starts with 1538, and contextualizes the Protestant regime's devaluation of the Virgin by examining key moments in the history of English iconoclasm over the next century. Thereafter it is divided into two parts. Chapters 2 to 4 look back at the Virgin's presence in late medieval culture. In Chapter 2, I focus on one of the crucial factors in the reformers' hostility to Mary, the alleged late medieval sexualization of the Virgin in theology, devotion, and popular culture. In Chapter 3, I examine her place in late medieval poetry, romances, and drama. Chapter 4 looks at Marian shrines and especially women's pilgrimages in the light of the emergence of late medieval Christocentrism and Erasmus's influential critique of pilgrimage, which contributed, however unintentionally, to the Dissolution of the late 1530s, a part of which was the conflagration of 1538.

Chapters 5 to 8 look at what I term the "fades" and "traces" of the Virgin in Protestant England, in ballads, poems, music, drama, as well as theological controversy, after 1538, as the Protestant regime tried to get the Virgin, as one early iconoclast put it, "out of their heads." My analysis shows, I believe, only the partial success of such an enterprise, as early modern England, even in its long and contradictory Protestantization, articulated a surprising nostalgia for the Virgin and what she was, or could be imagined to represent, in human life, even if she underwent multiple and contradictory transformations. Finally, I return to the theoretical "polylogue" I set up in my opening chapter and speculate why and how, four hundred years later, we might need to recognize, as Kristeva, the self-styled "Christian Atheist" does, the continuing power of the Virgin.

A Catholic friend remarked that for someone who has a great deal of skepticism about the Virgin Mary, I nonetheless seem to have been given a lot of work to do for (or, as my friend said, "by") her. I am not a professional (nor even an amateur) theologian, although some of my earliest publications were in theological journals and, as Terry Eagleton remarks in his 2008 Terry Lectures at Yale, the late 1960s in Cambridge was an era providing exciting theological explorations for impressionistic young minds. My fascination with the Virgin therefore goes back many years, even to when as an adolescent I read, equally avidly, a deliciously contradictory mélange of books on Marxism, Rationalism, and Kabbalistic mysticism in the presence of a very small and very cheap plaster reproduction of Michelangelo's *Pietà*. I have been grateful to have learned thereafter from those with different traditions of religious thought and experience, and none, including Peter Dane, Peter Erb, Bishop Richard Garrard (and Ann), Ken Larsen, Werner Pelz, Fr. Kenneth Prebble, and Bill Sessions (who introduced me to Medjogorie and may be pleased that that particular "madonnine" experience helped bring me back to the larger topic). In the latter stages of writing, Tina Beattie's Catholic feminist writings, both scholarly and popular, have been a continuing stimulus to my thinking, as my many references to her work will show. Regrettably, Jennifer Glancy's study of the "emotional sway" of Mary's sexuality, *Corporal Knowledge*, appeared too late to be discussed except in a few footnotes.

Over the years, many teachers, colleagues, and students have contributed much to this study, though I cannot blame them for its shortfalls or excesses. Many years ago, Professor J. C. Reid directed my first extended piece of academic writing; he would have been pleased by my return to the subject of Catholic devotion. At Magdalene College, Cambridge, I learned much from John Stevens and Jack Bennett, as I did from my students, most notably Andrew Brown and Michael Wheeler. I am very appreciative of the Pepys Librarian at Magdalene, Dr. Stephen Lucket, first, for (after nearly forty years) remembering me from earlier days, and, second, for permission to consult the library's unique copy of the Pynson Ballad. Elsewhere in Cambridge, I benefited especially from the kindness of Derek Brewer and L. C. Knights, and I was privileged to sit, if not at the feet of Raymond Williams, at least within earshot. More recently, Andrea Clough, Craig Dionne, and Susan Morrison have encouraged my work, by kindly reading early versions, especially of Chapter 2, while Michele Osherow has reminded me that Miriam of Nazareth was a Jewish mother before she was Christianized, allegorized, and given titles, shrines, and devotees. I am especially appreciative of Alison Chapman's help, both through her own research on the Walsingham ballads and Milton's hagiography, and for her perceptive comments on some very early draft chapters. My colleague Lenora Champagne's play *Traces/Fades* helped me formulate some of my thinking about the way I should describe the presence of the Virgin after the Reformation.

Drawing as it does on history, art history, literary criticism and theory, gender study, theology, and psychoanalysis, my approach is necessarily interdisciplinary and locates itself within cultural studies rather than in the traditions of empirical history or literary history. Despite (or rather, because of) that presentist bias, my work relies greatly on the extraordinary detailed historical research that has been carried out in the past generation on the late Middle Ages and Reformation periods in England, to which I am deeply indebted, both for educating me and for providing models of scholarship of which I am repeatedly conscious of falling short, thus exemplifying my old Cambridge and antipodean friend Richard Bosworth's insistence on the difference between a "real" historian and a cultural studies person (he also plays cricket better than I do). I think of those historical scholars to whom all of us working in early modern studies are indebted, such as Margaret Aston, G. W. Bernard, Patrick Collinson, Alexandra Cuffel, Eamon Duffy, Carlos Eire, Diarmaid MacCulloch, Arthur Marotti, Peter Marshall, Christine Peters, Miri Rubin, Ethan Shagan, Alison Shell, and Alexandra Walsham. My reliance on their and many others' historical researches will be obvious (and, I trust, is appropriately acknowledged) throughout. I have also drawn frequently, initially with amused skepticism and then with awe, on Edmund Waterton's enthusiastic 1879 collage of Mariological trivia, history, legend, and prejudice, the remarkable *Pietas Mariana Britannica*. I am grateful to many vicars, vergers, priests-in-charge, sacristans, friends, colleagues, and guides all across England, from east to west, from Walsingham and Castle Acre to Penrhys and Furness, who have over the years provided hospitality, fielded questions, commented on local legends, and tolerated my hunting around for the remnants of wells and holy trees, not to mention apparition sites, statues, wall paintings, places where the Virgin sat, leaned, or rested, many of which were stimulated by examples from Waterton's obsessive collection. Scilla Landale has been especially helpful for her expertise on (and providing easy access to) Walsingham, Binham, and Houghton-in-the-Dale. My wife and our son Philip have been extremely indulgent to me on such excursions. My older sons, Michael and Andrew, have tolerated accounts of their father's obsessions from a safe distance, and so this book is in part for their daughters (and my granddaughters), Dahlia and Kalina.

As the study developed, I joined a group of scholars who in 2008 met at the Shrine of Our Lady of Walsingham to share their research in that fascinating environment. My colleagues in that venture included Bradley Brookshire, Michael Carroll, Simon Coleman, Susan Dunn-Hensley, Carole Hill, Dominic Janes, Susan Morrison, Tom Rist, and John Twyning. Work in progress toward this book appeared in the volume of essays emerging from that meeting, *Walsingham from the Middle Ages to Modernism*, edited by Dominic Janes and myself, published by Ashgate. Early versions of some paragraphs appeared in the *Sydney Journal*, thanks to its encouraging editor Mary Ellen Lamb, and others in *Medieval to Renaissance*, edited by Konrad Eisenbichler, published by the Centre for Renaissance and Reformation Studies at the University of Toronto.

Research for this book was undertaken with the help of a number of grants from the faculty development fund of United University Professions, the Purchase College Foundation, and Greenwood/Labadorf Faculty Support Awards from the School of Humanities at Purchase, whose office staff, Rosalie Reutershan and Stephanie Acton, were always helpful. I also thank the staffs of the Cambridge University Library, the Pepys Library, the Folger Shakespeare Library, the Shakespeare Centre, Stratford-upon-Avon, the Robarts Library at the University of Toronto, and the Purchase College librarian Patrick Callahan and his wonderfully efficient and persistent interlibrary loan and visual resource librarians. I gratefully acknowledge the friendship and help of Purchase College's Associate Provost Bill Baskin, always willing to keep me updated on niceties of the calendar of the Virgin's feasts and festivals (as well as current apparitions) and former Provost Jennifer Clarke. A number of my students at Purchase aided in the preparation of the book, not least by listening (and contributing) in classes, notably Isabella Kyle and Sasha Piltser. I am extremely grateful for the generous and stimulating comments and suggestions by the two anonymous readers consulted by Cambridge University Press. At the Press, Andrew Brown, Linda Bree, Maartje Scheltens, Christina Sarigiannidou and the Press team of copy-editors, technicians, and designers have been remarkably patient, supportive, and generous.

My greatest debt is to my wife and colleague, Kathleen McCormick, to whom this book is dedicated, and of whom I confess I am close to being, despite the warning of the Laudian biographer of the Virgin, Anthony Stafford, both an admirer and an idolator. My devotions are directed to her not just for her courageous and creative explorations in her writings of many of the issues I try to raise, but for helping me understand more intimately through her life what Kristeva calls the "power and sorrow" of the Virgin Mary. One of Kathy's wonderfully outrageous,

CHAPTER I

1538 and after: the Virgin Mary in the century of iconoclasm

> Here is confounded and overthrown the foolish opinion of the papists, which would have us to worship a creature before the Creator; Mary before her Son. These wise men do not so; they worship not Mary; and wherefore? Because God only is to be worshipped: but Mary is not God.[1]

In 1538, in the late summer or autumn, in Chelsea or Smithfield or Tyburn, we can surmise – from both casual remarks recorded at the time and various histories and memoirs some years later – that one or more fires was lit and in it (or them) were burned statues, "images," of the Virgin Mary, most probably those that had been brought from shrines dedicated to her at Doncaster, Ipswich, Penrhys, and Walsingham.[2] Local records suggest that similar images from Caversham, along with roods from Bermondsey, Boxley, Islington, and others were added to this, or similar, fires elsewhere. In 1537, the reformist bishop Hugh Latimer had announced that in his own diocese there reigned "idolatry, and many kinds of superstition," and during what Helen Parish terms 1538's "long summer of iconoclasm," he also named the statue of the Virgin at Worcester a "devil's instrument." He gloated that the statue, along with "her old sister of Walsingham, her young sister of Ipswich," and statues from Doncaster and Penrhys, "would make a jolly muster" and, he added for good measure, unlike flesh-and-blood heretics, would not "be all day in burning." There are conflicting accounts on the date or dates on which such a "jolly muster" took place, and exactly when and what "idols" were destroyed, whether publicly or privately, but, Latimer pronounced, they were destroyed because they had "been the instrument to bring many (I fear) to eternal fire."[3]

---

[1] Latimer, *Sermons* II, 153.   [2] Parish, *Monks, Miracles and Magic*, 81.
[3] Frere, *Visitation Articles*, II, 12; Latimer, *Sermons*, II, 395. G. W. Bernard notes that the Ipswich and Walsingham images were reputedly "mustered" in July, Caversham's in September: *Henry VIII and the Remaking of the English Church*, 455. For Our Lady of Penrhys being "mustered" in September, see Chidgey, *Our Lady of Penrhys*, 10–11.

A series of invented traditions, differing according to whose records or reminiscences are followed and one's attitude toward the Reformation, have grown up over the centuries, to celebrate, denounce, or simply describe these acts. In 2008, nearly five hundred years later, an act of reconciliation or reparation for the burnings was planned, and the spot chosen was as ambiguous as the early records, "close to" the site of Chelsea Manor, once the home of Sir Thomas More, which, it was pointed out, had been given that same year of 1538 to Thomas Cromwell. The announcement came from the pointedly named Art and Reconciliation Trust, thus inviting both aesthetic and religious support. The site chosen for the new statue incorporated references to both Cromwell, the chief persecutor, and More, a most determined defender, of the Virgin's honor and much else of traditional religion, in the 1530s: "it was," said the announcement, "to Chelsea Manor that the Image of Our Lady of Walsingham was taken and burnt along with her other 'sisters'."[4]

The ambiguities surrounding the place and timing of the fires, and the number and identities of the victims, have been sufficient over the centuries to generate wish-fulfillment fantasies on behalf of some of the "images" that were destroyed, especially those of Our Lady of Ipswich and Our Lady of Walsingham. There are nostalgic sentiments, frequently expressed on guided tours, in booklets, websites, and even in relatively sober histories, that somehow they were mysteriously saved from the fire and smuggled away to places of safety, thereby to continue their work of (depending on one's viewpoint) miracle or idolatry. In the case of the Ipswich Virgin, Our Lady of Grace, it is possible that a medieval statue in the Italian town of Nettuno is of English origin. Stories of its miraculous arrival around 1550 have given devotees the hope that the Ipswich madonna escaped the fire. In the 1930s, there was even speculation that the Nettuno statue was the much-revered Walsingham image, and not a few accounts of Walsingham cherish the alternative, even more unlikely, possibility that somewhere, perhaps in the Norfolk village of Little Walsingham itself, waiting to reappear at some time during the triumphal revival of the shrine of the Virgin in the twentieth century, is the image that Erasmus called, as if disappointed by its appearance as opposed to its reputed miraculous powers and the opulence of its tributes and gifts of gold and jewels, "*Ostenditur imagincula, nec magnitudine, nec materia nec opere praecellens,*" cheap looking, not impressive, and not well constructed.[5]

---

[4] www.artandreconciliation.org/1000projects.htm.
[5] Smith, *The Madonna of Ipswich*; Erasmus, *Pilgrimage of Pure Devotion*, 29. Except where noted, I quote from this first (?1536–7) English translation of Erasmus's *Peregrinatio Religionis Ergo*.

These initial stories of event and legend, violence and nostalgia, expectation and mystery, with missing details and many variations and contradictions, provide an apt initial metaphor for this study of the Virgin Mary in English culture from the late Middle Ages until the mid seventeenth century, by which time the waves of iconoclasm had, at least on the surface of English life, died down. Rather ambiguously we have come to term this period "early modern," but it might as easily be called "late medieval," since its fades and traces were seen and felt long after the so-called Middle Ages were supposedly over. The burnings of Marian idols in 1538, in the middle of the process in the late 1530s by which the religious foundations, including many centers of Marian devotion in England, were shut down and most destroyed or wrecked, is my fulcrum. I move forward and back from that date, which is both historically important but more, of great symbolic significance. Reformation iconoclasm in England was, of course, not solely directed at the Virgin, but at certain times and with certain people, she became become an intense, even obsessive, focus of iconoclastic denigration and destruction.

In this study, I shall draw on the many closely documented historical studies of these events but I also attempt to ask about motive and desire, feelings and fantasies – matters that are not easily available to empirical verification, and overlap uneasily with conventional history and are more the province of psychoanalysis or theology. In what sense, for example, did the events of 1538, not only in Chelsea (or Smithfield or Tyburn) but across the country, mark the end of an era – not just in material terms but in men's and women's emotional allegiances and their deeply rooted, even unconscious, patterns of behavior? Why did the Virgin become a target of unusual Protestant violence in England in this decade and for the next century? To what extent did feelings about the Virgin disappear? Did the reformers, in their attempt to "control" Mary's role in salvation, end by banishing or tragically diminishing "maternal feminine symbolism" by their "commitment to an unambiguously patriarchal Father God," as the contemporary Catholic theologian Tina Beattie claims.[6] After the Walsingham "idol" had been burnt, Roger Townshend, one of Thomas Cromwell's Norfolk agents, wrote to him: "I cannot perceive butt the seyd Image is not yet out of sum of their heddes." To what extent did the image and all it stood for get out "of their heddes"? As Margaret Aston poses the question, "how are we to account for what seems like a transformation" of a society of "image-worshippers" into "image-breakers" and

---

[6] Beattie, "Queen of Heaven," 205.

"image-haters?"[7] Why did the reformers become so insistent on removing the presence of the Virgin from people's minds? To what extent were they successful? And what happened to the memory of Marian centers such as Ipswich, Penrhys, and (greatest of all) Walsingham, and (in a sense) to the Virgin herself, after the Dissolution of the late 1530s and the great fires of 1538?

"Iconoclasm was the central sacrament of the reform," states Eamon Duffy. It is an assertion that is more provocative than strictly accurate, especially in its dismissive use of the term "sacrament" in association with the Anglican Church, but many historians have persuasively presented iconoclastic extremism as a defining factor in the English Reformation.[8] The long struggle over "images" had broad and deep connections with the transformation of English society and the ideologies of selfhood, identity, gender, and sexuality that governed, or as Louis Althusser puts it, "interpellated," men and women into the grand narratives of their culture.[9] Today, some may say the picture of the world advanced by the reformers was maybe no less false, the idolatry of the Word no less pernicious than the idolatry of the Image. Yet Aston confesses that while she believes that historians are "not supposed to take sides," she finds it hard to "sympathize with the reformers' zeal for destruction … Doing without images is one thing, annihilating them another. Destruction may be exhilarating, but it has an eventual fall-out which is the opposite of life-enhancing."[10] My sympathies are similar but, nevertheless, from the 1520s onward a vociferous minority of English men and women did feel liberated by the revolutionary nature of Protestantism and its creation of a new sense of selfhood. Their enthusiasm and persistence (along with what Shakespeare termed in his Sonnet 115 the "million'd accidents" of history) intensified the pace of reform, animated the surges of iconoclasm of the next century, and eventually contributed to the Enlightenment project of a rational, autonomous, coherent self – a self, Beattie argues, that increasingly becomes "male through and through" in part because the Virgin "had been eradicated from Protestant consciousness."[11]

That claim (and the many qualifications to it I will gradually present) introduces a major focus of this study. Julia Kristeva calls the Virgin a "combination of power and sorrow, sovereignty and the unnnameable," making up "one of the most powerful imaginary constructs known in the

---

[7] Gillett, *Walsingham*, 65–6; Aston, *England's Iconoclasts*, 29.
[8] Duffy, *Stripping of the Altars*, 480.   [9] Althusser, *Lenin and Philosophy*, 174.
[10] Aston, *England's Iconoclasts*, 116–17.   [11] Beattie, *New Catholic Feminism*, 127; *Eve's Pilgrimage*, 138.

history of civilization."[12] It is Kristeva's "unnameable" by which I am primarily fascinated, both in relation to the Virgin herself (insofar as we can speak of "her" as dissociated from any construct of her), and in relation to the reactions of attraction and repulsion to the Virgin in early modern England. The force of that "unnameable" may at times be explicit, but more likely has to be inferred, forcing us to search for the non-saids and the unsayables as well as the saids, probing silences (what was not said) and the absences (what was not able to be said) of recorded events, records, and literary and other "cultural" texts.

I shall have more to say as I proceed on the difficulties of how we might go beyond what Sir Philip Sidney (not entirely fairly) calls historians being "captived to the truth of a foolish world" and thereby tied down to the evidence of "old mouse-eaten records."[13] I will be looking at many of the same records as well as drawing on many interpretations of them. But I will be looking at them with an unashamed, though (I hope) "lightly worn," presentist perspective.[14] I do not believe that the past can speak on its "own" terms, but only through and ultimately for the ever-changing present. To make my case, I draw on an eclectic selection of contemporary perspectives: cultural psychoanalytic scholars such as Kristeva herself, feminist theologians such as Tina Beattie, and sociologists of popular religion such as Michael Carroll. Beattie speaks of how we might "detour" or (as she quotes Luce Irigaray) "sidle" up to different struggles toward truth, discovering questions and issues from a variety of sources without committing to their overriding narratives.[15] I feel it is an apt metaphor. Naming the unnameable is not the easiest of human callings, and we may (perhaps must) inevitably fail; but it may be among the most important tasks we give ourselves (or have given to us) as human beings. Discussions of methodological "sidlings" will recur throughout this study, though usually with at least some warning. At one point in his study of Irish wells and pilgrimages, Carroll warns that "readers who like their history devoid of psychology, and in particular, readers for whom a good cigar is – under all circumstances and all conditions – never anything more than a good cigar may or may not wish to continue."[16] I will try to give equivalent warnings, most especially in Chapter 2 when I speculate about the underlying sexual contradictions of late medieval and Reformation idealizations and denigrations of the Virgin,

---

[12] Kristeva, *Tales of Love*, 237.   [13] Sidney, *Apology*, III, 113.
[14] I am grateful to Peter G. Platt for this phrase in his generous review of my *All's Well That Ends Well: New Critical Essays*, 495.
[15] Irigaray, *Speculum*, 36; Beattie, *New Catholic Feminism*, 10.   [16] Carroll, *Irish Pilgrimage*, 166.

or in the final chapter when I return to speculate, perhaps with a certain amount of wistfulness, about the continuing power of the Virgin in our culture. In some cases, what needs to be said can only be expressed through modern discourses, especially in such areas of intimacy and controversy as the Virgin's sexuality.

For the moment, however, as all readers of early modern culture must, I want to rely (and with deep gratitude) on the modern descendants of Sidney's historians to describe something of what was destroyed or obscured by what Duffy calls "generations of subsequent iconoclasm, first religiously and then aesthetically driven."[17] No other European country went through such a sustained period of struggle over images, representation, and the relationship of the material to the spiritual as England. The bonfires of 1538 were followed by a century of iconoclasm, consisting of both surges of destruction and a continuing undercurrent of state-encouraged iconophobia. It was by no means all directed exclusively at the Virgin, but because of her place in Catholic theology, liturgy, and devotion, she was given an unusual degree of hostile attention. The early reformers attacked, sometimes systematically and sometimes seemingly randomly, what they saw as superstitious practices, proofs that the medieval church had degenerated into a deceptive morass of idolatry and blasphemy, putting millions of souls over hundreds of years in jeopardy. At the core of their attacks was the belief that the sign and the signified should be kept separate, that the material world could not contain divinity, and they rejected and feared any suggestion that human instrumentality, the manipulation of objects of the material world – whether the bread of the Mass or images and relics – could influence or control the supernatural and give material things such as bread and wine "a life of their own."[18] The reformers' targets included not only unscriptural beliefs and devotional practices, but also many interconnected aspects of medieval religion, including papal authority, transubstantiation, the doctrine of works, along with the communion of the living and dead (and therefore the doctrine of Purgatory, a fond thing vainly invented, as Article 22 of the Church of England puts it). Key to their attack on sacramentality was a rejection of transubstantiation: the Mass was ridiculed as the ultimate foolishness and idolatry.[19] Near the center of their targets was the intercession of the saints, especially the power of Mary, who held the "special and leading place" within what Carlos Eire terms the "parapolytheism" of medieval Christianity. And it was, as I will discuss in

---

[17] Duffy, *Fires of Faith*, 3.   [18] Janes, *Victorian Reformation*, 15–16.
[19] Schwartz, *Sacramental Poetics*, 29–33.

Chapter 2, specifically the material, bodily nature of the Virgin that was intensely at issue. As Lyndal Roper states, the body of the Virgin was a "litmus test of the separation of the divine and the human" for Catholics and Protestants and what became their "radically different theologies of the body."[20]

All sides in the Reformation struggles agreed that deep and mysterious powers had been attributed to the Virgin and to relics and places especially associated with her. For Catholics such attributions were, with the exception of some marginal and pardonable exaggerations and a little corruption, truthful and reflected God's purposes; for Protestants such claims were false and demonic, slippages into paganism and evidence of the irredeemable corruption of the Roman Church. Reformers generally acknowledged Mary as God's chosen instrument, but rejected what Latimer saw as the "foolish opinion and the doctrine of the papists, which would have us to worship a creature before the Creator." The continental reformer Melanchthon regretted that "in popular estimation the blessed Virgin has completely replaced Christ"; Bishop John Jewel referred to the blasphemy of regarding Mary as "our lady and goddess"; William Perkins attacked the view of Mary as "a Ladie, a goddesse, a queene whom Christ her sonne obeyeth in heaven, a mediatresse, our life, hope, the medicine of the diseased"; it is, he thunders, a blasphemy that "they pray unto her thus."[21] The degree of hostility toward Mary varied greatly across Reformation Europe, in both time and place, with Lutherans more amenable to modifying rather than radically reducing her role, but a not uncommon note in Reformed polemic was that under papist superstition – in the words of the Puritan polemicist William Crashaw, who, along with his son Richard, will be mentioned frequently in this book – "the paps of a woman" were blasphemously "equaled with the wounds of our Lord, and her milke with his blood," even though "the holy scriptures speak no more of her, but as a creature," and, in a significant slur, as merely "a woman."[22]

Getting it "out of ... their heddes" took a long time. More drastic and immediate measures than polemic and exhortation were used, not just for the destruction of the idols themselves, but also for the bodily elimination of opponents. Eventually, what Christine Peters, quietly understating the process, terms an "adaptation" or "reshaping" of the Virgin's significance

---

[20] Eire, *War Against the Idols*, 12–13; Roper, *Oedipus and the Devil*, 178, 184.
[21] Heal, *The Cult of the Virgin Mary*, 53; Johnson, "Mary in Early Modern Europe," 364; Perkins, *Works*, 340.
[22] Crashaw, *Jesuites Gospell*, 32.

occurred.[23] Perhaps, as many Catholics (then and now) would maintain, both the virulence of the attempts to ensure forgetfulness and the length of time it took reflected the depth of attachment England had to the Virgin. But over the course of the next century, the Protestant cultural revolution was sufficiently successful that by the 1620s and 1630s, even moderate Protestants would feel uneasy about Archbishop Laud's imposition of what they saw as papist ceremonies and practices, not necessarily because they were a return to old ways, but because by then they were being seen as innovations. Even so "catholic" an intellectual as John Donne – who, it is surmised, kept a painting of the Virgin in his study – could preach in 1622 that by then, God had been "a hundred years" in his "repairing" of the Church, and had ordered "not a faint discontinuing of idolatry, but . . . utter destruction," and not just mentally or spiritually, but "the utter destruction of the very place, not a seising of the riches of the place, but the place it self."[24]

What lay behind the reformers' uneasiness about the place of the Virgin was not an upsurge of entirely new views. As Beattie comments, they believed indignantly that "the ancient goddesses and their female devotees still whisper[ed] and beckon[ed] in the cult of Mary," and saw their attacks as a return to the principles of the early Church. Concerns had often surfaced about excesses of popular devotion, false relics, and exaggerated claims of miracles associated with Mary, especially during the rise of what Erasmus, typically tongue-in-cheek, termed "thys new learnynge, whiche runnythe all the world over nowadays."[25] I will refer in Chapter 3 to Marian miracle stories, one of the most popular forms of creative non-fiction (or often purely fiction) in Christian history; one of Cromwell's agents, Richard Layton, wrote to him that he would send him "a book of Our Lady's miracles well able to match the Canterbury Tales," and his sneer reflects a dismissal of anything in excess of what could be verified and proven and which relied on tradition, or false imaginings, rather than being scripturally based. But as the English Reformation proceeded, in its zigzags, fits and starts, and eddyings (all currently favorite metaphors of modern historians), both within the factions that battled in the 1530s and 1540s and for the next century, there was no question, as Michael O'Connell comments, of merely "checking abuses and reforming excesses." The zeal of the reformers in the 1530s and 1540s was "directed against the entire system of worship and devotion."[26]

[23] Peters, *Patterns of Piety*, 208, 223.   [24] Donne, *Sermons*, v, 132–3.
[25] Beattie, *Eve's Pilgrimage*, 70; Erasmus, *Pilgrimages*, 19.
[26] O'Connell, *Idolatrous Eye*, 11, 50. For Layton's *Canterbury Tales* comparison, see Cook, *Letters to Cromwell*, 38.

Cromwell's agents, who were responsible for gathering up the super-stitious images that were burned in the summer (or autumn) of 1538, saw exposing false miracles and destroying feigned relics not only as part of the elimination of the religious houses, with the financial advantages that would bring the Crown, but also as the means to achieve much more deeply rooted changes. The reformers perceived the necessity of wholesale cultural revo-lution and (if possible) the rooting out not just the "structures," but the "feelings" attached to them, to use Raymond Williams's distinction.[27] Their goal was to destroy the images and idols within people's minds. Getting it out of their heads, not just destroying buildings and sending tens of thousands of monks and nuns out into the community, was therefore crucial to the revolution. But the "fantassie of idolatrie" might be so deeply rooted, the reformers feared, that "idolatrie will neaver be left till the said images be taken awaie." Cromwell instructed his agents to remove popular "idols" as discreetly as possible but to highlight what could be presented as obvious fakes, the "certain engines and old wire with rotten sticks," which could be used for propagandist purposes. Reformers jeered that the destruc-tion of some of the more dubious relics and images – the Blood of Hailes and the images of Our Lady of Walsingham and her sisters among them – did not provoke the once revered objects to respond, retaliate, or miracu-lously escape: 'Throw them down thrice, they cannot rise, not once to help themselves." With some successes in exposing "idols" and "false reliques," it became easier to make the case that all relics and images were fakes and needed, in the words of a 1535 Proclamation, "utterly to be abolished, eradicated and erased out." Some of the targets were easy, others made to appear ridiculous, such as the promiscuous veneration of "that ladye in that place and that ladye in that," a sneer that struck at one of the most common and comforting aspects of popular religion, the local saints and madonnas that we may today associate primarily with Italy or Mexico but which was before 1538 as naturalized a habit of English society.[28] From the other side of the ideological divide, traditionalists distinguished between true "Images" and false "Idols," affirming that when the images of saints are erected and properly venerated, the saints made intercession to God. In the reign of Queen Mary, looking back at what he saw as such blasphemous acts of desecration under Henry and Edward VI, James Brooks, Master of Balliol,

---

[27] Williams, *Keywords*, 288; Aston, *England's Iconoclasts*, 10.

[28] *Tudor Royal Proclamations*, 231. Carroll points out that we should, strictly speaking, speak of "madonnine" rather than "Marian" images, since there was only one Mary but multiple madonnas: *Veiled Threats*, 17.

condemned not just "the pulling down of God's houses and hospitals; the defacing of churches," but the "breaking down of altars; the throwing down of crosses; the carting out of images; the burning of tried holy relics."[29] Once Elizabeth became queen, the Church of England's homilies, first issued in 1547, were revised and reissued and became a key document for justifying official iconoclasm. The longest, 120 pages in four parts, Homily XIV, is headed "against peril of idolatry, and superfluous decking of churches." It was probably partly authored by Bishop John Jewel, and appeared first in the edition of 1562. It looks back to the recent return of papistry under Mary, the "corruption of these latter days," when "infinite multitudes of images" had once again "secretly and by stealth to creep out of private men's houses into the churches, and that first in painted clothes and walls." It provides a relentless compendium of biblical and historical precedents against images, assembles a didactic history of iconoclasm controversies in the history of the Church, and (having in mind that the Council of Trent was still in session) mounts a series of attacks on recent "reasons and arguments made for the defence of images or idols." Idolatry, the Homily thunders, is committed "by infinite multitudes, to the great offence of God's majesty, and danger of infinite souls," and is directly associated with "images set up in churches and temples, gilded and decked gloriously." These images, it pronounces with threatening finality, "be indeed very idols." More than twenty years after they had been destroyed, the images at Ipswich and Walsingham are still specifically mentioned by name as idols that had been reverenced by a previous generation in the mistaken belief that "decking and adorning of the temple or house of God" would seduce people to be "the more moved to the due reverence of the same, if all corners thereof were glorious, and glistering with gold and precious stones." What, asks the Homily, are such idols "but an imitation of the Gentiles idolaters, Diana Agrotera, Diana Coriphea, Diana Ephesia, &c. Venus Cypria, Venus Paphia, Venus Gnidia? Whereby is evidently meant, that the saint for the image sake should in those places, yea, in the images themselves, have a dwelling, which is the ground of their idolatry. For where no images be, they have no such means." The Homily's warning that, all too easily, "we like mad men fall down before the dead idols or images," is an anxiety about an ever-present threat inherent in human nature. Such blasphemous practices have, the Homily continued, echoing Calvin and Zwingli, whose influence on the revised Elizabethan homilies was pronounced, misled

---

[29] Brooks, quoted by Shagan, "Confronting Compromise," 65.

"the simple and unwise, occasioning them thereby to commit most horrible idolatry."[30]

It will be major part of my argument, especially in Chapter 2, that many of the attacks on the veneration of the Virgin and her shrines, relics, and miracles, were in part because she was, as William Crashaw emphasized, "a woman." Iconoclasm frequently has a distinctive misogynic caste – not just the chronically corrosive misogyny of medieval Christianity, which emerged from the struggles of the early Church in which, as Beattie puts it, the wrong side too often triumphed to the great detriment of Christianity itself – but a distinctive form of masculinist anxiety, a deep-rooted distinctively Protestant misogyny directed at women and female experience. Despite the thousand-year battle against "pagan" goddess cults, some of which affirmed rather than repressed women's experiences and especially sexuality, a deep-rooted need for the female had still managed to permeate popular Christian devotion. In fairness, that way of putting it would have been unthinkable to both Catholics and Protestants at the time, but in triumphing over goddess religions early in its history, it may be that Christianity nonetheless absorbed sufficient from them to allow for some degree of continuity in late medieval Marianization.

Going back to early Christian history, we can pick out landmarks of doctrinal and devotional experimentation that had attempted to give a conscious shape to such reactions – and to a largely repressed, alternate tradition of female-based religion. The Collyridians, a shadowy third-century heretical group, were reputed to have either grown from or adapted elements of a female goddess cult and to have made eucharistic offerings to Mary. Beattie argues that if the Collyridians had been welcomed into rather than rejected by the Church, that "women's religion" might then have helped create a less misogynic institution.[31] For the reformers, that absorption of such heresies had nonetheless happened and contributed not just to idolatry, but also to what they saw as the femaleness of the Catholic Church. Frances Dolan comments that many male saints – whether within the liturgy or in their representations in statues or pictures – survived the Reformation, but "wodden ... ladies" were a special target for the iconoclasts.[32] What they saw as the worship of Mary presented Protestants not only with an example of visible idolatry but also specifically with the further provocation of suspected worship of the female.

---

[30] *Certain Sermons, or Homilies,* 207.
[31] Epiphanius, *Panarion,* 353–4; Beattie, *God's Mother,* 63; Carroll, *Madonnas that Maim,* 41–8.
[32] Dolan, *Whores of Babylon,* 121.

To contextualize the continuing surges of Marian iconoclasm over the century following 1538, I will glance at three vignettes of state-sponsored iconoclasm directed at the Virgin: the desecration of the Lady Chapel of Ely Cathedral in the 1540s; the destruction of a statue of the Virgin and Child during the English invasion of Cadiz in 1596; and the rampages of William Dowsing in the 1640s as he scoured East Anglian churches, looking for remnants of papistry.

First, to Ely. The fourteenth-century Lady Chapel, one of the architectural glories of the Middle Ages, was the largest lady chapel attached to a cathedral in England, and on the eve of the Reformation must have presented a remarkable sight: dozens of brightly colored statues illustrating the life and biblical antecedents of the Virgin. In 1541, late in the process by which the monasteries were dissolved under the authority of the two Suppression Acts (1536 and 1539) and many local decrees, zealous local reformers in Ely, encouraged by Cranmer's decrees that local clergy destroy all shrines, pictures, paintings, and "covering of shrines," so that "there remain no memory of it," destroyed or severely defaced the chapel, mostly by crudely beheading virtually all the statues. In Articles sent to his own diocese of Canterbury, Cranmer had emphasized the point: such reminders of the old religion, he ordered, should be "utterly extincted and destroyed so that there remain no memory of the same in walls, glass windows, or elsewhere."[33] Today, looking at Ely's "glass windows," what O'Connell terms a "vast, almost bare interior space ... that has been drained of the warmth and color it once possessed" – an impression, I would add, not at all allayed by some, no doubt well-intentioned, modern sculptural and pictorial additions – it is hard to escape the impression of a vengeful giant fifty feet high, swinging maliciously at anything resembling a human, especially a female, figure. What likely happened was that local evangelicals rode their horses inside the chapel, beheading and mutilating all the statues they could reach, probably not without some guilt and fear mixed into their virulent indignation. Today, there are only four windows that have retained traces of their fourteenth-century origins – a few small angels, knights, and peasants overwhelmed by the eerily melancholy white light shining through the glass of this huge space – showing by their absence where the multiple colors of medieval glasswork would have once glittered. Modern comments referring to the "diabolical frenzy" and "satanic creation" of the desecrators are understandable, but frenzy is often accompanied or motivated by

---

[33] Frere, *Visitation Articles*, II, 67, 178.

resentment.[34] Curiously, none of the standard guidebooks available in the Cathedral mention who was responsible: the desecration is put euphemistically down to changes at the Reformation, without mention of the active oversight of Thomas Goodrich, the bishop who supported Henry's divorce and the Act of Supremacy, but also managed to conform under Queen Mary. All over England, Lady chapels such as that at Ely were destroyed or mutilated. At the Benedictine priory of Binham, near Walsingham, there were probably two chapels dedicated to the Virgin, one built in the fifteenth century; both were wrecked, and under the supervision of Robert Rich – at the time Cromwell's supporter (though later he assisted in Cromwell's fall and execution) – rubble and stone were taken from the site to build a house in nearby Wells-next-the-Sea.[35] After 450 years, Ely's Lady Chapel remains perhaps the most striking symbol of this destruction of a distinctively English aspect of medieval church architecture and, more broadly, of the iconoclasts' attempts to eliminate the presence of the Virgin from England.

Move on sixty years to an incident in which Queen Elizabeth – to some of her supporters England's triumphant Reformed Virgin, who actively sponsored aggressive anti-Spanish and anti-Catholic privateers – is seen to triumph over the figure and aura of the old Catholic Virgin. In 1596, a fleet of English mercenaries, led by the Earl of Essex and Lord Howard, invaded the port of Cadiz as part of the confrontation between Protestant England and Catholic Spain – each, of course, regarding the other as heretics and, as we might say today, terrorists. Essex, whose expressions of piety were rarely compromised by much sincerity, wrote that "if I be not tied by the hand, I know God hath great work to work by me." The immediate and material aim, as opposed to any spiritual crusade, was to cripple the Spanish fleet and replenish the Queen's treasury from merchant ships anchored in Cadiz harbor. Essex, however, was impetuous, sulky, and intent on using the incident primarily to forward his own standing with Elizabeth. Quarreling about whether to sack or occupy the city diverted him and his commanders, who included Sir Walter Ralegh, and a host of common soldiers and gentleman adventurers, including John Donne (both of whom will play parts in later chapters), until eventually, R. B. Wernham notes, the town was "portioned out among the English and Dutch officers and their troops to be systematically sacked." From then on, the invaders, by Ralegh's report,

---

[34] Collinson, *Birthpangs,* 98; O'Connell, *Idolatrous Eye,* 3. For Ely's Lady Chapel, Stanton, "On the Lady Chapel of Ely Cathedral," 310; James, *Sculptures in the Lady Chapel at Ely*; Stanbury, *Visual Object of Desire,* 1–3.

[35] "Binham Priory."

were "all running headlong to the sack ... tumultuous soldiers, abandoned to spoile and rapine, without any prospect of persons," a vocabulary of sexual violence totally unselfconsciously echoed in his later description of the invasion of Guiana as a "country that hath yet her maidenhead." The town was "pillaged to a farthing" some officers reported. After leaving Cadiz, the invaders called into Faro, in Portugal, which they also sacked and "left so demolished, as to yield no covering to their idols." They also seized paintings and books, some of which came eventually to the Bodleian.[36]

During the sacking of Cadiz, a statue of the Virgin was seized by the English invaders. They took it into the marketplace, cut the figure of the infant Jesus from the Madonna, stabbed at the statue's breasts, chopped off the arms, slashed the face, and nearly beheaded it. Some was probably just random violence, but to attempt to behead a statue and to attack obviously sexualized (or sexualizable) parts is at least some way toward anthropomorphizing it. In the long history of image destruction in Christianity, it has been three-dimensional figures, such as the Cadiz Vulnerata or the statues of Our Lady of Ipswich or Walsingham, that have attracted special hostility. The sexual and maternal characteristics of the Virgin are obviously more prominent in a three-dimensional figure because of its resemblance to a real body. Foskett suggests that heads include the mouth, which "opens to speak," and another lower orifice that "opens to receive," that can be identified with "allure and possession as well as pleasure and procreation," as if the invaders were, beneath their piety (or simple desire to loot), accepting as true the idolatrous identification of image and person. What comes from the mouth are not only secretions, scents, and seductive promises, but language – in the case of the Virgin blasphemous and false (and female) promises. Stow's *Chronicle of London* records similar behavior in London in 1601, when an image of the Virgin and Child that had been a repeated target of vandals, was defaced, stabbed in the breast, stripped of the figure of the Child, and almost beheaded.[37] At Vallodolid, the statue was rescued and eventually presented to the English College where missionaries for the re-conversion of the English were and are still trained. It is today known as the *Madonna vulnerata* and remains the focus for devotion of priests departing for England. It thus became an emblem of the fate of English Catholicism for expatriate Catholics, a "visual reminder" of the "wounds inflected by England's heresy."[38]

---

[36] Wernham, *Return of the Armadas*, 104, 100, 105; Williams, *The Later Tudors*, 350–6.
[37] Foskett, *A Virgin Conceived*, 40; for the incident at West Cheap, see Stow, *Survey of London*, 238–9.
[38] Shell, *Catholicism, Controversy*, 200–7; Redworth, *She-Apostle*, 83–5.

The violence directed against statues reveals the still nascent fears that perhaps lurked even in the most convinced of iconophobes, that the idols might not just tempt the ignorant into believing they were "real," but that they might respond and re-assert their power. Medieval (and later) saints' legends are full of weeping or bleeding statues, and one of the claims disputed by Catholics and Protestants was whether statues or relics might react in some way to real or threatened desecration. When the statues did not respond (and, in fairness, some Catholic propagandists publishing on the Continent or in Catholic Ireland asserted that many did, by weeping, bleeding, or miraculously disappearing), how did the iconoclasts themselves react? Such idols as the "sisters" over which he triumphed, sneered Latimer, were "not able to defend themselves,"[39] and while there must have been triumph at overcoming what the reformers believed to be hundreds of years of superstition, it is likely that some reactions included a residue of almost cosmic disappointment. Part of the triumph must have been seeing that no miracle occurred, and that it was possible to break free of the idol's power. But there must have been anguish that long-revered relics and images did not respond. When the magical world dies, its death may be mourned, even by the executioners.

The idols were often defiled and mutilated rather than, or before, being destroyed. Aston notes that "turning venerated images and consecrated objects to degrading secular uses was designed to shock by deliberate inversion" and "annihilating supposedly immaculate purity by inversion": altar stones and holy water stoups as kitchen tables, stools or toilets, for instance.[40] Such desecration – the throwing of images in ponds or holes, turning altars into tables, holy water fonts into pedestals or chamber pots, smearing holy objects with blood, ordure or other filth – showed the strongest disdain for the underlying beliefs. But desecration showed also that the iconoclasts were accepting, at least in part, the magic that the idols represented – as if, despite their convictions, they were afraid that the magical powers of the idols might in some sense still be effective.

Most idols were burnt, just as heretics were burnt. Turning a revered idol to dust by burning proved its falsity – and further decreased the likelihood that it would somehow revive. The dual ceremony to which Latimer refers in his celebrated letter to Cromwell – the May and July (or September) 1538 burnings of the friar John Forest, who had been Catherine of Aragon's

---

[39] MacCulloch, "Mary and Sixteenth-Century Protestants," 204–5; see also Simpson, "The Rule of Medieval Imagination," 19.
[40] Aston, *Faith and Fire*, 295.

confessor, and the idols of Walsingham and her sisters – was an auspicious symbolic start to the century of iconoclasm. Both heretic and idol were burnt in the same ritualistic space, and Latimer gloated over their common fate. The burnings of 1538 set a pattern: as Aston summarizes it, "from 1538 on, the ceremonial iconoclastic bonfire was an accepted part of the official reforming process in England." In the reign of Mary, "idols" were, of course, not burned; their places in the fires were occupied by heretics alone. The accession of Elizabeth in 1559 was also accompanied by public burnings in St. Paul's churchyard and across London of roods and other "idolatrous" statues, including those of the Virgin. Thomas Becon's *Catechism* (1560) wrote of the need for idols to be "burnt openly," as the Old Testament commanded: "ye shall destroy their alters ... and burn their graven images with fire" (Deut 7:5). In 1578, on progress with the queen in Norfolk, Richard Topcliffe discovered a statue of the Virgin which, he ordered, must be "commanded to the fire." In 1583, William Fulke looked back at nearly fifty years of iconoclasm and proclaimed that "though they were as ancient and goodly monuments ... it is to the great honour of God that they should be despised, defaced, burned, and stamped to powder."[41] Reprobates and papists would burn in hell; burning them or their idols participated in their divinely ordained punishment.

My third, brief, vignette is from the last major phase of English iconoclastic vandalism, in the 1640s. By the 1630s, the Church of England was gradually – depending on one's point of view, then and now – opening itself to increasing tolerance or backsliding toward papistry. Anthony Stafford's *The Femall Glory*, an Anglican celebration of the Virgin – carefully cautious about papist associations in some areas, warmly responsive to Tridentine and even earlier medieval Catholic emphases in others – was published in 1637; in Cambridge, at Little St. Mary's, Richard Crashaw, the son of a notorious Puritan campaigner against Marian devotion, was reviving the cult of the Virgin, and producing some remarkable poetical tributes to her, written when he was still an Anglican, before he converted to Rome and became a canon at the shrine of Our Lady of Loreto. Laudianism, with its emphasis on ordered externals and traditional ceremonies, was becoming increasingly influential. The 1640s, however, saw a renewed wave of image destruction. In 1641 and 1643, Parliament issued ordinances for the removal and destruction of any remaining idolatrous images. In 1644, a Committee for the Demolition of Monuments of Superstition and Idolatry commenced

---

[41] Eire, *War Against the Idols*, 157; Miles, *Image as Insight*, 107; Purkiss, "Desire and its Deformities," 6; Michalski, *Reformation and the Visual Arts*, 45.

work in London. "Images" were not its only targets: they went along with painted glass, communion rails, church furnishings, symbolic renditions of lions and lambs, church organs, vestments and even, in places, the Book of Common Prayer.

Among the most (in)famous acts of iconoclasm were those perpetrated by William Dowsing – whose name, three hundred years later, would be associated with a satirical society in Cambridge mocking architectural and aesthetic excesses – who was appointed by the Puritan Earl of Manchester to enforce Parliament's ordinances in East Anglia. Julie Spraggon comments that Dowsing's attacks were the continuation of a century of systematic extermination; they were "an almost ritualistic destruction of symbols representative of the enemy ... the Puritan theology-in-action of a godly and reforming army." Dowsing's journals record a dogged attempt to root out the remains of popery. He purged over two hundred churches in East Anglia, meeting some resistance in Cambridge, where academic indignation and sophistry were no match for army-backed brutality. His records vary from the quasi-statistical to a frantic obsession with the very objects he hunted down. Over and over he recorded such details as that "in the church, there was on the roof, above an hundred jesus & mary [and] a glorious cover over the font."[42] Spraggon picks out the last phrase as revealing: she comments that "the art vandal turns out in each of his several guises ... to be a peculiar category of art lover." Even in his obtuse brutality, Dowsing records the images' potential to move him. A century before, 1520s, the German Protestant Andreas von Karlstadt had likewise become more vehement a destroyer of idols when he noted his own fear before the images: "a harmful fear," he records, "has been bred into me" from which he would be delivered, "but cannot."[43] Those sentiments haunt the century of iconoclasm and epitomize the "traces" and "fades" of the Virgin in England.

From these vignettes and the ongoing surges of state-sponsored iconoclasm that became part of the dominant ideology once Elizabeth came to the throne, from the attacks on relics, feigned miracles, and idolatry, there emerges a picture of the created universe which the reformers wished to bring into being. The Virgin Mary had been the center, the prime creation, of the medieval Catholic universe. It was a magical universe, not in the sense that Protestants saw the term "magic" as distinct from "religion," a dichotomy made famous in our time by Keith Thomas's classic study, *Religion and the Decline of Magic*; rather, it was a sacramental universe in which the

---

[42] Spraggon, *Puritan Iconoclasm*, 201; Morrill, "William Dowsing," 12.
[43] Spraggon, *Puritan Iconoclasm*, 52; Mangum, *Reformation Debate*, 39.

supernatural was embodied in material creation, including the human body, and able to be influenced by human actions in accordance with traditionally approved rites and rituals.[44] It is the slow and spasmodic and by no means complete disintegration of this magical universe with the Virgin at its center that this study traces.

Throughout the century, iconoclasm expressed itself in a distinctive rhetoric of sexualized misogyny. Thomas Bilney, "little Bilney," who was burned as a heretic under Thomas More's chancellorship, called Our Lady of Willesden (one of the Marian shrines to which More made a pilgrimage) "the chefe Lay maistres" and "common paramour of baudry." Roger Hutchinson compared Christ's presence in the Virgin's womb as like sunshine shining upon a "filthy jakes." The homilies refer to "the idols of our women-saints" as "nice and well-trimmed harlots."[45] Latimer's diatribes against pilgrimages, relics, and images have a special edge when commenting on the Virgin and the place of the female in religion. MacCulloch comments that Latimer's "campaign to sweep out the remnants of the once-mighty English cults of Our Lady" betrays an "uneasy mixture of derision and gynaecomorphism." In his biblical commentaries, Latimer attacks Mary for what he sees as pride, bad manners, arrogance, and – in an extraordinarily revealing remark given the history of Christianity and its emphasis on motherhood – for reprimanding Jesus "like a mother." As MacCulloch comments, the very phrase forms "a clue to Latimer's unconscious feelings," especially his need to neutralize or destroy specifically female or motherly power.[46] But Latimer clearly was not unusual. Sexual polemic, often graphically involving references to the reproductive and excretory functions of the Virgin, was (as I will discuss in Chapter 2) a tradition dating back to medieval controversies among Christians, Jews, and Muslims and continued throughout the Reformation period. His "unconscious feelings" were rather acting out a much wider revolutionary cultural unconscious.

In his *Actes and Monuments*, John Foxe's rhetoric frequently takes on a peculiarly sexualized tinge, especially when attacking the sexual corruption of the papacy. He waxes indignant at Sixtus IV's alleged propensity for brothels, sodomy, and sexual indulgence; he mocks Sixtus's establishment of the Feast of the Immaculate Conception; and he saves particularly vicious

[44] Carroll, *Madonnas that Maim*, 112–28.
[45] Aston, *England's Iconoclasts*, 163–4; see also Davis, "Bilney." For Willesden, see the website listed under Willesden, Our Lady of.
[46] MacCulloch, "Mary and Sixteenth-Century Protestants," 204–5; Simpson, "Rule of Medieval Imagination," 19; Foxe, *Actes and Monuments*, 780.

negative rhetoric for the fifteenth-century Dominican theologian Alanus de Rupe who had a vision in which the Virgin fashioned a ring of her hair for him, "betrothed herself to [him] . . . kissed him, and gave him her breasts to be fondled and milked and, finally . . . gave herself to him as familiarly as a wife customarily does to her husband." As Thomas Freeman notes, Catholic commentators on Alanus praised his poetic vision; but to Protestants such as Foxe, they seemed "manifestly ludicrous . . . the delusion of a dirty old man."[47]

For these and other Protestant polemicists, the scatological and sexual rhetoric was an attempt, in Robert Scribner's words, to "desacralize the numinous and withdraw it from the realm of religious veneration."[48] But this continuing tradition was not confined to religious polemic. It occurs as a commonplace in tracts, fiction, poetry, and drama. In the last years of Henry VIII's reign, around 1546, one William Thomas, sometime tutor to Prince Edward, recorded a supposed conversation with "certain Italian gentlemen" on Henry's reform of the English Church, and what the Italians call the king's "wicked life and doings" and the fulfilling of his "his devilish desires." Thomas attacks feigned miracles, including those of the Blood of Hailes, and pilgrimages, the "running to this or that image with candles, torches, lamps, incense, bells, and a thousand other tricks," which is "so foolish a thing that me seemeth it rather meriteth to be laughed at than spoken against." Henry is praised for finding out "the falsehood of these jugglers, who led the people into this idolatry of worshipping of saints, believing of miracles, and going on pilgrimage here and there." England, laments Thomas, "in times past . . . hath been occupied with more pilgrimages than Italy," and just as Italy has "our Lady in so many places . . . even so had we our Lady of Walsingham, of Pennice, of Islington . . . And here and there ran all the world." The images of "these our Ladies" in England were, laments Thomas, even less authentic than those in Italy. Some had "engines in them that could beckon, either with their heads and hands, or move their eyes . . . to the purpose that the friars and priests would use them." The deluded pilgrims had included even Henry himself who, until "God opened his eyes, was as blind and obstinate as the rest." As the argument heats up, Thomas gives a ringing peroration on the sexual corruption of the popish Church, drawing the conventional parallels with Sodom and other cities God has destroyed. He describes the Catholic Church and the papacy in familiar sexualized terms: the Romish "Mother, Holy Church" is "an arrant whore, a fornicatress, and an adultress," just as the

---

[47] Freeman, "Offending God," 228–38.   [48] Scribner, *For the Sake of Simple Folk*, 94.

Pope, the "son of the devil, your god on earth, in fornication engendereth on your whorish Mother Church all the bastards of perdition that believe remission of sin in him by ignorance and superstition." He points with prurient satisfaction to the king's abolition of the resorts of friars and nuns who had been "whores and thieves in the open street."[49]

Fifty years after Latimer, Foxe, and Thomas, a similar rhetoric can be observed in a virulent attack on the cult of the Virgin in a sermon which William Crashaw preached at Paul's Cross in 1607, and repeated in his anti-papist polemic, *The Jesuites Gospell* (1612). He rejects the traditional Catholic doctrine, the "strange and fearefull doctrine of poperies," that "Images were good laye men's bookes," or that "Images are better and easier bookes for the laye people than bee the scriptures": the veneration or worship of images, thunders Crashaw, is "a fearefull doctrine, maintaining horrible idolatrie." He ridicules "execrable" and "incredible" statements by Catholic theologians on the intercessory powers and the status of the Virgin. He points in horror at the heresy of appealing from God to a mere creature, misnamed "the Queene of heaven," and establishing thereby "2 divine Courts: the one of Iustice, and that is Gods; the other . . . a Courte of Mercie, and that is Maries." Papists see, asserts Crashaw, "the pappes of a Woman equaled with the wounds of our lord, and her milke with his bloud." A doctrine that "Almightie GOD, (as farre as it is lawfull) hathe made his Mother fellowe and partaker of his divine power" is seen as especially blasphemous. Crashaw is derisive of the key phrase "as farre as it is lawfull," variations of which had been used in the initial phases of the establishment of Royal Supremacy in the 1530s. It is a prevarication, he asserts, which "grossly abuseth the reader and containeth horrible impiety against God."[50] He repeats the common slur that the Catholic Church turns the Virgin into a pagan goddess and "the Psalmes from *Dominus* to *Domina*, from God to our Ladies." There is a distinctively misogynic and prurient edge in Crashaw's hostility to any belief in the Virgin's intercessory powers. Not only does such a doctrine "divide" God's kingdom "with a creature," he rants, but also very specifically, "yea with a woman." Attacking the Roman Church, he vows not to "spare to discover her skirts, and lay open her filthinesse to the world; that all men seeing her as shee is, may detest and forsake her."[51] It is tempting, as MacCulloch observes on Latimer, to see such outbursts as subjective pathology. Melanie Klein comments that developmentally, the "bad parts of the self" are characteristically projected

---

[49] Thomas, *Pilgrim*, 37–44.   [50] Crashaw, *Jesuites Gospell*, 32.
[51] Crashaw, *Sermon Preached at the Cross*, 84.

in infancy upon the source of pain and repulsion, and are frequently expressed in terms of the infant's most immediate experiences of ingestion and excretion, and directed primarily against the mothering figure.[52] But with Crashaw, no less than with Latimer, we are not dealing merely with individual dyspepsia but a cultural unconscious revealing itself. Sexualized abuse of Catholicism, often intensified by association with the Virgin, in short, is a commonplace of Protestant polemic throughout the period, and we need to qualify Christine Peters's claim that "Mariolatry did not feature strongly in anti-Catholic polemic." Indeed, as Dominic Janes points out in his study of nineteenth-century iconoclasm, anti-Catholic polemic continued over many centuries to point to what continues to be seen as the inherent sexualization of Catholicism and Mariolatry in particular well after the Reformation.[53]

"Against whom," asks Carlos Eire, "or what, did iconoclasts vent their fury when they destroyed the images and altars? Was it in fact the 'idols' themselves . . . or was it the church and the social system that supported it?" Or was it something in themselves? What happened to the emotions and allegiances associated with the loss of those images? To what extent did they survive? To what, if anything, were they transferred? If it is "simplistic," as Peters warns, "to see the Reformation as involving the 'loss' of the Virgin Mary," what was done, or already had been done, to dissipate her apparent powers?[54] Were those powers a delusion? Were they, as reformers argued, part of a diabolical design (along with relics, the Mass, prayer for the dead, and indeed the whole superstructure of medieval Catholic devotion) to keep men and women in ignorance and lead them to damnation? And when the light of the gospel, and the flames of the fires, burnt brightly, did liberation and truth show forth?

The iconoclastic vehemence of the reformers – what Diane Purkiss terms their unleashing of "the death drive in a series of aggressive and repetitive acts" of destruction – was perhaps in part caused by their realization that the accounts of human purpose and salvation they had been told by the Church, and which they saw as lies and legends, existed at deeper levels in human experience than destroying an image or two, or thousands, would remove.[55] The reformers were, in effect, trying to construct new stories, more truthful, less elaborate, more reflective of a changing sense of the universe in which, as they saw it, God had a more central and powerful place that the medieval Church had neglected.

---

[52] Eire, *War Against the Idols*, 157; Klein, *Envy and Gratitude*, 25.
[53] Peters, *Patterns of Piety*, 228; Janes, *Victorian Reformation*.
[54] Peters, *Patterns of Piety*, 207–8, 215.   [55] Purkiss, "Desire and its Deformities," 6.

To put the matter that way and speak of competitive "stories" in the Reformation is not a formulation that any of the combatants would have easily accepted, and I therefore now come to one of those moments about which I warned those readers who like their history verifiably documentable and presented in the discursive conventions of what we used to call the "texts themselves." In my introductory remarks, I described my approach in this book as "lightly worn presentism." Texts are, as Tony Bennett points out, always "texts in use"; inevitably, we pose questions that come from a particular ideological formation, which is, however slightly, always shifting. Furthermore, in trying to focus on the deep-seated ideological changes brought about by the Reformation, we are necessarily reading at the edges of dominant cultural practices, in the gaps and fissures, seeking for the unsaids, even the unsayables, as well as the saids. At times, therefore, the safety of empirically based historical and textual exegesis must be supplemented, even replaced, by some degree of speculation within discursive frameworks, Bennett's "reading formations," that were not available to those at the time.[56] Madeline Caviness, writing on medieval art, points out that some aspects of a culture can only be understood or even evoked by later discourses since "Western culture has been slow in bringing them to words."[57] In her history of the interactions of witchcraft, sexuality, and religion in early modern Europe, Lyndal Roper similarly argues that we need somehow to acknowledge the "importance of the irrational unconscious in history," not as deduced from documents but as experienced in the bodies of men and women,"[58] and we may have to wait for adequate words to become available, and always be prepared to rethink and tentatively re-state our speculations.

In puzzling over the transition from the overwhelming presence of the Virgin Mary in late medieval culture to her "re-negotiation" or "disappearance" in Protestant England, I have found two modern discourses in particular up to which I have "sidled," to repeat Beattie's appropriation of Irigaray's phrase, and which have helped formulate my questions. Neither is especially fashionable in combination with traditional historicist scholarship. One surfaces fitfully, usually in a highly mediated form, in literary and cultural criticism, especially when it interacts with cultural, not merely clinical, analysis, and that is psychoanalysis. The second is also rare in literary criticism, except where denominational or confessional allegiances are explicit, and that is Catholic feminist theology. I am not an advocate for

---

[56] Bennett, "Texts, Reader and Reading Formations," 3–7.
[57] Caviness, *Visualizing Women*, 7.   [58] Roper, *Oedipus and the Devil*, 3.

either – I claim no master discourse in this study – but I have found the questions posed by these sometimes contradictory, sometimes overlapping, discourses invaluable for opening a discussion – both with others and within myself. Written records, even historical events, may appear open to inspection and analysis; the bodies and the feelings that animated them within a different ideological framework are less accessible. In this case, the notion of "body" is further complicated by one of the bodies in question being an extraordinarily mythologized body which still, today, excites a huge range of emotions ranging from absolute devotion, even voluntary "slavery," to scorn and denigration. Both of these discourses have, therefore, allowed me to pose questions to my subject that older historicisms would have felt were illegitimate, undocumentable, unverifiable, but without which I could not shape my argument – or, in the metaphor that keeps surfacing, and with which Kristeva makes so much suggestive play, my own "stories."

From the late 1980s, the sociologist Michael Carroll has been a pioneer in the application of psychoanalytic models to Christian and specifically Catholic popular religion, yet only rarely has his work impacted on literary and cultural criticism. Andrew Greeley, the American Catholic priest, sociologist, and novelist, calls him " a dragon slayer . . . a major force in the sociology of religion, more of an influence than he himself may realize because the dragons have not fought back."[59] In the 1980s, Carroll puzzled over the inexplicable "failure of psychoanalysis to take any significant interest in the study of popular Catholicism," and his early attempts to correct that failure remain a challenge to those of us attempting to work in this often fraught area. His studies of popular religion have been primarily focused on Italy. Some of his early work has been criticized for an unmediated and over-simplifying Freudianism, but he points out that while many of the hypotheses and observations of Freud and his followers may be outdated, the Freudian model retains an uncanny power as a tool of cultural analysis, and is particularly well suited to popular religion, since we are looking at the shared desires and fears of a local community. As he puts it, "what otherwise seems problematic about popular Catholic beliefs and practices becomes intelligible" when they are "viewed through a psychoanalytic lens."[60] Carroll's later work has moved further afield, both theoretically and geographically, to Ireland, the Americas, and, most recently, to late medieval England, focusing less on the differences across Europe in popular religion than the similarities. Carroll's work is all the more impressive for its reverence toward its often sensitive subject matter, and he

---

[59] Greeley, "[review of] *American Catholics*," 101–2.   [60] Carroll, *Irish Pilgrimage*, 167.

frequently gives credit for the tone he adopts to the pioneering studies of the early twentieth-century Jesuit Herbert Thurston.[61]

Working in the same tradition, particularly in his stimulating analysis of St. Rose of Lima, Frank Graziano has explored what he terms "cultural psychology," which uses psychoanalysis but sees symptomatic behavior and fantasies not as aberrations but as "truths of the speaking subject" within specific historical and social formations. He sees the cultural historian's position not as "demeaning or displacing the studied culture," but rather "adding another interpretive layer on what anomalous manifestations – corporal or psychological – can mean when disparate cultures come into contact." It would be, he argues, an unnecessary "handicap" to not use "theoretical and scientific advances that have radically altered human knowledge" and "given us the interpretive capacity to understand these texts in ways not previously possible."[62]

Klaus Theweleit's related blend of sociology and cultural psychoanalysis, derived from Deleuze and Guattari rather than Freud, has a similarly nuanced discussion of authoritarian "soldier-males" in Western history and their attitudes to the female. His now classic study, *Male Fantasies,* is of special interest when we consider the cultural context of devotion to and revulsion from the Virgin in the late medieval and Reformation period. Theweleit focused on the proto-Fascist *Freikorps* in 1920s Germany, but his findings were continually directed toward an ominous wider context, and include some powerful observations on the psychological patterns of masculinity in late medieval and early modern Europe, and in particular the place of the Virgin in the period's characteristic "male fantasies." Theweleit sees European history as illustrating a continuing male obsession with the female body that manifests itself in a simultaneous desire for and fear of fusion with that body, "as if two male compulsions were tearing at the women with equal strength. One is trying to push them away, to keep them at arm's length . . . the other to penetrate them, to have them very near." [63] Theweleit argues that we are not dealing with individual "male fantasies" but broadly shared social and cultural tendencies, the dominant ideology of masculinization in particular historical periods – the ways by which the masculine self is constructed by education, social structures, and in the case of the medieval and Reformation periods, especially through the multiple apparatuses, repressive and ideological, of the Church. He observes that in

[61] For early reactions to his work, see Carroll, "Interview: Praying the Rosary"; for a particularly positive view, see Andrew Greeley's reviews of *Madonnas that Maim* and *American Catholics.*
[62] Graziano, *Wounds of Love,* 18–19.   [63] Theweleit, *Male Fantasies,* I, 196.

looking at the medieval idealization of the Virgin, we are observing what men "loved first – woman and mother," becoming "that which they must learn to despise in others and suppress within themselves," with the denigration of the female developing as "a permanent reality which derives from the specific social organization of gender relations in patriarchal Europe."[64]

In that direction, I think, lies the basis for understanding important aspects of early modern controversies over the Virgin, and I will sidle up to all three scholars in the course of this book. The second area of intellectual exploration to which I am indebted in formulating my approach is contemporary feminist Catholic Mariology, especially the writings of Tina Beattie, whose books, essays and incidental papers since the mid 1990s have stood out for their boldness, clarity, and above all their challenge to the dominant masculinist history of Catholicism. Beattie's writings have been particularly helpful to me in searching for what in Chapter 2 I introduce to the discussion as alternate views of sexuality and gender identity in the late medieval veneration of the Virgin. In the Reformation, she argues, we watch Mary the mother–queen–goddess being replaced by the meek and obedient vehicle of the father's will, and yet the history of Christianity shows where quite different, more woman-centered, decisions about sexuality, the body, and the Virgin herself might have been made.[65]

Third, in a sense touching on, if not by any means reconciling, all these diverse worlds of psychoanalysis, history, and feminist theology, is the work of Julia Kristeva. Beattie comments that it is odd that Christianity and psychoanalysis have not come together more frequently to pose the questions of being since they both claim humanity is "marked by originating experience of catastrophic loss that gives rise to an insatiable yearning for restoration and wholeness."[66] Throughout her extraordinary career as psychoanalyst, philosopher, feminist, novelist, and public intellectual, Kristeva has made that a major project. The self-styled "Christian Atheist" has been fascinated by stories of the Virgin and what they might open up for women and, indeed, for men. In addition to her celebrated essays on motherhood, abjection, and women's language, in her lectures, *In the Beginning was Love*, given to students at l'École Sainte Geneviève, a Catholic school in Versailles, Kristeva offers some powerful insights into the place of Mary in Western history. Religion, in her view, may be "nothing less than illusion," but it is "a glorious one," an "unrealistic construct" which through its stories can nevertheless give us accurate representations of the "reality of

---

[64] *Ibid.*, i, xvi, 79.   [65] Beattie, *God's Mother*, 4, 38–39; *New Catholic Feminism*, 10.
[66] Beattie, *God's Mother*, 45.

its subjects' dreams" as we "destabilized" human subjects search for stabi-
lization.[67] Kristeva asserts that although the image and associated stories of
Mary constructed by the Church may have been a primary means by which
it has tried to keep potential power of the female under paternal control, and
so helped to "infantalize half the human race by hampering their sexual and
intellectual expression," we should nevertheless consider that the stories
embodying such religious beliefs are projections of fantasies which reveal
the primal bedrock of our identities, and therefore should be listened to
with care.[68] Quoting Philippe Sollers, Kristeva puns that the "hole" of the
Virgin, both the genital gap and the "empty space left for Mary" around
which "the members of the Christian Trinity revolve," is the center of the
most profound of human fantasies. That (w)hole represents where we come
from and where we will return.[69]

In such remarks, Kristeva poses the question with which I started this
study and which continues to fascinate me, just as I believe it does our time,
and perhaps every time, in Western history: what are the stories which we
have projected upon the elusive figure of the Virgin? And to what extent
were there alternate stories that might have been more liberatory than
repressive? One on which Kristeva focuses is the "censorship of Mary's
sexuality" which, she asserts, has been the most devastating erasure of
human pleasure and fulfillment in our history. Another powerful story of
which the Virgin has been the center and by which our history has been
haunted, is the fantasy that we can overcome "the unthinkable of death by
postulating maternal love in its place," and so move beyond the rule of the
father.[70] The bodies of women, Kristeva proclaims – echoing an ancient
view of the apotropaic power of women's sexuality – provide a "strange
intersection," a meeting place of physical and spiritual fantasies which are
focused on "the *jouissance* of" the "reproductive body."[71] The questions
posed by Kristeva in such remarks will recur throughout this study as
I probe the literature and some aspects of the popular culture of the
transition, in England, between the medieval and early modern worlds.

Is a revitalization of the image of the Virgin possible? Or is a study of the
Virgin, especially a historically rooted one, merely an exercise in nostalgia? It
is a question which has been, in all honesty, never far from my mind as
I started this work. As I will discuss in my final chapter, when I revisit some
of these more general questions, in her optimism that a historically rich
image can have a further life if we reach behind its hitherto repressive stories

[67] Kristeva, *In the Beginning was Love*, 19.   [68] Kristeva, *Feminine and the Sacred*, 76.   [69] *Ibid.*, 78.
[70] *Ibid.*, 76; *Tales of Love*, 22.   [71] Kristeva, *Feminine and the Sacred*, 178.

and ask what further ones lie at deeper levels in our individual or collective unconscious, Kristeva differs from the verdict of Marina Warner's celebrated conclusion to her classic, richly detailed but finally grimly pessimistic study of the Virgin, *Alone of All Her Sex,* that there are no eternal myths, and that today the Virgin has been emptied of any moral significance and "will lose its present real powers" to both "heal" and "harm."[72] Kristeva takes a more optimistic view – and one not just directed to women. Near the end of her exchange of letters with Catherine Clément, she observes that women "perhaps, stand at that intersection in a more dramatic, more symptomatic manner, in a more unknown manner in the future that is upon us. I say 'perhaps' because there is always the surprise – and often even a happy surprise – of the 'feminine' in men as well."[73]

Beattie rejects Kristeva's move beyond Christianity. From the margins of that debate, I would comment that these great master discourses are understandably rivals, but together they do help many of the great questions of our existence to be posed. A re-envisioning of the Virgin might, as the Liberation theologians put it, bridge the gap between Mary and ordinary women, something I see especially occurring in late medieval and early modern England, although in multiple and contradictory ways, not least in medieval drama (Chapter 3), Petrarchan love poetry (Chapter 6), and in Shakespeare's *The Winter's Tale* (Chapter 7).

This book, then, is offered as a dialogue between – or rather since there are many involved, a polylogue among – many voices, read from a shifting present, centered on how English writers from the later Middle Ages to the mid seventeenth century both venerated and denigrated a body, probably a historical, certainly a mythologized, body, multiple "images" of which were burnt, in the summer or the autumn of 1538, publicly or privately, certainly at the order and possibly at the house of Thomas Cromwell, in London. That seemingly definitive act, however, remains ambiguous, and did not by any means end the presence of the Virgin in the life and feelings of England. Catholic historians and theologians have argued that Cromwell, Latimer, and their generation of reformers created a huge and perhaps unhealable wound in the collective psyche of early modern England, creating a "disembodied and defeminized Culture."[74] The extent to which this is true, and why, and how we might construct the many stories that tried to account for it, will be what I explore in the following chapters.

---

[72] Warner, *Alone of All Her Sex*, 339.   [73] Kristeva, *Feminine and the Sacred*, 178.
[74] Beattie, *Woman,* 135.

The Virgin Mary in late medieval culture to 1538

CHAPTER 2

The sexualization of the Virgin
in the late Middle Ages

Conflicts over the nature and power of the Virgin Mary have shaped Christianity from its beginnings, but likely never more strongly than the long period of transition in England from late medieval to early modern. Both the physical body of the Virgin and its representations and symbolizations become matters of intellectual controversy, powerful feelings and, all too frequently, conflict and violence. At the heart of the Catholic theological tradition, Tina Beattie maintains, is a symbolic space centered on the Virgin so central that its version of Christianity "is not fully coherent without it."[1] That was emphatically not the view of the reformers, who believed vehemently that the medieval Church had sexualized that space and filled it with sinful fantasies and idols. In this chapter, I will sketch out the issues of sexuality, physical and metaphorical, related to the Virgin which became central points of conflict, raising questions not only of how she was depicted, venerated or denigrated, but also the implications for real women, and for the men who responded to them, too often in ways that used a fantasized account of the Virgin's body and sexuality to denigrate them. The subject of this chapter is female bodies, one an intensely mythologized body, the subject of many stories, especially concerning its generative and maternal functions, but as well, I will argue in this and subsequent chapters, impacting deeply on the bodies of female pilgrims and worshippers, and of women's bodies generally.

In their everyday devotions, Eamon Duffy comments, when ordinary late medieval men and women prayed, they usually prayed to the Virgin.[2] Theologians might point out that Mary's role in salvation was strictly intercessory, and that we go through her (as we do lesser saints) to God, but, as Michael Carroll asks of Italian popular religion, what is it, "or rather *who* is it, that holds so many people, both rich and poor, from their homes every year, and that pulls them to ... distant sanctuaries?

---

[1] Beattie, "Redeeming Mary,"107; *God's Mother*, xi, 6.   [2] Duffy, *Faith of our Fathers*, 101.

31

It is not usually a saint, and is certainly not Christ. It is Mary." Popular piety stressed that access to the Virgin was quite independent of her Son: even so traditional a Catholic historian as Hilda Graef acknowledges that late medieval Mariology became "an independent subject in which pious imagination was allowed to run riot."[3] In the so-called Pynson Ballad, a poetical guide to the great shrine of the Virgin at Walsingham, the miracles that are celebrated, which include even the raising of the dead, are attributed not to Christ, but quite explicitly to his mother. The ballad's striking claim for the powers of the Virgin would have appalled the reformers. She is, in a startling (though for the fifteenth century, an unexceptional) phrase, the "Chyef pryncypyll and grounde of oure saluacyon."[4]

Richard Marks points to the "massive expansion" of representations of the Virgin in fourteenth- and fifteenth-century parish churches. But Madonnas, he points out, "not only multiplied," they also "diversified." Sir Thomas More pointed out to reformers such as Tyndale that the various ladies – such as those of Walsingham, Ipswich, and, nearer to his home in Chelsea, at Willesden, to which he made a pilgrimage just before he was imprisoned – were "but the images of our Lady herself."[5] With their origins in the stories generated by hundreds of years of popular religion rather than orthodox theology, the multiple Madonnas of medieval England played different roles in various localities: they stood guard over individual and collective lives, worked miracles, cured and appeased the sick and suffering, warded off disasters, offered special intercession for the living and dead, and made constant interventions, experienced by men and women as favors or punishments, into every moment of space and time. In doing so, these local Madonnas stayed close to the everyday experiences of local Christians. The explosion of Marian devotion in the later Middle Ages reveals an increasingly humanized Virgin who embodied what Teresa Coletti terms the "material fact of divine carnality," rather than the austere, powerful Queen of Heaven who had dominated the art and devotion of the High Middle Ages.[6] This emergent Virgin can be observed, as Chapter 3 will show, in poetry, prose romance, and drama, as well as in art and everyday devotion, showing the centrality of the Virgin within the structure of feeling

---

[3] Graef, *Mary*, I, 65; Carroll, *Madonnas that Maim*, 25.

[4] The unique copy of the Pynson Ballad is in Magdalene College, Cambridge, Pepys Library item 125; Dickinson, *Shrine*, 127–9.

[5] Marks, *Image and Devotion*, 121; More, *Dialogue concerning Tyndale, Works*, VIII, 164. For More's pilgrimage to Willesden, Mitjans, "Thomas More's Veneration of Images," 67–8.

[6] Coletti, *Mary Magdalene*, 204.

of the late Middle Ages, and making her supposed disappearance in England in the next century all the more intriguing.

Afraid that the Virgin's powers meant that she and not her son would be believed to be the intercessor between mankind and God – "putting her beades in the balaunce" is Cranmer's scornful phrase[7] – the reformers attempted to remove, or at least severely curtail, both the theology and the popular devotional practices through which the late medieval Church celebrated the Virgin. As they saw it, Mary, not Christ, had disproportionately become the focus of people's deepest yearnings. Why, asked Luther, was Mary venerated when her role was at best an example of obedience, and essentially that of providing Jesus with a womb for nine months? Or, as it was put more disparagingly by Latimer and others, when she was but a pudding sack or a "bag of saffron . . . when the spice was out," a slur that was sufficiently *au courant* in 1536 to be specifically named and banned as heretical.[8]

The reformers believed that medieval theology and devotion had sexualized the Virgin by excessive, idolatrous attention to her body, and by venerating the material details, however trivial or apocryphal, of events in Mariological history. As Donna Ellington puts it, "Mary's bodily human nature was the cornerstone of the entire medieval edifice of the Virgin's cult."[9] At a further level of idolatry, the veneration of bodily and material objects associated with Mary's body – hair, milk, girdles, for example – was accorded, in the eyes of the reformers, a blasphemous magic simply because of their alleged physical proximity to her or even, because they had been touched, to a relic of hers. They attacked the "fetishization" of individual parts and accoutrements of the Virgin's body – a term that might appear as a modern anachronism but which was, in fact, already becoming current among Protestant polemicists to deride what they saw as superstitious religious practices of pagans and Catholics alike.[10]

The reformers, were, on the one hand, at least on a superficial level, accurate in their perception of the medieval sexualization of the Virgin. Although Mary was encoded theologically as a woman outside ordinary sexuality, and therefore sealed off from the intimate details of female bodily functions, she was in fact nonetheless insistently sexualized in medieval devotion, art, and popular culture and, not least, within theology. However

---

[7] Cranmer, *Short Instruction*, 23.
[8] Strype, *Works*, I, i, 442; A.G., *Widowes Mite*, sig F. See also Fissell, *Vernacular Bodies*, 25. For Mary in Lutheran theology, see Kreitzer, *Reforming Mary*.
[9] Ellington, *Sacred Body to Angelic Soul*, 31. See also MacCulloch, *Reformation*, 639.
[10] For the background of "fetish" in the late Middle Ages and early modern period, see the seminal essays by Pietz.

hard the Church tried to isolate Mary from ordinary human sexuality, there repeatedly surfaced what the modern liberation theologian Mario Ribas terms "an infused sexuality in relation to the sacred mother."[11] But, on the other hand, the intensely sexualized language and violent actions of the reformers themselves betray a high level of their own uneasiness before the body-centeredness of Christianity, what the Marian Bishop Bonner called the "receyvynge of our nature and flesshe."[12] In doing so, they were, arguably, not only dramatically shifting the underlying basis of Christian theology and devotion, but also denigrating their own sexuality and bodily natures. Quite apart from the question of the truth of the diverging traditions of Christianity, the Protestant view of Mary, argues Beattie, "easily lends itself to the denigration of the female body," not only "its sexual and maternal functions," but also as the basis for both individual and relational being.[13] That dual claim – that the reformers were, in effect, empirically correct about the medieval sexualization of Christianity but at some deeper level mistaken about human sexuality – will be a major suggestion of this study.

In her discussion of the art of the High Middle Ages, Madeline Caviness comments on the hidden "gynecological power" underneath the "heavily draped idealized figure" of the Virgin.[14] I use the similar term *gynotheology* to refer to a high degree of concern, sometimes seemingly obsessive, within medieval (and later) Mariology, with the gynecological, the female sexual and reproductive apparatus and functions. It is an emphasis shared, paradoxically, by both late medieval Mariology and its Reformation opponents. Whether it involved deeply misogynic revulsion or the attribution of a level of mystical power rooted in the details of being female – and, as Freud taught us, often such idealization and denigration are found together – the common thread is a level of detailed concern with the significance of the gynecological. When, in his semi-fictional account of a visit to Walsingham, Erasmus's character Ogygius is asked whether he wishes to see the "secrets" or "pryvytes" of the Virgin, and he pauses coyly before commenting that he wasn't quite sure what was meant by the phrase, we should see not merely a risqué joke but a serious theological and broader philosophical issue.[15]

"Gynotheology" elevates a mythologized biology of being female to a universal metaphysical and material principle.[16] It is a term that may be met

[11] Ribas, "Liberating Mary, Liberating the Poor," 135.
[12] Bonner, quoted in Tydeman, *Mary Tudor's Church*, 87.   [13] Beattie, *God's Mother*, 131.
[14] Caviness, *Visualizing Women*, 2.   [15] Erasmus, *Pilgrimage*, 64.
[16] For an earlier and more summary discussion of "gynotheology," see Waller, "The Virgin's 'Pryvytes.'" For comment on the term, see Morrison, "Waste Space," 58. Beattie, *God's Mother*, 156–8, advocates a "gynocentric" [sic] reading of Marian symbolism; Althaus-Reid, *Indecent Theology*, 47–63, discusses the "vulvic" symbolism of Marian apparitions and representations of Our Lady of Guadalupe; Jane

with surprise, perhaps on the grounds of taste, a criticism similarly directed against one of the modern works of scholarship on which I draw, Leo Steinberg's classic study of the representation of "Christianity's greatest taboo," Christ's sexuality, *The Sexuality of Christ in Renaissance Art and Modern Oblivion*. As Rosemary Ruether notes, "to ask about the sexuality of Jesus is for most Christians to border on blasphemy. Even for Protestants the basic image of Jesus is that of sexlessness." Steinberg comments that "normative Christian culture has disallowed direct reference" to Christ's sexual organs or sexuality: he notes, by contrast, the willingness of late medieval and Renaissance artists "to place this interdicted flesh at the center of their confession of faith." He argues that modern discussions of the fusion of the erotic and the theological are characterized by what he terms "modern oblivion" – although the issues at stake in fact go back to the early Church's controversies over the representation of divine personages. Deep in the history of Christianity, Steinberg argues, there lay a battle with the docetic heresy that saw Jesus as divine but not fully human. Pointing to the remarkable number of late medieval and Renaissance representations of him as a baby with an erect penis, including many where it is being fondled or displayed by the Virgin and sometimes his grandmother St. Anne, Steinberg raises the question in relation to Christ, asking – akin to my posing the questions about Mariological gynotheology – is there "a genital theology" implied by these representations of Christ? What is the relationship between the theological and the genital, not just as represented in the art work, but also apprehended in the viewer's mind and emotions? In their revulsion from the human body, he suggests, theologians in the dominant Augustinian tradition may have too often drifted toward docetism; it was the artists who pulled them back.[17]

As Frank Graziano comments, in the 1980s Steinberg's views provoked much polemical scholarship concerning the relationship between theology and eroticism. Carolyn Walker Bynum argued indignantly that medieval viewers of Christ's flesh did not understand the art as sexual: they did not see the representation of Christ's penis in sexual terms, and they viewed the Virgin's breasts "primarily" as food.[18] A lot of weight rested on "primarily"

Caputi, "Naked Goddess," 186, calls for the "holy sites" of "gynocentrism" to be reclaimed; Glancy, *Corporal Knowledge*, 127, speaks of "theology from the womb." I am grateful to the anonymous readers for Cambridge University Press for suggestions on an early version of this chapter.

[17] Steinberg, *Sexuality of Christ*, 16, 219, 238, 110; Ruether, "The Sexuality of Jesus," 134–7.

[18] Graziano, *Wounds of Love*, 10–12. Martha Easton summarizes the "famously acrimonious debate" between Steinberg and Bynum in "Was it Good for You, Too?" 3. For specifics, see Bynum, *Jesus as Mother*, *Holy Fast*, 79–117, and "The Body of Christ in the Later Middle Ages," 79–117; Steinberg, *Sexuality*, 364–89.

in this argument, and subsequent iconographical readings have sided with Steinberg. Explicitly erotic references or representations of Christ may point toward spirituality but they remain erotic. Considering the Virgin in this context, what Ribas terms her "divine vaginality," and Erasmus, half jokingly, her "pryvytes" may, however, all too easily provoke even more extreme modern "oblivion." Boss echoes Steinberg's observation that "the modern aversion from Mary's physical motherhood" is accompanied by "a certain embarrassment of some commentators in the face of descriptions of pregnancy and parturition."[19] In her reading of the Gospel of Matthew, Jane Scharberg comments on a reviewer's indignation that she should discuss intimate details of Mary's pregnancy as a topic inappropriate for "polite company."[20]

Medieval literature and popular culture are certainly full of erotic representations of the genitalia of ordinary women. They are imagined, described, evoked, joked about, celebrated, in the work of jongleurs, galliards, in Chaucer, in popular ballads, in plays. In *Le Roman de la Rose*, the poem's pilgrim-lover draws back the curtain, suggesting the opening of the labia, and breaks down the barrier in the "little opening." The much sought-after rose lies inside the sanctuary and in the final lines of the poem "opens up" after a few drops of "dew" are sprinkled on it.[21] But it is, after all, the Virgin's apparent independence of such sexualization that supposedly makes her acceptable as the Mother of God and Queen of Heaven. Mary's vagina is perpetually sealed, her vulva discreetly closed, her hymen unbroken, her clitoris barely if ever mentioned. But her sexual organs are not totally invisible. "Although," as Miri Rubin comments, references to the "most private feminine part . . . strained propriety," and were linked to the womb's associations with "disorder" and "pollution," nonetheless the Virgin's "pryvytes" appear over and over in symbols right across the culture, tinged with religious significance and often the object of awe and devotion.[22] The vulva-shaped mandorla, often accompanying or enclosing representations of the Virgin herself or the Virgin and Child, is widespread across medieval (and later) art; the numerous Sheela-na-Gigs (representing, it is widely suggested, the repressed goddess which the early Church theologians saw the Virgin transcending) in gargoyles and other church decorations, and even the pattern of Gothic church architecture itself with its open arch and long narrow interior, opened or, as Caviness puts it, the

[19] Ribas, "Liberating Mary," 135; Erasmus, *Pilgrimage*, 64.
[20] Scharberg, "Feminist Interpretations," 32–3. See the perceptive discussion in Glancy, *Corporal Knowledge*, ch. 4.
[21] Lewis, "Images of Opening, Penetration and Closure," 215–42.   [22] Rubin, *Mother of God*, 343.

displaying or "disemboweling" of the Virgin "in the entrance to the architectural space of the Church-as-Mary."[23] The architectural historian Dan
Cruickshank makes the case for the association of the Order of the Garter
and the *visica pisces,* the sign of the fish representing the Virgin's genitalia as
"both the symbolic representation of the generative power of the female and
the place through which the saviour of mankind entered the world." Susan
Morrison, drawing on many studies of pilgrimage art (a matter which will
be further discussed in Chapter 4) points to the common representations of
holy (and parody) female genitalia in pilgrimage souvenirs and badges,
many of which refer to the Annunciation and Nativity.[24]

Add to this ubiquitous symbolism, with its stylized but explicit representations of the Virgin's sexual organs, the increasingly realistic artistic
representations of her pregnancy and the Nativity itself, many of which
show the pain, exhaustion, and at times coming close to what a modern
Catholic writer calls a "genuine childbirth, with the mother's customary
pains and post-partum blues and the child's pollution," and the suckling
and nurturing of the Christ child.[25] Margaret Miles, Madeline Caviness,
and other art historians have shown how early medieval representations of
the nursing Virgin attempt to stress the theological rather than any erotic
significance. Before the thirteenth or fourteenth centuries, the Virgin's
breasts are usually severely de-eroticized (thus of course acknowledging
the lurking presence of potential erotic associations) by displaying only
one breast – often strangely disembodied, as if lying loosely on the upper
chest close to the collarbone, like a compressed sack, with the other side of
the chest flat. Over time, however, representations of Mary's breasts become
increasingly eroticized, turning, Easton comments, into "a multivalent
symbol of motherhood, femininity, and erotic longing." Celebrated examples are the fantasy-visions of the Virgin's milk being squirted through the
air to St. Bernard, or projected toward sufferers in Purgatory, angels and
humans catching drops while the Virgin is nursing, or (in a favorite motif of
the Virgin's intercessory role) having her exhibit her breasts as part of her
pleading with God the Father or her son, thus adding a suggestion of incest
to the exhibitionism motif. Increasingly anatomical accuracy of representations became more prevalent in the century prior to the Reformation, often

[23] Caviness, *Visualizing Women,* 1–30. For the sexual symbolism of the mandorla, see Blackledge, *The Story of V,* 52–4; Rubin, *Mother of God,* 63, 340. For the sheelas, see Easton, "Was It Good for You, Too?" 15–16; Weir and Jerman, *Images of Lust.*

[24] Cruickshank, *Britain's Best Buildings,* 57–69; Morrison, "Waste Space," 53–61; Whittington, "The Cruciform Womb," 9–10.

[25] Neyrey, "Mediterranean Maid," 65–75.

with the outline or even the full exposure of a second breast at a time when representations of women's breasts were intensely eroticized in portraits or frescoes for rich clients.[26]

Caviness argues that the increasing realism of depictions of the Virgin in the later Middle Ages and Renaissance dramatically increased their potential sexual suggestiveness so that "subjects that were not erotic in the abstract modes of representation of Romanesque art became disturbingly sado-erotic in the more and more graphic representations of physicality" of the later period. Easton comments on naked images of St. Catherine, and her point can be extended more broadly, "it must have taken an unusually resistant viewer" to not experience the erotic attraction, "beyond the theological," of such evidently sexual images.[27] A frequently cited landmark late in the period is Fouquet's use of Agnès Sorel, the king's mistress, in a *Madonna lactans* pose, her femininity and sexuality boldly foregrounded. Caravaggio's use of a notorious prostitute as the model for the Virgin is well known; another famous merging of sexuality with the representation of the Virgin and Child is the fresco pained by Pinturicchio for Pope Alexander VI's bedroom, where the model for Virgin was the Pope's eighteen-year-old mistress, Giulia Farnese.[28] By the mid sixteenth century, it is clear that many reformers (both Protestant and Tridentine) felt unease, even distaste and revulsion, at certain kinds of intimate representation of the Virgin, and that they sensed a degree of indulgent sexuality in devotion, art, and theology that did not accord with the orthodox unease before the sexualized body.

Evidence for extending Steinberg's argument to representations of the Virgin's sexuality at the level of popular culture is therefore not hard to find and has been frequently documented. But he is wrong to say that such popular and artistic flirtations with anatomic speculation were not also found in serious theology or in the evolving dogmatic pronouncements of the Church. The physicality of Mary's body parts became a matter of pious yet frank discussion once the early Church moved to interpret Mary's virginity. At the Councils of Constantinople (553) and Lateran (640), the Church decided to particularize the anatomy of the Virgin Birth, specifically decreeing that Mary's hymen remained intact, before, during, and after Christ's birth. For a thousand years (and more), theologians explicated this decision. A theological decision preceded but needed to be authenticated in

---

[26] Miles, *Complex Delight*.   [27] Easton, "Was It Good for You, Too?" 4, 9.
[28] Caviness, *Visualizing Women*, 36; Holmes, *Fra Lippo Lippi*, 191, 207; Rubin, *Mother of God*, 177–82, discusses the increasing realism of late medieval Marianization.

the physical. The hymen was seen as the most reliable part of the body by which to authenticate her perpetual virginity. It was as if the womanly nature of the Virgin was open for men to probe and cast their curious or prurient eyes into the heart of a mystery.[29] Beattie argues that the theologians largely accepted a "fundamental incompatibility between sex and God" rather than embracing the transformation of the flesh and therefore the inherent goodness of the body as represented in the Mother.[30]

What is at issue here is something more than metaphors of idealized eroticism, which was certainly a strong tradition, especially in high medieval court culture. The Virgin was certainly often described by some theologians in idealized erotic terms – when St. Bernard, for example, speaks of her as a "girl" who "I do not know by what caresses, pledges, or violence, seduced, deceived, and if I may say so, wounded and encaptured the divine heart." But medieval gynotheology goes beyond such idealized effusions to speculate on the supposed physical details of the Virgin's sexual and reproductive anatomy in the context of her perpetual virginity – her womb, birth canal, vagina, hymen, and capacity to generate moisture were all legitimate subjects of pious speculation. The womb could be rendered primarily as a symbol since it was sufficiently interior to her body to permit appropriate discussion. Her more external sexual parts and functions became more awkward to mythologize. Most especially, it was the Virgin's hymen, and not just what it represents but its physical nature – in effect what "it" looked (or, as I shall suggest in my discussions of late medieval Marian drama in Chapter 3, felt) like – that above all else is repeatedly fetishized.

The belief that Mary gave birth without breaking the hymen or (to be more anatomically accurate) making physical changes to the birth canal involves, of course, a level of primitive and anachronistic anatomy that was pre-determined by the theology, and was blatantly entangled with gynophobic, misogynist, and what Jane Caputi labels as "frankly infantile" (predominantly, perhaps exclusively, male) fantasies. There are alternate stories that the Christ Child miraculously just appears, perhaps in a burst of light in the way a magical universe in a child's fantasy operates. To adapt an observation of Michael Carroll's, today any adult patient in an analyst's care telling such stories would probably become the subject of professional care and invited to partake of a variety of therapies, be given some elementary biology lessons, and be counseled not to confuse the surface world of Harry

---

[29] For discussions of the existence of the hymen in the early Church, see Sissa, "Maidenhood without Maidenhead," 339–64.

[30] Beattie, "Queen of Heaven," 206–7.

Potter or Narnia with reality. But however anachronistic or even patholog-
ical such obsessions appear today – and in fairness, many in effect appeared
so to many reformers, both Protestants and even a few Catholics – the effect
was not to distance but intensify the obsessive concern with the Virgin's
sexuality. By intensifying its focus on the Virgin's body, medieval gynotheology accorded the sexual/reproductive apparatus and functions of the
Virgin, what Theresa Coletti terms her "boundaries and openings," a level
of mystical power that made them obsessively central to salvation.[31]

Beattie's Catholic feminist analysis of the early Church fathers is
extremely helpful in this respect. There was, she argues, a debate in the
early Church or, as she puts it, "at least in embryonic form" a "dual
theology" regarding women's place in salvation history that included giving
female sexuality a more central and creative place. The orthodox understanding of the Virgin attempted to exclude any explicit affirmation of
ordinary female sexuality. Augustine's attributed phrase of graphic revulsion
against gestation and birthing as degrading (we are "born between faeces
and urine") and the transmitter of original sin to each generation, or
Chrysostom's diatribes against female physicality ("nothing less than
phlegm, blood, bile, rheum, and the fluid of digested food") are not
aberrations. The inherent sinfulness of bodily functions – sexuality, ingestion, secretion, elimination – echoes throughout medieval theologies of the
human, especially the female, body. For Tertullian, woman's overt physicality proved she was the gateway of the devil, and, he accused, "you
destroyed so early, God's image, man. On account of your desert – that
is, death – even the Son of God had to die."[32]

There are, for example, incessant solemn discussions that have seemed
"at best simplistic and at worst crude" to later historians on whether the
Virgin ingested ordinary or "heavenly" food, and whether she excreted.
Another recurring question about female anatomy that specifically brought
the gynotheological to the fore is: did the Virgin menstruate? In many
societies, menstrual blood has been held (at least in the male imaginary) to
have uncanny powers, linking women's bodies to supernatural forces, and
therefore at once fascinating and contaminating, provoking what Kristeva
terms "abjection," the mixture of fascination and horror at extreme and
marginal experiences, most of which are associated with the female body.[33]

---

[31] Caputi, "On the Lap of Necessity," 4; Carroll, *Catholic Cults*, 3; Coletti, "Purity and Danger," 86.
[32] Ellington, *From Sacred Body to Angelic Soul*, 48.
[33] Kristeva, *Powers of Horror*, 54; Glancy, *Corporal Knowledge*, 109–18. For medieval attitudes to
menstruation, see Wood, "The Doctor's Dilemma."

Aquinas, following Galen rather than Aristotle (who saw the woman's role in procreation as essentially passive), argued that in sexual intercourse the heat of desire brings menstrual blood to the female genital area to achieve conception, but any blood used in the conception of Jesus could never have traveled for such a reason: "on the contrary," he affirms, "the operation of the Holy Spirit brought completely pure and untainted blood directly to the Virgin's womb." As Beattie ironically notes, commenting from within the Christian tradition, Christianity "has never accommodated the fertile, sexual, bleeding female body into its symbolic life."[34]

Such discreet references are as close as theological discussion seems to get (except in modern feminist theology or cultural studies) to any recognition of the Virgin's possession or use of the female organ of sexual pleasure, the clitoris. Karma Lochrie points out that, as with most aspects of women's sexual and reproductive anatomy, medieval Europe had a "messy and incoherent flux of ideas" about the clitoris. Greek and Arabic traditions did provide medieval medicine with some information, but the organ was primarily seen as pathological (when large) or leading to uncontrollable female sexual pleasure, neither of which states would be linked with the Virgin.[35] But to formulate an argument against the Virgin's experiencing sexual pleasure, even to oppose it, involves thinking, even negatively, about the functioning of the Virgin's most private areas. Likewise, even if it is denied that the Virgin excreted, menstruated, or produced bodily fluids from sexual excitement, nonetheless the possibility of her doing so had to enter the mind of the curious theologian. Since so many aspects of late medieval theology, devotion, and popular culture were increasingly stressing the humanity of the Virgin and Child, invariably the natural mechanics of birth – bleeding, pain, tearing, and changes in other bodily functions – became part of the contemplation, even if only to deny they happened.

Such speculations show a distinctive, and again we might add infantile and predominantly male, fascination with and abhorrence of the pollution and impurity of the female body. As Alexandra Cuffel has recently shown in her pioneering study of medieval religious polemic, that sense of revulsion generated a tradition of scatological and gynocological abuse going back to the early Church (and which we saw in Chapter 1 animates reformers' polemics) which continually used detailed references to the Virgin's intimate bodily functions to abuse religious opponents. Polemicists – Christian, Jewish, Muslim alike – attacked one another by using "parturient

---

[34] Ellington, *From Sacred Body to Angelic Soul*, 51; Beattie, *Woman*, 118–19.
[35] For the clitoris, see Lochrie, *Heterosyncrasies*, 76–89.

and menstrual blood and excrement to denigrate the beliefs of those with
whom they disagreed." In all these arguments, Cuffel notes, the "primary
issue" is the functioning of Mary's body, and on either justifying or
ridiculing the paradox of "pure divinity" within "a filthy human body,"
and centered on "the dirt of Mary's body rather than Jesus." Even in
denying her sexuality, an intense level of sexualization was occurring.[36]

Virtually all these discussions of the Virgin's body, Beattie points out,
were "mediated and authenticated by men." Ironically, "the celibate man"
needed "the female body to provide the metaphors for his love of Christ."[37]
Miri Rubin likewise argues that medieval devotion to the Virgin took its
characteristic shape in part because she was constructed by isolated, celibate
men who were not only imitating Mary by "making" Christ's body every
day at the altar, but were projecting their own histories and psychological
profiles upon her. "Might not," Rubin asks, "their yearning for Mary" echo,
at least in part, the "nostalgia for the sounds of childhood, the warmth
of kindred bodies, for the incomparable acceptance of the maternal
embrace?"[38] While these approaches may seem somewhat reductive, the
Virgin has unquestionably been a scaffold on which male fantasies have
been hung and identified as universally true. At this point in the discussion,
I return to the work of Klaus Theweleit, whose important study of "male
fantasies" I introduced in Chapter 1. In his discussion of the formation of
Western masculinity, Theweleit suggests that the medieval idealization of
the Virgin provided a fantasy of re-absorption into the Mother; by contrast,
the Reformation rejection of the Virgin involved a violent attempt to
achieve a radical differentiation. Images and fantasies of the Virgin, as
well as relics and devotional aids, had functioned as transitional links
between the individual and the outside world and between the Child and
the Mother which might, experienced more gently, eventually enable a
healthy degree of self-actualization. Theweleit's formulation of this pattern
is, I believe, helpful here when he argues that we are not dealing with
individual "male fantasies" but broadly shared social and cultural tendencies, the dominant ideology of masculinization in particular historical
periods – the ways by which the masculine self is constructed by education,
social structures, and, in the case of the medieval and Reformation periods,
especially through the multiple apparatuses, repressive and ideological, of

---

[36] Cuffel, *Gendering Disgust* 3, 6, 12, 27, 58–9, 108, 117, 121, 123–4; cf. Rubin, *Mother of God*, 59: "The
polemical terrain between Jews and Christians involved the issues of Mary's body."

[37] Beattie, *God's Mother*, 21; Beattie, *Woman*, 126.

[38] Rubin, *Mother of God*, 363.

the Church. He observes that in looking at the medieval idealization of the Virgin, we are observing what men "loved first – woman and mother," becoming "that which they must learn to despise in others and suppress within themselves," with the denigration of the female developing as "a permanent reality which derives from the specific social organization of gender relations in patriarchal Europe." The "not-yet-fully-born" – a profile that he sees pessimistically as the dominant pattern of post-medieval Western masculinity – struggles unsuccessfully for release from the fanta-sized Mother, and turns its rage upon its (near universal) inability to break free from her upon all women. What the child seeks, Theweleit notes, "its whole life long, if need be, is unification with maternal bodies, within which it can become 'whole,' born to completion," an experience of unification with the maternal body from which it was expelled. To advance the process of being fully born is a perpetual challenge for Western males: when freedom from the Mother comes prematurely, as Theweleit argues it almost universally does, it may be intensely painful, and so the suffering ego turns its negativity into violence against the female. Such a pathology is partly built upon a male fear of women's sexuality and incorporates such fantasies as the fear of the alleged insatiability of the female sexual appetite and the fearfulness of her sexual organs. It is, asserts Theweleit, the Virgin's apparent independence of these threats that make her acceptable as an ideal and a symbol of reassurance. Her vagina is perpetually sealed; it will not engulf, emasculate, or threaten a man. Her "female body," he argues, is denied so she may more safely "function as a terrain for male fantasies."[39]

A major fantasy structure of late medieval Mariology is scopophilia – an obsession with looking. The reformers sought to restrain idolatry by restricting the power of vision and controlling the worshipping gaze. Removing or destroying images, whitewashing walls, removing heads from statues, were all designed to destroy the temptation not just to touch and achieve physical domination, but of sight. "Loss of sights and seeing" made a fundamental change not only in the "visual apparatus of worship," but also in the apprehension of the self: it was, says Aston, an assault on the idea that holiness could be "physically located" and openly used to educate the illiterate through visual means.[40] The recurring com-mand in medieval devotion had been that we "see," attempt to visualize intensely the Virgin's physical features and functions as well as evidence of

---

[39] Theweleit, *Male Fantasies*, I, xvi, 134, 196; II, 211–13, 252, 259.
[40] Aston, "Public Worship and Iconoclasm," 9.

her spiritual virtues. Marian shrines frequently originate in an apparition vision, and thereafter the believer is invited to observe, look, visualize, witness, and see evidence of her power through history; Books of Hours characteristically illustrate the scenes on which to meditate during prayer; devotional anthems and poems likewise require their readers (or listeners) to visualize their object of adoration.

Within modern cultural theory, the psychosocial dynamics of scopophilia and the gaze have been much debated. The standard viewpoint, represented by the work of Tania Modleski and Laura Mulvey in film studies, has focused on the male gaze as the normal subject position for the viewer of classic cinema, and the need to develop an alternative point of view, especially for women viewers. On the other hand, Gaylyn Studlar has argued that, on the contrary, many films assume a male viewing position not simply based on the desire to over-see and dominate, but rather on a masochistic fear/desire of being dominated and absorbed themselves by women.[41] Both analyses, of course, are pointing to the variety of ways by which the dominance of the male subject position has been reinforced, and both domination and fear of being dominated are central to medieval scopophilia. Modern clinical studies have shown how intense gazing may involve an insecurity or even rage that returns us to a very primitive level of experience, to when we were forced to give up our early maternal identification, while evoking a fear of being trapped, and a consequent need for revenge that she put us in this predicament. She is both the mother from whom we have been expelled and yet to whom we continue to desire. We have been thrown alone into the world, yet finding ourselves inevitably drawn, in reality or fantasy, back to her, puzzled yet reassured by the familiarity of our tortures.

The gaze, therefore, is a way of detoxifying the viewed object, and obsessive gazing is a way of temporarily relieving the voyeur of fear. In devotion to the Virgin the scopophilic impulses arise from the obsession not just with seeing her in person, in apparitions, but more easily, to view what represents her – paintings and frescos, statues, and a huge variety of objects of devotion, whether for use in private, or at public devotional sites such as chapels or shrines, parish churches or abbeys. Central to our understanding of this process is therefore a predominantly male (or male-created and authorized) fantasy, what Stoller terms the premier male "perversion," a complex, deeply rooted, psychological reaction formation that seeks to come to terms with the fear of the beloved's

---

[41] Mulvey, *Visual and Other Pleasures*; Studlar, *In the Realm of Pleasure*.

overwhelming power. That is fetishization, the intense focus on particular details of a beloved's or desired object's physical presence that are chosen by (or presented to) the worshipper as substitutes for the absent object of devotion.

Developmentally, fetishes acquire their power from childhood fantasy structures that may in adulthood be reactivated and elaborated, their origins long lost under the accretions of later narratives but their power still latent. The analyst Louise Kaplan comments that "the extravagant sexual theories" of childhood "may be outgrown and forgotten but they are never entirely given up. They are repressed and temporarily banished from consciousness but persist as unconscious fantasies that are ready to return,"[42] and can be re-activated unpredictably, or deliberately as parts of an elaborate ritual. Fetishization is thus a normal part of human relationships, and a fetish may be any ordinary object that the erotic imagination imbues with metonymic power – shoes, clothing, pets, portraits, locks of hair, odors, sounds. The devotee of the Virgin will seek out and use familiar inanimate objects associated with her – not just relics such as hair, milk, garments, but statues, badges, even seemingly neutral objects such as the pictures in a Book of Hours – and, like every normal fetishist, believes they will have or can be used to generate a certain amount of her power. The belief in Mary's bodily assumption (not yet dogma but an increasingly dominant view) meant that relics sought by her devotees had to be primarily clothing and minor detachable body parts such as nails, hair, or milk, and their derivatives, which became the focus of numerous cults and devotions across medieval Europe. These included pieces of clothing such as her veil (as at Chartres), and the multiple copies of her girdle or sash, famously tossed to (Doubting) Thomas as she ascended to heaven, copies of which were housed all across Europe, with the "original" at Prato in Tuscany. A major Marian relic in late medieval England across Europe was the Virgin's milk. Erasmus's views on the Virgin's milk at Walsingham which, his fictional pilgrim is assured, came directly from the Virgin's breast, will be mentioned in my survey of Marian pilgrimages in Chapter 4. Lollards, evangelicals, and reformers were appalled by both the proliferation of such objects, and as the iconoclastic urges of the Reformation gathered momentum, their use (as in the case of girdles in childbirth) forbidden, and they were, wherever possible, destroyed. Less easily destroyed were the habits of mind and the emotional attachments that went with them. Those were harder to get out of "their hedds."

---

[42] Kaplan, *Female Perversions*, 35.

The fetishist's goal is to find a remnant of the beloved's power, and to treasure it, since that may be all he can be given of her. Sometimes, clinical studies suggest, the fetish is chosen for just the right intensity of the beloved's power with which the worshipper can deal, at least for the moment. Since her full reality cannot be faced, the Virgin can be accommodated by the worshipper's mind only if she is accorded less than full presence because the gap between her immaculate purity and freedom from corruption and ordinary men and women is so vast and her claims on him so overwhelming. The more she is contemplated, the more what Robert Maniura terms "the aching void at the core of Marian devotion" serves "to make the devotee's longing ... all the more intense."[43] The fetish therefore allows the worshipper to experience her in miniature; he chooses or is permitted, to be, Stoller suggests, the "possessor of selected parts or qualities" only; he compulsively "anatomizes" them, typically in endless lists and ritual recitations. He extols her beauty, her virtue, her role as mother, queen, empress of heaven and hell and her power as intercessor – or, in the case of the Virgin's girdle, its power to protect a woman's body and child in the dangerous experience of childbirth.[44] This complex partial presence/ absence paradox is a version of Freud's classic *fort/da* game, in which the child pushes the toy away in order to have the pleasure of having it come back (and also, as the game acquires more elaborate fantasies, to punish the object for its power over him). These stories, told over and over, become therapeutic, taking on the function of a cure or at least creating a holding pattern by which the devotee (or patient, we might say today) may persist in living functionally or, hopefully, creatively.

In this scenario or "script," the object of devotion, in this case the Virgin, absolutely cannot herself be blamed for the devotee's pain or frustration. That is crucial: she fulfills a necessary blameless, "immaculate," role. She remains untouchable, causing pain even when most loving. She is at once merciful and solicitous and yet immaculate and unapproachable. Such intense devotion inevitably involves, as Graziano puts it, a degree of "self-negation and suffering," with the blamelessness of the imagined Other always protected so that the dominant "partner" is, or is imagined to be, continually needing to be "re-won with endless acts of submission and self-sacrifice."[45] Part of such masochistic pleasure arrives in delayed or denied gratification, the pleasurable pain of subsequent repetition, the need to earn favors by returning, day after day, to dedication, repentance, and

[43] Maniura, "Image and Relic," 211–12.   [44] Stoller, *Observing the Erotic Imagination*, 31–2.
[45] Graziano, *Wounds of Love*, 169.

continually repeated devotion. The worshipper is inevitably and repeatedly drawn to her, and to embodiments, even brief reminders of her, and is perpetually aware of his inadequacy before her. The masochist, Stoller notes, "waits for pleasure as something that is bound to be late, and expects pain as the condition that will finally ensure (both physically and morally) the advent of pleasure." Frustration is balanced by hope, the love of God by the lure of the world, passivity by restlessness, the hope of salvation by the fear of damnation. The relationship between the Virgin's transcendence and the worshipper's suppliance creates a state of deliciously anxious fluidity, in a world that is unpredictable, uncertain, and always threatening. Such contradictions and paradoxes are central to this experience – as they are, not coincidentally, in Petrarchan poetry, as I will suggest in some detail in Chapter 6.

The Argentinian theologian, Marcella Althaus-Reid, pushes the parallel even further by asserting that the "top–bottom relationship" of sado-masochism "is a master sketch ... symbolic of the greater religious submission of Christianity."[46] Such a parallel may appear as shocking as Steinberg's discussion of Christ's sexuality, but it is an attempt to locate the distinctive combination of pain and worship which is central to Marian devotion in observable human patterns of emotion and behavior. The "pain" involved in this never finally fulfillable relationship could be the relatively mild discomfort of scapulas or hairshirts – the mother of St. Edmund, it is recorded, wore "herde heyre for our Ladie's love"[47] – to self-abasement and self-abuse. The practice of referring to oneself as a "slave" of Mary, most prominently associated with the seventeenth-century saint, Louis de Montfort, and in certain contemporary cults such as the Slaves of the Immaculate Heart of Mary, is observable from as early as the ninth century and was given ecclesiastical approval in the thirteenth. As Mark Miravalle notes, several popes, including the Renaissance Pope Paul V, proclaimed themselves "slaves of the Mother of God." "We belong to Mary," Louis de Montfort was to declare repeatedly, "completely and exclusively," and "can expect nothing." The slave has no rights, even of life and death; the slave-owner, he states, can kill the slave "as he would kill his horse." Finally, whereas "a servant is in his employer's service only for a time," a slave is "for always." The pursuit of such abjection, notes the psychologist Roy Baumeister, typically involves devising elaborate and repeatable rituals and scripts designed to

---

[46] Stoller, *Perversion*, 99, 105; Marcella Althaus-Reid, *Indecent Theology*, 153.
[47] Waterton, *Pietas Mariana Britannica*, II, 121.

stress the nullification of the devotee's personal and social identity except in relation to the dominator.[48]

Kristeva is helpful at this point in her discussion of abjection. The attraction/repulsion syndrome that the debate over Christ's genital theology provoked, the startling mixture of sexuality and spirituality in many medieval mystics, especially women, and my discussion of Mariological devotion in terms of common "perverse" psychological patterns as discussed by Carroll, Stoller and others, all have in common what she describes as a blurring of attraction and repulsion "for the desirable and terrifying, nourishing and murderous, fascinating and abject" especially when it is associated with the "inside of the maternal body." In its most intense form, disease, violence, death, putrefaction, sexual extremities, and especially liquids and excretions of all kinds, play into abjection, to produce a paradoxical pleasurable pain in an "erotic cult of the abject." As Kristeva comments, "one of the insights of Christianity . . . is to have gathered in a single move perversion and beauty as the lining and the cloth of one and the same economy."[49] In her important work on Waste Studies, Susan Morrison notes that our history has conditioned us to see not only the excremental body as repulsive, but also the processes of ingestion, digestion, secretion, and elimination. The story of Mary's being fed by angels was clearly meant to exclude her from the processes of ordinary human functions – it was believed that if the food was "uncorrupt," she would not have to process and excrete it.[50] But St. Catherine of Siena (1347–80), St. Maria Maddalena de' Pazzi (1566–1607), St. Rose of Lima (1586–1617) and many others, mainly though not exclusively women, are recorded as having abased themselves by eating and drinking excrement, pus, and other bodily effluvia. Just as extreme intimacies of smell, taste or touch play a part in the "normality" of human sexuality, so the mystics and other devotees who threw themselves into the abject were, as it were, accepting the infamous "*Inter faeces et urinam nascimur*" and turning its intensity into ecstasy.[51]

To discuss Marian devotion in terms of fetishization, masochism, and abjection is not simply reductive "presentism." Although using different vocabularies, such judgments are very much in line with those the reformers

---

[48] Montfort, *True Devotion*, 47–8; Baumeister, *Social Psychology and Human Sexuality*, 303. For the "slaves of Mary," see Miravalle, *Introduction to Mary*, 155; Perry and Echeverría, *Under the Heel of Mary*.

[49] Kristeva, *Powers of Horror*, 54, 55, 125. Here and also in the analysis of Richard Crashaw's poetry in Chapter 8, I am indebted to the persuasive (though at times slightly reductive) discussion of Kristeva in Sabine, *Feminine Engendered Faith*.

[50] Morrison, *Excrement in the Late Middle Ages*.

[51] For a brief survey of "abject" religious behavior, see Morrison, "Strange Miracles," 129–44.

made. The term *fetisso* originates in Portuguese gold and slave traders in the late Middle Ages to explain what were perceived as "superstitious" religious practices.[52] The term is adapted in sixteenth-century Protestant controversy to describe what were perceived as analogous Catholic devotions. Belief in the power of relics was vilified as "intolerable superstition and abhominable idolatry"– such as the "stinking boots, mucky combs, ragged rockets, rotten girdles, pyld purses, great bullocks' horns, locks of hair, and filthy rags, gobbets of wood … and such pelfry, beyond estimation," observed in a monastic inspection, or the similar list by the first English translator of Erasmus's colloquy on pilgrmage, the *Peregrinatio religionis ergo*, puts it.[53]

Nor, emphatically, is my argument that (unlike what the reformers, within their own discursive formations, certainly thought) Mariological cults or devotions ought to be added (at least directly) to the list of common paraphilia, along with coprophilia, kleptomania, or exhibitionism, though all these "perversions" may play a part in religious devotion, as they may in any normal human interaction. Such a classification – and indeed the popular pejorative associations of "perversion" or "pervert" – can all too easily turn into a moralistic dualism such as "normal" and "patholog-ical." On the contrary, as Freud noted, "a certain degree of fetishism is … habitually present in normal love, especially in those stages of it in which the normal sexual aim seems unattainable or its fulfillment prevented."[54] The intensity and longevity of Mariological devotion was (and, indeed, remains) rooted in some of the major fantasies of patriarchal gender assignments which, if not universal, at least have been historically remarkably consistent, as if they were, as Theweleit would have it, seemingly permanent aspects of the Western male psyche – or, as a Jungian would say, archetypes of the male unconscious. I have no predisposition to these or other meta-discourses: I am probing to find how we might, at least in part, explain the powerful hold the Virgin had on late medieval men and women, why the reformers' reactions against the Virgin's power (and her bodily nature) were so strong, and (in later chapters) what the manifestations of that mixture of attraction and repulsion were after the 1538 conflagration. My hypothesis is that some of these matters can be accounted for, at least in outline, by our knowledge of how certain male fantasies operate.

However, it will perhaps be noted that I have started to insert an important qualification into my argument. Although I believe my analysis

---

[52] Pietz, "Fetish."   [53] Frere, *Visitation Articles*, II, 59–60; Erasmus, *Pilgrimage,* 6–7.
[54] See the discussion of Freud's consideration of "normal" fetishization in Freikel, "The Shakespearean Fetish," 117.

points in the right direction, it is predominantly a model focused upon the male construction of what is fantasized as the mystery and horror of the female body. What is the place women – real women, not the constructs of the male imaginary – occupied in the fantasy structures of late medieval gynotheology? Insofar as we can consider medieval women outside the male-dominated economy of sexual roles and exchanges, we need to ask how women's experiences of the Virgin and their own bodies in relation to her might have tended to be distinct from men's. The Virgin depicted in mainstream medieval theology offered limited roles for women, essentially that they accept their places (the rigid Althusserian formulation of "inter-pellated" or "summoned into" a subject position does not in this case, at least on the surface, seem excessive) either as being outside the sexual economy as religious, or within the patriarchal family structure, as mothers, wives, and daughters. Above all, their religious experiences and insights as women were overwhelmingly repressed.

Some modern theologians, as a consequence, have called for an alter-native Mariology that is more responsive to female perspectives. There exists, argues the German theologian Elisabeth Gössman, a "women's counter-tradition to Christianity," and consequently we need "a new pic-ture of Mary," one that acknowledges "unashamedly," argues Mario Ribas, that it was through "the breasts and vagina of the Virgin" that God "chose to communicate Godself to the world."[55] Uncannily, these theologians –not, it needs to be acknowledged, necessarily among the contemporary main-stream – are reaching back to many of the practices of pre-Reformation devotion to the Virgin and, they would argue, attempting to find stories which will explain differently from the predominantly male-authored ones how both women and men are constructed as human subjects. Beattie argues that victory in the early Church's ideological struggles over the place of women was achieved at enormous cost and contributed to the near-elision of women's experiences and the enormous cultural burden of the Church's revulsion from sexuality. The Council of Ephesus, which declared Mary *Theotokos*, Mother of God, looks like a triumph for the place of the Virgin and for women's sexuality in Christian theology and devotion, but Beattie suggests – in line with Michael Carroll's observations on the formation of the Marian cult in the first four centuries of the Church – that it was, in fact, a "decisive act of curtailment." The affirmation of the perpetual virginity of the Mother of God took a stand against a background not only of pagan cults which emphasized violent and often

---

[55] Gössman, "Image of God," 26–56; Ribas, "Liberating Mary, Liberating the Poor," 135.

sacrificial sexuality and ostensible virginity, but also a number of Christian communities relatively independent of patriarchal norms which advocated, within limits, venerating Mary as the Christian goddess. Beattie suggests we read the much-quoted (and maligned) Collyridians as a part of what she terms "Marian Christianity" and that the Council's acceptance of Mary as *Theotokos* paradoxically set back "the possibility of an independent women's movement developing alongside male Christianity" within the Catholic Church. But the impetus for an alternative account of Christianity does not necessarily die out. While the Church may have taken over and christianized some aspects of the pagan cults, what was never given a place in the patriarchal theology that dominated the Middle Ages was the sexual female body, and Beattie concludes that "to this day it is the woman as body who remains outside the boundaries of Christian symbolization, even though the woman as maternal feminine has found a place at the heart of the Church's symbolic life."[56]

There are, however, more than a few hints of the breaking of those "boundaries." Karl Whittington has elucidated a thirteenth-century manuscript depiction of female sexual physiology – arguably, he claims, meant to represent the Virgin's own – which is schematically projected upon a diagram of the crucified Christ to suggest both information about the mysterious inside of the female and its symbolic connection to salvation. It reinforces those strands in medieval incarnational theology that female flesh could be seen as a path to God rather than an obstacle. The shared bodiliness of ordinary women and Mary would allow women, Whittington suggests, to think of themselves as like Mary not only negatively but also at least potentially in more positive ways. Hence, at least potentially, "the manner in which ordinary women related to Mary's experience of the incarnation" may have gradually become more intimate, especially as artists and writers "emphasized more than ever Christ's real birth from a real woman."[57] There were, therefore, ways by which women could identify positively with both the Virgin's and their own experiences of childbirth, motherhood, and, by extension, sexuality and thereby become agents of resistance, creating what Elizabeth Dreyer terms the "creative by-passes" required to survive "when one belongs to a marginalized group." Catherine Driscoll points to the alternate social contexts given by tableaux of the Virgin in medieval representations of the Annunciation – most stress her passivity and reticence, a pose that reappears in Shakespeare's Ophelia – but

---

[56] Beattie, *God's Mother*, 63; Carroll, *Cult of the Virgin Mary*, 41–8.
[57] Whittington, "Cruciform Womb," 1–2, 15, 17.

there are also representations of Mary as, in effect, the empowered social activist, a stance inherent in the Magnificat, the hymn of praise as Mary contemplates the raising of the poor and oppressed and the social consequences of the Incarnation.[58]

Recent scholarship on women writers in the period, including recluses and mystics such as Julian of Norwich, has emphasized how frequently the images of the spiritual life are drawn from their erotic experience. Anne Marie Dalton argues that "their experiences, while cloaked in conflicting rhetorics, provide a text of women's bodies as the loci of spiritual transformation."[59] Julian's is a strikingly Christocentric vision, but Mary is still "in worth and grace above all that God made." Julian provides an extraordinary model of an alternate bodily centered theology, using the language of mothering, birthing, and, especially in her imagery of Jesus-as-Mother, correcting (with some sense of her own heterodoxy in a time when Lollards were especially viciously hunted) the dominant Augustinian emphasis on sinfulness and the corruption of the female body.[60] Other mystics evoke their experiences more explicitly in genital coupling: Mary as Jesus's bride, Mary united with God in divine marriage, seducing or even copulating with God. As early as the tenth century, Hildegard of Bingen's poetic meditations on the birth of Christ describe the event in terms of the Virgin's own erotic experiences, the "paradox of the initial bypassing and then ultimate passing through of the female genitalia" from the security of the "closed gate" of her virginity to the warmth of impregnation, the engorging of her genitals, and the explosion in what Judith Peraino terms "the opening of her vagina and the orgasmic salvational ejaculation ('*Et Filius Dei per secreta ipsius quasi aurora exivit*': And the son of God came forth from her secret passage like the dawn)." Hildegard, suggests Peraino, sees the birth as a "reverse penetration."[61] There are frequent accounts by female mystics of their own sexual ecstasies or their own virginal breasts dripping because of the ecstasy of imagining themselves breastfeeding the Christ Child. There is also a level of sexuality in many *pietà* lyrics, as in those in which the Virgin grieves for the death of her Son, that goes beyond conventional piety. Sarah Stanbury describes the recurring "formal tableau" of the Sorrowing Mother as a motif that breaks somewhat with the conventional positioning of the woman's body as the stern object of the admirers' gaze, and more as one that

---

[58]　Dreyer, "Whose Story Is It?" 158; Driscoll, *Girls*, 143.
[59]　Dalton, "Challenge of Violence."　　[60]　McEntire, "The Likeness of God," 20–7.
[61]　Peraino, *Listening to the Sirens*, 32, 46; Rubin, "Mary," 3; *Mother of God*, 147–8; Hildegard, *Symphonia*, 1–6.

provokes an excitation that is "both erotic and maternal . . . legitimized by maternity and eroticized by its transgressive sexuality."[62] The feminization of Christ's body, especially through the vulvic imagery of the "side-wounds" at the crucifixion, is also, as a number of scholars have suggested, a recurring motif in the age's literature and devotion.[63]

Do these breaking of the "boundaries" add up to a continuing tradition? Or is there, even, as Kristeva and others have argued, a level of the pre-conscious beyond male-dominated discourse which women inhabit and which patriarch attempts, often desperately, to repress? Are there distinctively female patterns of experience that we can observe without falling into an ahistorical essentialism? Given that most of the texts that have come down to us from the later Middle Ages (and, indeed, the whole historical period with which I am dealing) are written by men, how might we bring such an emergent tradition out? In Chapter 4 I will attempt to pose some of these questions relating to women's religious and sexual experiences when I look at that most distinctive of medieval popular activities, the pilgrimages to Marian shrines. I shall take up the sociologist Simon Coleman's observation, that even within a rigidly supervised society, pilgrimage provided a "splendid diversity," a polyvalent symbolic space, able to accommodate "varying" or "discrepant" discourses," a prompt "for private, sometimes ironic, even subversive narratives," able to accommodate alternate "pathways."[64] His views echo Beattie's insistence that there was implicit in, though repressed from, early Christian responses to Mary an alternative tradition of body-centered experiences that could have led to an alternative account of women's place in salvation – and, indeed, to our understanding of women more generally.

The reformers, however, saw only perversion and idolatry as they contemplated these or any sexualizations of the Virgin and her "womanly" nature. Their reactions to the rich and complex world of late medieval Mariology motivates what Theweleit terms the iconoclastic "tension-and-explosion," as the absolute transcendence of the God of Protestant theology seemed to give Protestants the pretext for repudiating the Mother, attempting to be released from the maternal body by a savage wrenching away from its power – and by turning violently upon it.[65] But as I shall show in Chapter 3, on the apparent margins of society, alternate pathways, adapting

[62] Stanbury, "The Virgin's Gaze," 1088.
[63] See e.g. Julian of Norwich, *Showing of Love*; Lochrie, "Mystical Acts, Queer Tendencies," 180–200.
[64] Coleman's "Tradition as Play," 279; "Do You believe in Pilgrimage?" 359, 360; Coleman and Elsner, "Pilgrimage to Walsingham," 192–3.
[65] Theweleit, *Male Fantasies*, 1, 44.

Coleman's phrase, were being mapped out that were centered on the possibilities of a repressed but not entirely invisible female sexuality. From the cultural margins – popular religion, song, drama, as well as the visual arts such as painting and sculpture – there were indeed "traces" that show us what Raymond Williams called "pre-emergent"[66] possibilities, alternatives in which the figure of the Virgin, despite hundreds of years of repression and exploitation, might have forwarded an affirmation of the body and a more positive endorsement of human sexuality that could have been associated with, not differentiated from, Mary.

---

[66] Williams, *Marxism and Literature*, 126.

CHAPTER 3

The Virgin's body in late medieval poetry, romance, and drama

"This matere here mad is of the modyr of mercy," announces the character Contemplacio at the beginning of the so-called "Mary Play" that is found interleaved into the miscellaneous collection of biblical dramas from East Anglia we term the "N-Town" plays. The "matere" is not only the life, but the power, of the Virgin Mary and the need to revere her as an essential figure in the drama of creation and salvation. Following the Resurrection play in the same collection, Jesus announces of Mary:

> Al this werlde that was forlorn
> Shal wurchepe you both evyn and morn;
> For had I not of yow be born
> Man had be lost in helle.[1]

It is particularly in the popular drama that we see the extraordinary extent to which devotion to the Virgin was central to the everyday life of the later Middle Ages in England. But we can also sense, lurking behind (or in Irigaray's metaphor, "sidling" up to) the ideological (and state) apparatuses of what in many ways was a rigid and repressive society, possible alternate readings of Mary, despite her being coded very carefully by the Church as created outside human sexuality and its (apparent and incessantly emphasized) discontents. In this chapter, I shall examine the presence of Mary in late medieval popular culture – poetry, romance, and story – but the main focus will be on the drama, especially on plays where she provides a major role in events that in many cases would come to be seen by the reformers as an idolatrous, pagan, and blasphemous feminization of Christianity.

The material environment of late medieval England, whether in the countryside, villages or towns, gave men and women recurrent reminders of Mary's omnipresence in their lives through the daily Offices, prayers, devotions, feasts and festivals, images and statues, and in innumerable

---

[1] Sugano, *N-Town Plays*, 287.

material details of their everyday lives. This intense "Marianization" of late medieval society, as Rubin puts it, also provided poets, musicians, and story-tellers "seemingly endless opportunities for display of cleverness and inventiveness."[2] Mary is praised, petitioned, celebrated, implored, and beseeched, in order to help men and women through the brutality of this "false, fickle world." Solemn hymns such as the *Mater Dolorosa* and thousands of playful, didactic, moralistic, or narrative poems, lyrics that are ecstatic, soulful, joyful, erotic, all have the Virgin at their center. In poem after poem, as she is in devotions, she is "Queene of the Trinite," "queene ... of paradis," Noah's dove, Sinai's bush, David's sling and stone, Solomon's temple; she is compared to biblical heroines, fulfilling biblical prophecies that a thousand years of Christian exegesis had insisted were represented in Judith, Rachael, Esther, Sarah, and Eve. Virtually every phrase in the Old Testament that could be applied positively to a woman was allegorized and turned to the Virgin's praise and place within the sweep of history. In Walsingham's Pynson Ballad, she is addressed, among other epithets, as "Cypresse of Syon and Ioye of Israel, / Rose of Jeryco and Sterre of Bethleem."[3] To the reformers, the myriad of roles and titles given to Mary, except of course the basic "virgin" and "mother," were irresponsibly extra-biblical. The Old Testament heroines were dissociated from Mary by the reformers and seen rather as exempla of heroic, obedient, and faithful women, virtuous Protestant witnesses for the faith.[4] For medieval Christians, however, Mary was omnipresent in the Bible as it was mediated through the Church, just as she was in daily life.

As an example of a medieval poet whose work was especially focused on the Virgin, we might glance at John Lydgate. His long (6,000 lines) verse life of the Virgin, written 1416–22, survives in over forty manuscript versions; it first appeared in the new mode of print in 1484 and was reprinted even as late as a few years before the process of Dissolution commenced. It is largely a paraphrase in rhyme royal of material from the *Pseudo-Matthew*, a later derivative from the *Protevangelium*. Lydgate affirms the conventional narrative of Mary's life that she is "of all wymen, / by hir self alone," both Virgin and Mother: "O blissid lady, flour of virgynyte: / We prayen ichone, o welle of our welfare / Like a mother net thy milke to spare." He praises her maternal role, giving detailed if conventional descriptions

[2] Rubin, *Mother of God*, 367, 268.
[3] Luria and Hoffman, *Middle English Lyrics*, 178, 43, 170, 173. For a useful survey of Mary's poetical and devotional titles and their historical origins, see Haskins, *Who is Mary?* 12–20.
[4] Osherow, *Biblical Women's Voices*, especially ch. 1, on the Bible's first woman prophet, Miriam.

of her bodily functions, which are mainly abstract but have occasional details that draw on the gynotheological obsessions of medieval Mariology. Her milk is "hevenly licour of her pappes small," as she feeds the child whose "yong face between thy pappes couche"; her womb is "the closter virginall . . . closed and shutte."[5]

To take a shorter (and justly better known) example, the much praised celebratory lyric, "I singe of a Mayden," uses the similarly conventional metaphor of dew falling from heaven to convey the incomprehensible event occurring in Mary's body at the Annunciation: "He came as still / Where his mother lay / As dew in April / That falls on the spray." Perfectly orthodox in its theology, the poem quietly and elegantly celebrates the Incarnation, avoiding any indelicate physical detail. Mary's womb is not so much a female organ as a symbol of fertility, purity, and redeemed nature.[6] Yet elsewhere, especially in fifteenth-century poetry, we sense more signs of the gynotheological dimension of medieval devotion emerging strongly and unselfconsciously. In many of the poems on Mary, there is an explicit level of unembarrassed sexuality on display, celebrating what Rubin terms her "secret places . . . full of music, ablaze with chastity, yet moist with saving dew." [7] Much of the imagery in this more explicit poetry is mediated from the Song of Songs, especially focusing on metaphors for the Virgin such as "a fountain sealed" (Song 4.12), "a closed gate" (Ezek 44.1–3) through which only the God of Israel may enter, as Joseph finds in the cycle plays (discussed later in this chapter) when he returns home to find Mary's door locking him out.[8] By the twelfth century, the Song was widely adapted into litanies and poems, with the metaphors – enclosed garden, well of living waters, flower of the field, lily among thorns, and others – read as prophetic allegories of the Virgin. Especially potent was the juxtaposition of the richly sexual metaphors of a woman's lush, well-irrigated garden with the forbidden locked, enclosed, and sealed nature of the garden, a paradox that (as Chapter 6 will explain) had parallels in Petrarchan love lyrics. Mary becomes exhibited as "transformatively vaginal," Rubin comments: she both "had" and "was" a rose, which is both physical and mystical, to be celebrated as the Gate of Heaven, the mystical gateway of the Incarnation; she quotes a poem which even imagines God so at home inside the Virgin's womb that he is tempted to return and "unmake the Incarnation."[9]

---

[5] John Lydgate, *Life of Our Lady*, 71, 76–7, 103.
[6] Luria and Hoffman, *Medieval Lyrics*, 170.   [7] Rubin, "Mary," 3.
[8] Ellington, *From Sacred Body to Angelic Soul*, 69–70.
[9] Rubin, *Mother of God*, 212, 299. See also Beattie, "Queen of Heaven," 300; Haskins, *Who is Mary?* 19.

The poems at which I have glanced all underline, as has often been noted, the importance medieval devotional culture afforded to visualization. Lydgate's poem on the Virgin continually invites us, as do the myriads of statues and paintings in shrines and churches, doorways, and wall niches, to look, watch, see, and marvel at this paradox of transcendent virtue, beauty, duty, and power. The need for clear and concentrated sight is a frequent topic. Poem after poem invites the reader to see and marvel at the Virgin's body – paradoxically, uniquely immaculate, impenetrable, and intensely spiritualized and yet, frequently, eroticized – with each limb and feature dwelt on, functions such as lactation praised, the "rose" of her impenetrable vagina and hymen verbally if not visually displayed. Scopophilia is, as noted in Chapter 2, inevitably associated with frustration: Lydgate also comments on the paradox that we both need to look at the Virgin and yet acknowledge our human inability to fully see her, since "we may not have full the blissednesse" that is required.[10]

If the poetry of the later Middle Ages is saturated with richly metaphorical references to the Virgin, so is that most ubiquitous literary form, the romance, whether folk story or tale, whether in verse or prose, written or oral. Carroll points out that "medieval sermons were typically built around stories" taken from such fictional sources as the saints' lives in the *Golden Legend* or John Mirk's collection of sermons, the *Festial*, what Judy Ann Ford terms the "most widely read vernacular sermon collection of late medieval England."[11] Outside the strictly religious stories, in the long tradition of idealized heroic or erotic romances that dominated court taste from the twelfth century onward, the Virgin is often a powerful background presence, with the religion of love and the religion of devotion becoming frequently intertwined. Stories of knights and ladies, love, valor, honor, making incidental references to the Virgin (as in the case of Arthurian legends such as those on Sir Gawain, described as Mary's own knight, who has the Virgin's picture on the inside of his shield to remind him of his ideals) are among courtly society's most popular stories. She appears primarily as a presiding aristocratic lady, frequently alluded to as an inspiration, or as the final goal of a quest, as when Arthur goes to Glastonbury to die under her protection.

But Mary had her own genre of romance stories that highlighted her miracles and interventions in human affairs. What we might term the

---

[10] Lydgate, *Life of Our Lady*, 445.
[11] Ford, *John Mirk's Festial*, 9; Carroll, "Robin Hood." For a popular compendium of the Virgin's medieval miracles, see Herolt, *Miracles*.

Marian romance becomes a major popular genre throughout the Middle Ages, transmitted orally but also written down and copied over and over. Originating in the early Christian era, these compositions echo and some-times intertwine with the extraordinarily popular Greek romances, with their comparable structures of human loss and devastation, passionate and often highly eroticized adventures, unpredictability, coincidence, and cli-mactic miracle. Rubin summarizes what she terms "the quintessential Marian story" as a "transgression and return" story. [12] There are countless tales of the Virgin's interventions into events great and small, public and personal appearances, followed by conversions (especially of Jews and other infidels) as well the redemption of persistent and undeserving sinners. As Chaucer's "The Prioress's Tale" makes clear, the Virgin may well support reprobates, even criminals, who give her only a passing prayer, dispensing a kind of unpredictable justice "dayly," more typical of folklore and fairy tale than providential history. Thieves try to steal gold and gems from a statue of the Virgin and Child which closes its arms around the child to protect him, thus explaining why "even to this day, in proof of this great miracle, our Ladye enfolds her arms around her Divine son." St. Edmund places a ring on the finger of a statue of Our Lady, and it is miraculously found on his own finger at his death. An apparently undeserving sinner is miraculously saved from death. A knight, fleeing from his enemies, prays to the Our Lady of Walsingham as he approaches the walls of her shrine, and is miraculously transported through a tiny gate. [13] In such stories, the Virgin could some-times be unpredictable, even vindictive, but typically produces the reassur-ance of a benign resolution in which she shows her authority and, often, simply her power to be at the center of a gripping narrative.

The reformers ridiculed such stories. The Protestant antiquarian William Lambarde reports on "a Popish illusion" that Our Lady of Chatham "arose by night," and went to complain to the local parish clerk that the look of a recently dead person offended her; she accompanied him to the churchyard and the "whole track of their journey" remained forever a "green path" before "our Lady shrank again into her shrine." Such a story, commented Lambarde, although not without a little wistfulness, was characteristic of an age "prone to believe illusions," and now "declining to oblivion." [14] Robin Hood stories came under special disapproval because, in many, Robin is

---

[12] Rubin, *Mother of God*, 183.
[13] Waterton, *Pietas Mariana Britannica*, II, 61, 121; Price, "Re-membering the Jews," 439–63; Dickinson, *Shrine*, 128.
[14] Lambarde, *Perambulation of Kent*, 324–6.

presented as particularly devoted to the Virgin. In the *Gest* of Robin Hood, we are told that every day Robin hears three Masses in honor of God, the Holy Ghost, and the one "he loved all ther moste," to "Oure dere Lady." Carroll makes the further point that in these stories there is a Mariocentricity that stresses not that Mary's power is intercessory, but rather shows her devotees regard her "in the same way she was regarded by many Italian and Spanish Catholics, as an independent powerful supernatural being who deserved attention in her own right, and who was far more important than Christ." Robin had always been treated with some suspicion – a "scripture," a biblical story, complained Sebastian Brant in his *Ship of Fools* (translated into English in 1509) would be all too easily dismissed in favor of "a folysshe jest of Robyn hode"– and the reformers readily associated such tales with popery and superstition.[15]

Stories are another variant of the Marian romance of Mary's own miraculous childhood, descended mainly from the *Protevangelium Jacobi* and its derivatives. This extraordinary non-canonical but immensely popular compilation of stories, written in Greek but transmitted to later readers in Syriac, exists in well over a hundred manuscripts, the earliest from about the third century, most of the rest copied and in some cases augmented around a thousand years later, especially in the expanded version, known as *Pseudo-Matthew*, which adds such oft-repeated stories of the tree (date or cherry) that willingly bends over to refresh Mary on her trip to Egypt. The original authorship of the *Protevangelium* is uncertain, though in the Middle Ages it was generally attributed to James, the brother (or half brother) of Jesus, and its title implied it was a prior or at least early gospel and therefore had historical reliability. Some of its stories are based on canonical gospels, others arise from different sects and traditions in the first two centuries. Many of its stories were composed to intervene in early Christian debates and today it is commonly regarded as reflecting the early Church's wrestling with the place of Mary in salvation history against Jewish and Docetic attacks on the claims of Jesus's divinity and his miraculous conception. The stories seem deliberately chosen to emphasize the miracle of a virginal childbirth, and (especially strongly emphasized) Mary's perpetual virginity. The *Protevangelium* also gives us the vivid picture of Joseph as an elderly widower (dutifully even more concerned with Mary's offences against purity laws than his own honor), the nativity of Jesus in a

[15] Stock, "Lords of the Wildwood," 240, 248; Brant, *The Ship of Fools*, 72; Ohlgren, "The Marchant of Sherwood," 180. I am grateful to Michael Carroll for sharing an early version of his forthcoming paper on Robin Hood.

cave, and the remarkable story of the visit of the midwives to attend Mary after the birth.[16] Later accretions turn her into a medieval lady, with an educated upbringing, fashionable clothes, and as Susan Haskins points out, as the legends are re-written in different regions of Europe, she adopts the look of local ideals of beauty. Scorned by the reformers, the *Protevangelium* constituted a major source of belief about the miraculous powers of the Virgin.[17] Its stories also contained sufficient contradictions to indicate how alternate traditions regarding sexuality and the female body might well have survived or re-surfaced throughout the late Middle Ages – especially, as I am about to show, in the popular drama.

Medieval poetry may overwhelmingly command its readers to watch, see, and observe the Virgin, and medieval tales may have asked their readers and hearers to visualize her amazing life and powers, but the art form that had sight as its fundamental principle in the later Middle Ages is the drama. It is a cliché of Shakespearean and Elizabethan scholarship that audiences went to "hear" a play; that is arguable, but unquestionably medieval drama was primarily incorporated into the economy of sight. While the guild-sponsored cycle plays have received most attention from modern scholars, as more account books, play scripts, and town records have been analyzed, we have become aware of the variety and number of individual and local performances of plays, entertainments, processions, and festivals that have arisen. The upsurge in late medieval dramatic activity is traditionally attributed to the instigation of the Feast of Corpus Christi and the subsequent activities by guilds in towns such as York or Chester, but games, revels, entertainments, and plays were common pastimes, often in or sponsored by local churches, or associated with local saints. Such local events might be designed for fund-raising, instruction, the establishment of community or, as Penny Granger notes, simply to put a "town or village on the map."[18] Christopher Marsh points out that while such religious festivals celebrating, for instance, the Feast of the Virgin's Assumption, were primarily occasions for church services, "the line between the sacred and the secular" on such occasions "seems impossible to draw."[19] Nor should be overlooked the entertainments provided for local magnates or the court, where we see, well before the rise of commercial theater in the 1570s, early signs of semi-professional troupes of entertainers and actors.

---

[16] Gaventa, *Mary*, 105.   [17] Haskins, *Who is Mary?* 30; Amirav and Kirn, "Theodore Bibliander," 161.
[18] Granger, *The N-Town Play*, 9.
[19] Marsh, *Popular Religion in Sixteenth-Century England*, 98–9.

Like the poetry and romances of the period, late medieval drama was preoccupied to an unusual extent with the Virgin. This is particularly the case with the "N-Town" plays, a collection arranged more or less as a sequence like other cycle collections, but made available for staging in parts by local groups, traveling players, or even for private reading. Peter Meredith has argued (with general if not universal scholarly agreement) that it even includes a composite "Mary Play," possibly by a single author, which draws on the tradition of legends and devotions derived largely from the *Protevangelium*, lives of the saints in the *Legenda Aurea*, and the *Meditationes Vitae Christi*. Its episodes include the stories of Mary's conception by her parents, Joachim and Anna, her presentation in the temple, the betrothal to Joseph and Joseph's doubts about her virtue (which includes the episode known in some of the cycles as Joseph's Troubles with Mary), the Parliament of Heaven which meets to consider initiating the Annunciation, and the episode of Mary's visit to Elizabeth. N-Town also includes other plays that involve the Virgin as a supporting character – especially the plays on the Nativity, Christ and the Doctors, the Crucifixion, the burial and the risen Christ's appearance to his mother.[20]

N-Town has a special focus on the Virgin, but Martin Stevens suggests we can usefully view the other major collections of medieval plays – York, Chester, Wakefield, for instance – as structured as much by Mary's life as by Christ's, with the ongoing narrative of the life of Mary, constructed to mirror her son's, providing the first deliberately constructed subplot in the history of English drama.[21] The Marian plot is centered on the Annunciation and the Nativity which, however they may have become sentimentalized in a secularized Western world, have long possessed a power based on the intermixing of theology with the sheer physicality of human conception and birthing. The various speculations on how Jesus was born, the shepherds, the no-room-at-the-inn episode, the three magi or wise men, were all developed in elaborate narratives and drew on themes and motifs from fairy and folk sources, and the Nativity plays predictably exploit these associations and the stories' immediacy and narrative charm. The Wakefield Second Shepherds' Play is rightly praised as one of the great masterpieces of the period. It is reverent and reticent about the divine birth: despite the earthy language in the story of Mak and the stolen sheep, the play alludes only indirectly to the actual birthing of Jesus. In York and N-Town, however, the physical details of birthing are boldly foregrounded

[20] Meredith, *Mary Play*.   [21] Stevens, *Four Middle English Mystery Cycles*, 245.

vividly in the story of the two midwives who visit the Virgin and Child after birth in a play which I will treat in detail later in this chapter.

In the Marian "subplot," typically the birthing plays are followed by powerful scenes presenting the Massacre of the Innocents, the Purification of the Virgin and the presentation of Jesus in the temple, all of which have Mary at their center. The N-Town play on the Purification includes a traditional Candlemas ritual in which mothers in the audience would likely have taken part: three birds are presented to the temple along with a candle representing Mary's virginity. The occasion draws attention to the intimate bodily nature of birthing and the supposed uncleanness of a woman after childbirth. Of course, because of her perpetual virginity, Mary should have no need to be purified; instead, the incident is designed to stress her obedience to the law. Gibson argues that the drama of Candlemas, both in the liturgical ritual and in the plays, was one of the many occasions in popular piety that stressed the "centrality of bodily feats of the Virgin"[22] with which the women of the community could readily identify.

The next event in the conventional sequence of plays which is centered on Mary is the biblical anecdote from Luke in which Jesus is presented to the temple. But even though it does have a scriptural basis, the event is elaborated in the *Protevangelium* and was also depicted in many visual representations including a remarkable painting by Simone Martini which shows a defiant, almost surly Jesus glaring at the parents whose control he had temporarily escaped. In N-Town, Towneley, York, and Chester, the episode is designed to show Jesus's knowledge and wisdom, but the plays give glimpses of Mary's contradictory parental emotions as she worries over her son's upbringing. Jesus goes off to the temple, where he claims to the skeptical doctors to be both motherless and fatherless, and when he does not return home, she is anxious: "Alas, myn hert is wo! / My blyssyd babe awey is went! / I wott nevyr whedyr that he is go!" She asks Joseph if he sent him "Out on herrande to any place?"[23] As usual, Joseph has been falsely accused, and feels abused and misunderstood as she scolds him and makes him follow her in her quest to find her son. In the York version, Mary's emotions show a flash of intense realism, as she insists, despite her husband's reticence, on her motherly rights to challenge authority and discover the whereabouts of her child. Acting out the conflicting familial emotions – adolescent assertion of independence, fatherly awkwardness in public and

[22] Gibson, *Theater of Devotion*, 167, 196.   [23] Sugano, *N-Town*, 172.

before authority, the righteously assertive mother – would bring immediate recognition from parents in an audience.

Mary tends to be a side player in the Crucifixion and Resurrection plays – but though small, her role is crucial, and the sorrowing mother was the subject of some of the most moving lyrics and hymns in the repertoire of medieval popular devotion. She is presented as beside herself with grief, and in some collections (York, for instance) questions the meaning and necessity of her son's death in a direct and no doubt, for mothers (and fathers) in the audience, all too understandable way. The narrative line of the plays thereafter focuses on the aftermath of Christ's Resurrection, stretching out to the culmination of salvation history in the Day of Judgment. But the N-Town and York collections both contain a number of pieces on Mary's later life, culminating in her death, ascension, and coronation as Queen of Heaven. Theologically, these events are presented as the culmination of God's decision that Mary has been uniquely chosen to be the peak of creation, and a demonstration that, as the N-Town Assumption play triumphantly announces, "God, throw Mary, is mad mannys frend." Because of its particular Mariological focus, N-Town's narrative is typically the most detailed, but York adds a touching moment when the Virgin appears to the Doubting Thomas to comfort him – and leaves her girdle in his hands, a moment in the *Protevangelium* that initiated a major chain of fetishization, the multiple copies of the Virgin's girdle located in churches and shrines all over Europe, about which the reformers, in their zeal to denounce and destroy false relics and superstition, would become particularly derisive. The York Assumption play, which was used in 1486 for an official welcoming of Henry VII, and the final York play, on the Coronation of the Virgin, could evidently be very elaborate productions, marking the theatrical climax of the Virgin's progress from creation to her cosmic role as Queen of Creation. The N-Town Assumption play is likewise presented as one of the culminating moments of the collection. Preceded on the manuscript by a prayer to God the Father and his mother, it demonstrates the centrality of the Virgin in the popular medieval mind. It repeats the rough humor of the play of Joseph's doubts about Mary, with a rapacious bishop who wants to kill and burn her; it includes a visitation from an angel, echoing the earlier scene of the Annunciation and bringing her news of God's intention that she will ascend to heaven; farewells for John, Paul, Peter, and a chorus of angels, virgins, and apostles. The persecuting bishop is made to repent, the evil princes converted, the shouting devils confounded, and the play ends on a triumphant note that the reformers would undoubtedly have found blasphemous:

GOD: Yow to worchepe, moder, it lykyth the hol Trinyte
Wherefor I crowne you here in this kyndam of glory
Of alle my chosyn, thus schul ye clepyd be
Quen of Hefne and Moder of Mercy.[24]

The reformers, however, in their zeal to distinguish between stories that were scriptural, and therefore really happened, and stories that were part of tradition and therefore merely legendary and at best matters of indifference, at worst blasphemous and idolatrous, had no patience with the story of Mary's Assumption, let alone the multiple girdles scattered across England and the rest of Europe, or other "superstitious things, to be occupied about the woman while she laboureth" that the Protestant authorities were to forbid.[25]

This overview of the Virgin's roles in the N-Town and other cycles shows how the familiar narrative of Mary's life was highlighted by scenes and emphases that – without undermining what Victor Scherb terms the "staging of faith"[26] – manage to humanize the Virgin and her reactions to ordinary domestic and familial experiences. Elizabeth Witt argues that French Marian plays of the period portray a Virgin who is notably more humanized than in the English plays, expressing maternal anxiety and some degree of irrationality – "stereotypically female" in the conventions of a patriarchal world, on occasions "obstinate, bossy, unreasonable, weak, and emotional," more in line with Eve, or Noah's wife than an idealized portrait of a near-goddess. French cycle plays, she argues, tend to avoid the episodes in which Mary is the subject of miracles such as her birth and upbringing, assumption or crowning as Queen of Heaven.[27]

If French plays on the Virgin reflect the fifteenth-century shift right across the arts toward portraying her less as a goddess and more as a woman and mother, a similar increase in naturalism can also be seen in the domestic scenes of the English plays. Even when the plays focus on occasions of high theological significance such as the Annunciation and the Ascension, the treatment of Mary is frequently staged within recognizably domestic and familial situations. In the episode of Mary's childhood, there is a touching gesturing at parental worries about the child's bewilderment beneath her confidence, with Mary presented as both reluctant to leave her parents and yet determined to fulfill her destiny. As Carole Hill has shown, devotion to St. Anne, the Virgin's mother, was an especially widespread cult in East Anglia, part of the emphasis on "holy kin" in the churches around

---

[24] Simpson, *Reform and Cultural Revolution*, 520–3; Sugano, *N-Town*, 329.
[25] Frere, *Visitation Articles*, II, 59.   [26] Scherb, *Staging of Faith*.   [27] Witt, *Contrary Marys*, 4, 97, 131.

Walsingham.[28] A. J. Tassioulis terms the scene between Anne and the young Mary in the N-Town play as "one of the most successful portraits of the holy child throughout all medieval literature," with theology merging harmoniously with narrative verisimilitude. As a young girl, her shyness or vulnerability may be seen as reflecting "theological" virtues of modesty or obedience, but there are hints of her life as a housewife and mother or, when visiting her cousin Elizabeth, as part of an extended family. Even the Annunciation scenes are typically written to show her humor; she teases Joseph when he tries to discover who has fathered her child; and in her role as mother concerned about her son, she initiates their decisions on marriage and child rearing, displaying a range of emotions from annoyance to anguish, and being both defiant and forgiving in the trial play when she has been accused of immorality. Staging the Virgin brought Mary into realms that many women in the audience would have recognized as like their own. The closer the dramatists of these plays brought their scenes to ordinary reality, the more integrated into the everyday the biblical story might become. The Virgin has come among them; divinity and the process of individuation and separation is not something remote, but present and at hand.[29]

Beyond the plays in which Mary has a role, there are domestic dramas centered on other women who prefigure her: Eve, Mrs. Noah, Elizabeth, and the slaughtered infants' mothers. In these plays the women "set into sharp contrast the exhaustion, blindness, and sometimes the brutality of men."[30] Many focus on marriage. Many of the husbands – Noah and Joseph among the most prominent – are shamed by their wives, and inept at negotiating, or even understanding, what is going on around them. Even when men control or even attack women, Simpson suggests, the plays "articulate a larger truth about male vulnerability" that the audience's men might find acceptable but which the women might have applauded.[31] Emma Lipton has argued that the plays on the marriage and trial of the Virgin were written in part in response to ongoing controversies over marriage. It is noticeable that Mary, she suggests, like other Jewish girls, is expected to marry but (as the early Church fathers argued) her marriage with Joseph is not based on sexuality but rather on spiritual unity, a mistake that both Joseph and the detractors make in their initial shock at her pregnancy. Yet while such patriarchal structures are left firmly in

[28] Hill, "St Anne and her Walsingham Daughter," 99–112.
[29] Tassioulis, "Between Doctrine and Domesticity," 231.
[30] Simpson, *Reform and Cultural Revolution*, 520.   [31] *Ibid.*, 520–3; Sugano, *N-Town*, 329.

place, at the same time, as James Simpson points out, male authority is often criticized and "quietly revealed as a structure designed to disguise male impotence and exhaustion."[32]

Not that the plays are without explicitly misogynic sentiments. Women are repeatedly described (by men) as sluts and slovens, threats to good government and God's will. The woman taken in adultery from the New Testament story is a "hore and stynkyne bych clowte"; Mary's detractors scoff at her vow of virginity and point out that "However it be her womb doth swell," and speculate about the cause:

DETRACTOR 2   Ya! That old shrewe Joseph–my trowth I plight–
                Was so anameryd upon that mayd,
                That of hyr bewté whan he had syght,
                He sesyd nat tyll he had her asayd!

DETRACTOR 1   A, nay, nay, wel wers she hath hym payd!
                Sum fresch yonge galaunt she loveth wel more
                That his leggys to her hath leyd!
                And that doth greve the old man sore![33]

But like Shakespeare's strong heroines – to whom the women of medieval drama have some definite resemblance – these heroines are witty, defiant, and seemingly undisciplinable, even while at the same time they work to hold together a family, society, and, in Mary's case, human history and salvation.

A thoroughgoing Althusserian approach to medieval drama might view it as a clear instance of an Ideological State Apparatus (Althusser's ISA) serving to maintain the dominant Christian ideology, creating and reinforcing subject positions for actors and audiences alike, and attempting rigidly to exclude alternatives.[34] According to this view, the plays' presentation of the Virgin was designed to represent her special status, her self-denial, obedience, silence, self-effacement, and her sexual purity, manifested not as renunciation so much as the absence of sexuality. But such a view, that the role of the drama was primarily to celebrate and confirm faith rather than question it, has been challenged from many sides in recent years.[35] Yet, even while acknowledging the orthodox intentions of the English Marian plays, we need to note that the dramatic form itself is inherently encouraging to alternative, even oppositional, ideas. In the theater,

[32] Simpson, *Reform and Cultural Revolution*, 521; Lipton, "Performing Reform," 407–35.
[33] Sugano, *N-Town*, 125.   [34] Althusser, *Lenin and Philosophy*, 137.
[35] The most thoroughgoing view of the plays as affirming orthodoxy is Scherb, *Staging Faith*; see also Witt, *Contrary Marys*, 57, 61, 81.

Peter Lake notes, "we are confronted with a sort of playpen in which participants could adapt and lay aside, ventriloquise and caricature, try on for size and discard a whole variety of subject positions, claims to authority, arguments and counter-arguments."[36] Except for closet drama – one of the alternatives to the stage favored, if briefly, by some regimes both Protestant and Catholic – by its very nature, the drama works by the staging of varied points of view and the opening of multiple possibilities of response from its audiences. Medieval drama's lack of any "fourth wall," its constantly drawing attention to itself as theater through the use of historical anachronism, and its location at once "here" and "there," both in the world and transcending it, represented a liminal space in which multiple perspectives could interact, for "staging" not only "faith," but faith's contradictions.

By the late sixteenth century, suspicion of drama becomes associated with what comes rather loosely to be called Puritanism, but throughout the previous centuries, actors and acting were also subject to ecclesiastical and civic suspicion. In one of the few records we have of an audience's reception of a medieval play, in 1431 a play on the Virgin's funeral was acted but it was abandoned after a petition from the Masons that "the subject matter of this pageant was not contained in the Holy Scriptures," and that it caused "laughter and shouting rather than devotion."[37] Given the blurring of physical realities and theological explanations in these plays, "laughter and shouting" rather than simply solemnity might well have been common responses and therefore a measure of many of the plays' theatrical success – but also an encouragement to the emergence of meanings not foreseen by the Church. In scenes in which Mary's body is the center, even with a closely controlled, heavily didactic script, the place of the human body and the "sacramentality" of the female body in particular is unavoidable.[38] When the Protestant regimes in England eventually gave up on reforming the traditional religious drama – a process which took until late in the sixteenth century – it was not just the objectionable level of papistry in the plays to which they were opposed, but the theater's uncontrollability.

Of course, the plays do not consistently spell out any oppositional or alternate traditions through explicit sexual suggestion. Typically, it is the comedy of the plays that leads to the questioning of religious conformity. Even at their most solemn moments – Creation, Fall, Incarnation, Nativity, Crucifixion, Ascension – a rough and engaging humor acts to subvert any

[36] Lake and Questier, *Antichrist's Lewd Hat,* 379.
[37] Coulton, *Art and Reformation,* 394.   [38] Beattie, *New Catholic Feminism,* 4, 141–2.

monovalent response. Nor is humor restricted to the diabolical or disruptive characters. The association of raucous comedy with evil (Satan sitting on God's throne, Herod shouting at his "knights") is obviously a disarming note in many medieval plays: it is hard to not to enjoy and respond enthusiastically to the devils' heroic bluster, let alone to fire crackers exploding from their backsides. But it would be naïve to say that enjoying the evil characters shows how we all share in humanity's fallen nature – not merely because such an explanation unquestioningly takes an orthodox interpretation of the events for granted, but because the kind of subversion encoded in performance is that it does not necessarily provide instantaneous opposition, but operates rather at a level that may influence later thinking and action. By the very nature of theatrical performance, members of an audience may have immediate reactions very different from those "intended" (always a question-begging concept with staging a play) and may develop quite different responses after the performance. Epilogues, such as occur at the end of the N-Town Assumption play, are often used to attempt to claw back meanings into the consciousness of an audience so that they leave with an orthodox viewpoint.

Nonetheless, many alternate meanings could easily arise from the multiple interactions of audiences and performers as they watched the staging of these plays. In being affronted by what they saw as the sexualization of Mary, the reformers may have been stripping "the sexual body of its overtly religious significance," but as Caviness comments, it was as if the reformers accurately sensed "the gynecological power" of the Virgin that percolated under the surface of late medieval culture.[39] This palimpsest of orthodoxy and alternate views permeates the Mary plays. When, in the N-Town play of the Creation and Fall, Eve and Adam have their eyes opened to their nakedness, the playwright cannot resist exaggerating and prolonging their discovery of their genitals:

> I se us nakyd before and behynde–
> Oure Lordys wurd wold we not drede.
> Therefore, we be now catyvys unkynde!
> Oure pore prevytes for to hede–
> Summe fygge levys wolde I fynde,
> For to hyde oure schame.
> Womman, ley this leff on thi pryvyté![40]

The audiences had unquestionably been taught not to doubt the official explanations of the mysteries of divine conception and maternity. But they

---

[39] Caviness, *Visualizing Women*, 2.   [40] Sugano, *N-Town*, 41.

were also able to compare them with their own bodily experiences. In a
society where loss of virginity, sexual intercourse, and birthing were continually highlighted as of cosmic significance, they would nonetheless have
unavoidably compared the Virgin's experiences with their own, which
(despite the official views of fallen sexuality) cannot always have been
unambiguously painful and humiliating or experienced as sinful, and
would have been intimately bound up with multiple bodily pleasures.
The experience of sexual contact, orgasm, and, not least, feelings of joy
and fear associated with gestation were bodily realities – and find an echo in
Mary's apprehension and cries of joy as she feels the child move inside her.
Like the Renaissance artists painting the Virgin's breasts or the Christ
Child's erect penis, the dramatists were moving theological abstractions
toward a degree of empirical testing against the real bodies that they knew –
their own. Because women have been so continually and consistently
identified with the body, when the real bodies are represented – on stage,
in the flesh – then the spectators find themselves testing the representations
against their own bodily realities. In the physical concreteness of drama –
with the Virgin being acted by and before neighbors – the physicality of
sexuality and birthing was thrust into the daylight where women (and no
doubt a few men) recognized the experience. There is an undercurrent of
affirmative sexuality in these scenes that challenges the dominant view of
the Virgin as totally "other"– impassably immaculate, impossibly ideal –
and of women as grotesque and fearful. They would recognize both their
own and the Virgin's sexuality, not just through the abstractions of
theology but in the play space of stage or street, physically present in
the bodies of the actors from the community playing amongst their
fellows.

In searching for an alternate tradition of the place of the female in
salvation history in the late medieval drama, it is important that we not
focus only on the Virgin, but on Eve, and glance at the plays about the Fall.
The orthodox medieval understanding of Eve, which is consistently
reflected in most dramatizations of the story, is that, as the Chester pageant
puts it, "my licourouse wife hath bynne my foe,"[41] that Eve's disobedience
was responsible for the exile of mankind from primal innocence and into an
awareness of sexuality and death – to be reversed only by Mary, the second
Eve. Was, however, Mary a symbol of Eve's condemnation or her redemption? That had been an active question in early Christian theology and the
concept of Mary as the New Eve can be traced back to early in the second

[41] Hussey, *Chester Mystery Plays*, 19.

century.[42] However, it was the heavy Augustinian emphasis on Eve's responsibility for original sin – the concept that Beattie terms "one of the greatest scourges of the Western Christian tradition"[43] – which predominated in medieval thinking about Eve and in large part determined the place women occupied in creation and society. Yet the redemptive role of Mary in restoring the original redemptive goodness of Creation and the equality of humanity was also woven into that tradition. The theological paradox of *felix culpa*, the fortunate fall, is echoed in many Marian lyrics of the period and is celebrated in the plays not only in the narrative of Mary's life and assumption to heaven as the symbol of the restored order, but even in the occasional hints of assertiveness and power of Eve herself.

The connection between Eve and Mary is particularly brought out in Annunciation plays. In the plays' main source, the *Protevangelium*, there is a strong emphasis, more than in the account in the Gospel of Luke, on Mary as the new Eve. In N-Town's words, "this name *Eva* is turnyd *Ave*." The Towneley Annunciation play stresses that "Man for man, tre for tre, / Madyn for madyn; thus shal it be." Mary will redeem mankind and she is hailed: "of all vyrgyns thou art queen."[44] In the Cornish mystery plays, the relationship between Eve and Mary is a major motif. In the Fall scene, Eve asks the serpent to bend down the branch of the apple tree for her, anticipating the scene in which the cherry tree bends for Mary when she is pregnant, thus making a connection "between the loss of paradise" and the "winning of salvation" through Mary. As Evelyn Newlyn points out, the Cornish *Ordinalia*, in effect a compressed version of a mystery cycle, distinguishes between women characters resembling Mary, who are dutiful, chaste, and theatrically passive, and those like Eve, such as Bathsheba, who are active, sexual, and also (not incidentally) theatrically attractive. But rather than rigidly separate the two, the text goes out of its way to stress the connection, making the "fortunate fall" central to the play, "carefully moving," Newlyn argues, between theological orthodoxy and "likely audience expectations."[45]

The joyful affirmation of the place of the female in salvation is also emphasized in the confidence and serenity, as well as the sense of humor, that Mary displays in her teasing of Joseph in the York and N-Town plays when he accuses her of adultery and tries to pry from her the identity of her child's father. In the Visitation scenes, when she visits the elderly Elizabeth

---

[42] Haskins, *Who is Mary?* 11.   [43] Beattie, *Woman*, 98.
[44] England, Pollard, and Kölbing, *Towneley Plays*, 87; Sugano, *N-Town*, 108.
[45] Newlyn, "Between the Pit and the Pedestal," 126–7, 133; for Eve, see also Glancy, *Corporal Knowledge*, 86, 93.

and we see two repletely pregnant women congratulating and admiring each other, the echoes of the Magnificat serve as a retrospective and prophetic affirmation of the place of the female body in salvation. Some post-patristic medieval theologians saw the praise of Mary as a sign that a woman's body was to be celebrated as central to the transformation of nature. That tradition of affirmation culminates in the various Assumption plays; York has a series of three, staging the appearance of the Virgin to Thomas and her Assumption and Coronation. N-Town's emphasis is similarly strong and sums up the narrative of Mary's life:

> At fourten yer sche conseyved Cryste in hire matere clere,
> And in the fiftene yer, sche childyd, this avowe dar I,
> Here lyvyng wyth that swete sone thre and thretty yere.
> And after his deth in erthe, twelve yer ded sche tary.
> Now acounte me thise yeris wysely.

In the York Weavers' play, the Appearance of Our Lady to Thomas, we are given the origin of the relic of the Virgin's girdle:

> I schall the schewe
> A token trewe,
> Full fresshe of hewe,
> Mi girdill, loo, take thame this tokyn.[46]

Not only Mary's body but her accoutrements have a transformative quality.

Arguing that women's experiences played a central place in both the production and reception of medieval drama is perhaps complicated by the apparent fact that, in England at least, for the most part women did not act in them. I state what used to be a firm scholarly assumption, but as more records come to light, the evidence is that women did often appear in local parish entertainments, parades, and plays. James Stokes suggests that, from evidence in Somerset parishes, we can include not merely parish games and dancing, but village and even itinerant performances as activities in which women may have sometimes participated. There is a little, admittedly slight, evidence for some women taking part in some of the cycle plays: records of a procession of virgins, a young girl playing Mary in a midsummer staging in London in 1523; Mary and Elizabeth played by "two maidens" in 1519; virgins scripted as participating in the *Killing of the Innocents*; the Chester Assumption play organized and possibly acted in by the town wives; the Killing of the Children play's requiring a procession of young girls, and a record of a celebration of the Festival of Lights at Candlemas by

---

[46] Sugano, *N-Town*, 313; Smith, *York Plays*, 486.

town women.[47] Given the scarcity of the surviving evidence about the plays overall, more women may have acted than we have generally assumed. Certainly, women frequently participated in dramatic performances on the continent. Tydeman quotes an account of a performance of the Presentation in Avignon in 1372 that called for "a young and most beautiful girl about three or four years old, who shall represent Mary [and any most beautiful woman, aged about 20, who shall be called Ecclesia and who shall] represent the Church."[48]

The question of whether women acted in plays is, however, less important to our understanding of how traditional gender roles might have been put into question by performance than the awareness that most of the women's roles were probably played by young men and boys. We are used to thinking of the complexities of gender bending raised by male actors playing female roles in Shakespeare's plays. Most notably in *As You Like It* or *Twelfth Night*, cross-dressing disrupts gender expectations, raises questions about sexuality and about "playing," not just on stage but in the wider society by members of the participating audience. But the thrill of transgression may well have surfaced even more strongly when the part of the pregnant Virgin was acted. Even a small detail such as costuming also raises the question of cross-dressing and therefore the blurring of gender lines. Meg Twycross comments on a cryptic manuscript remark about borrowing a gown for one of the Marys: it sounds unthreatening, she comments, if the character Mary Cleophas had been played by a woman, but if we think of the actor as a man it moves into a whole area of gender ambiguity. As Lesley Ferris comments, "transvestite drama – cross dressing in performance . . . forces the reader/spectator to see multiple meanings in the very act" of watching a performance.[49] These are issues that are all the more important in a drama supposedly designed to reinforce theological orthodoxy on matters of sexuality and gender.

Women's issues, in multiple senses, then, are central to these plays. In particular, there is a significant gynotheological strand in those plays dramatizing events that come close to the physical and sexual intimacies of the Virgin, especially the Annunciation and Birth, plays which, in Gibson's words, "stage the secrets of Mary's body."[50] Theresa Coletti's study of Mary Magdalen in medieval drama argues that it is Magdalen who brings

---

[47] Stokes, "Women and Performance," 25; see also Hill-Vasquez, *Sacred Players*, 160–1.
[48] Gibson, *Theater of Devotion*, 211.
[49] Twycross, "Transvestism"; Ferris, *Crossing the Stage: Controversies on Cross-Dressing*, 8. See also Normington, *Gender and Medieval Drama*, 66–7.
[50] Gibson, "Scene and Obscene," 18.

sexuality into the plays, but, less explicitly, the Virgin herself also brings female sexuality into performance.[51] Gibson has written eloquently on how the plays concerning Mary bring out the "mostly unstoried history of ordinary late medieval attitudes towards the pregnant body," not least because they put sexuality into public discourse. The very centrality of Mary's specifically female physical characteristics in the salvation narrative, the fact that as Gibson puts it, "the symbolic and ritual center of this drama was a woman's body," and that there were women's bodies in attendance, in the audience, along with men's bodies which in turn knew, carnally as well as theologically, those female bodies, may well have made the gynotheology of the Mary plays as exciting, and disturbing, as they sometimes appear today.[52]

The scenes that best illustrate these observations are the plays on Joseph's "troubles" with Mary and the midwives scene of the Nativity play. Their subject is the Virgin's impregnation, gestation, and birthing, and her perpetual virginity – before, during, and after birth. The scene of the marriage of Mary and Joseph is often preceded by a scene or even a separate play in which the members of the Trinity debate and decide on their actions. But these plays are not solemn theological expositions. They combine popular theology with the broadest of humor, and add not a little melodramatic prurience. Lipton points out that earlier versions of the life of the Virgin generally paid little attention to the details of the marriage between Mary and Joseph, and because these plays also go well beyond even the details provided by the *Protevangelium* and the *Golden Legend*, which were their major sources, the dramatists were clearly taking a special interest in the theatrical possibilities of the event.[53]

First, Joseph's so-called troubles with Mary. The story was dramatized in all the extant collections, and it is possible that the N-Town compiler drew on the York play. The audience is continually brought into the action by the use of gender stereotypes. Joseph repeatedly appeals directly to the anxieties of men in the community with young wives. His doubts are reinforced by the wonderfully direct dialogue of the two detractors. Their scorn of Joseph and cynicism about Mary is at once outrageously insulting but theatrically disarming:

DETRACTOR I   Such a yonge damesel of bewte bryght,
              And of schap so comely also
              Of hir tayle ofte tyme be light
              And rygh tekyl undyr thee, too!

[51] Coletti, *Mary Magdalene and the Drama of Saints.*   [52] Gibson, "Scene and Obscene," 18.
[53] Lipton, "Performing Reform," 407.

DETRACTOR 2   That olde cokolde was evyl begylyd
To that fresche wench whan he was wedde!
Now muste he faderyn anothyr mannys chylde
And with his swynke, he shal be fedde.[54]

When Joseph is accused of impotence, the action seems designed to make the orthodox theological point that their marriage was a spiritual not a carnal one, and that he and Mary did not have sexual relations. But the lesson is undermined by being presented as comedy so effective that it constitutes a counter-discourse. As Lipton notes, in "the spectacle of the actors holding up wands to see whose will bloom we are being given a graphic image of phallic sexuality," the effect is warm-hearted ridicule of male impotence and (de)tumescence. With theological mysteries brought into the flesh, the scene enacted is hardly going to be a theatrical flop (as it were) and enables, without forcing, the audience to take a critical stance toward the theology. Joseph is not simply a pious symbol, but one of the great comic figures of frustration and confusion in drama. He grumbles about his impotence and the humiliation his wife's obvious pregnancy brings him. He evokes the common fear that men often have of women's unpredictable and uncontrollable sexuality, their reputed vulnerability to other men, and the humiliation of being an old man with a voluptuous and supposedly sexually aggressive young wife. He laments his lot to his wife's maids, and is annoyed by their mocking insistence that an angel has been responsible for her pregnancy: "It was sum boy began this game / That clothyd was clene and gay, / And ye geve hym now an aungel name!" His language to Mary is crude, direct, and continually draws attention to the physical details of the sexual act: "And I cam nevyr ther ... so nyh thi boure." Even when finally reassured, he is not reduced to a theological stereotype, but takes on the comic role of the henpecked male with a controlling, even petulant, wife.[55]

It is important to stress that the scenes in which Joseph confronts Mary are not to be read but acted. This distinction may appear elementary but we may tend to overlook the enactment of the plays as a bodily experience. The actors would gesture, touch, push, spit, insult, as the script demands, with the implied actions serving to physicalize and bring out the scene's gyno-theological impact. The detail in which both York and N-Town develop the scenes suggest that they were – like Noah and his wife or Satan in Eden – crowd favorites. Even when Mary and Joseph have triumphed in their trial,

---

[54] Sugano, *N-Town*, 125.   [55] Lipton, "Performing Reform," 413; Sugano, *N-Town*, 113–14.

are enthusiastically hailed, and the backbiters have begged Mary's forgiveness, the comedy encourages a degree of indulgence in at least the possibility
of probing into forbidden mysteries. Joseph's repentance may underline the
lesson of Mary's perpetual virginity, but in the process the audience has
entered into speculations about what Erasmus, in his coy way, was to refer
to as the Virgin's "pryvytes." As spectators we have been privy to those
secrets and inevitably relate them to our knowledge of our own. Male
members of the audience must have felt especially reinforced for their
curiosity about women's sexuality, even simply about the details of female
anatomy. In the trial scene, Mary is surrounded by male lawyers, judges,
bishops, and detractors, in a space where there are no other women to
support her – except those in the audience. Women might well have
identified with her and sympathized; for men, such intense interrogations
might easily have intensified the fantasies in which they peered into the
mystery that was female sexuality.

The Midwives scene in N-Town (and also in the Chester collection
where the stage direction speaks of the two "obstetrics" touching the
Virgin's "*sexo secreto*") brings out the contradictions of medieval gynotheology in an even more startling way. The Chester stage direction reads: "*Tunc
Salome tentabit tangere Mariam in sexu secreto, et statim arentur manus eius, et
clamando dicit.*"[56] The plays make public "those secret orifices of the female
body that have become theological mystery" by having the birth take place
not in the accustomed secret female space, but publicly. It is, Gibson says, a
"stunning transgression of social order," a "birthing that violates decorum at
every level."[57] Today, it the scene that (from the experience of directing it)
can still shock: it is as if the bodily reality of the scene subverts the
theological purity of the concept. One of the reasons the *Protevangelium*
was rejected from the canon, in fact, was because it included the story of the
midwives. Jerome criticized its depiction of the Virgin lying on a bed,
referring to childbirth, suffering pains. Rather, said Jerome, "those pictures
should be promoted which show the birth of Christ in which the Blessed
Virgin Mary with arms folded and on bended knee before her little son, as
though he was just now brought into the light." But the story had, van der
Horst comments, "an enormous influence in Patristic literature till far into
the Middle Ages." It extends the Lukan narrative of the birth of Christ to
stress "a graphic post-partum gynecological exam," and was probably
written as part of an earlier invented tradition to establish the Virgin as

---

[56] Lumiansky and Mills, *Chester Plays*, I, 118. For a helpful discussion, see Bicks, *Midwiving Subjects*, 19.
[57] Gibson, "Scene and Obscene," 18.

having no less dignity and magical powers than rival pagan goddesses, and possibly to counter stories of her illegitimate pregnancy.[58]

In the play, dutiful Jewish husband that he is, Joseph – who, as a man, would be conventionally excluded from attending the birthing – has set about to find a midwife to assist his wife during and especially after the birth. Midwives occupied positions of authority in medieval communities, often taking on a "judicial function" to verify virginity, rape, infanticide, or adultery.[59] The midwives therefore become authoritative witnesses to the postpartum miracle of Mary's continuing virginity:

> With honde now lete me now towch and fele
> Yf ye have nede of medycyn
> I shal yow comforte and helpe ryght wele
> As other women, yf ye have pyn.

Mary asserts, in accord with sound theology, that "peyne nere grevynge fele I ryght non," and invites the midwife to "tast with youre hand yourself." Zelomye affirms that "A fayr chylde of a maydon is born ... His modyr, nott hurte of virgynité." In awe, she points out the miracle of the Virgin's flowing milk: "Beholde the brestys of this clene mayd / Ful of fayre mylke how that thei be." The other midwife, Salome, expresses skepticism that "a mayd milke have" and states that she will never believe it "but I it preve / with hand towchynge." Mary invites her to carry out a vaginal inspection: "To put you clean out of doubt / Towch with your hand and wele assay, / Whether I be fowlyed or a clene mayd."[60] Salome touches Mary and finds her hand dried up and, in pain, is forced to admit the miracle. The miracle of Mary's miraculous virginity is therefore attested by authorities recognizable to the watching community.

Theatrically, this story of "doubting Salome" [61] is a tour de force. The inspection is the culmination of a traditional fictional genre. Like the heroines of countless stories of threatened heroines in Greek romances or virgin martyrs threatened by rape, stories full of "virginity tests, near seductions, and threats of rape,"[62] Mary has been made holy, set aside by her virginity and her precarious position in a skeptical community when she seems to be both sexually active and pregnant. Historically, as many biblical

[58] Johannes Molanus, *De Imaginibus Sacris*, quoted by Neyrey, "Mary: Mediterranean Maid and Mother," 66–89. For the influence of the story in the *Protevangelium*, see Zervos, "Christmas with Salome," 90–3, van der Horst, "Sex, Birth, Purity and Asceticism," 64–5.

[59] Ryan, "Playing the Midwife's Part," 435, 444; Mills, *Recycling the Cycle*, 174.

[60] Sugano, *N-Town*, 139–40.   [61] van der Horst, "Sex, Birth, Purity and Asceticism," 79.

[62] *Ibid.*, 70.

scholars have indicated, a girl in Mary's condition at the time would not have been married off but almost certainly stoned to death. Her appeal is that of the heroine of a romance tale, a vulnerable heroine poised between innocence and sexuality, entrapped by her female nature and rescued only by miracle – and then, in this wonderfully outrageous scene, with the "evidence" of the shriveled hand and the doubting midwife's acknowledgment, shown quasi-empirically, to be miraculously "whole." The shriveled hand of the intruder is meant to be the real proof of divine intervention, with Mary's perpetual virginity being a mysterious theological or magical rather than a gynecological reality. But the effect in performance may well have been the opposite – to invite spectators to imagine precisely what is occurring, including the insertion of fingers or hand into the Virgin's vagina.

The effect of sexual and gender dislocation would no doubt have been intensified when the part of the Virgin was played by a boy. Staging these scenes today – and the midwives scene in particular – may still produce a similar combination of intense fascination and, to some, considerable shock. The audience is being invited to (almost) see into the heart of the mystery – of sex, woman, and the origins of life, in the title of Courbet's famous painting, *L'Origine du Monde* (1866, Musée D'Orsay, Paris). Because the scene is literally embodied, the nature of the Virgin's private parts becomes publicly imaginable and discussable, and the more convincing the acting, the more the physicality of the acts is foregrounded. In a three-minute scene, the gynotheological basis of medieval Mariology is – if not exposed – at least rendered as an extraordinarily present absence. It is as if one is watching some of the most fundamental physically sensitive stories of our culture exposed. The center of the episodes are the sexual organs of the supposedly least sexualized figure in Christian history. Marian plays were understandably among the first censored or removed as the Reformation attempted to eliminate the idolatry of the community biblical dramas.

The midwives scene came in for some predictable criticism from reformers. That it was a sensitive matter can be seen from the Chester banns that were posted after the Reformation: "Yf the scriptures a waarant not of the Mydwyfes reporte / The Author telleth his Author then take it in sporte."[63] The Puritan Christopher Goodman made a list of blasphemies and absurdities in the Chester plays, which ceased by 1575 since they contained, according to Archbishop Grindal of York, "sundry absurd & gross errours &

[63] Bicks, *Midwiving Subjects*, 69.

heresies joined with profanation & great abuse of god's holy word"; prominent among them were the magi honoring "the virgin in place of Christ," and specifically directed to the midwives scene, "two midwives to Christ Tibill & Salome"; and, specifically directed at the playing of the Virgin, "the miracle of drying up of Salomes hands & the restoring of the same."[64] As I noted in Chapter 2, some contemporary Catholic theologians have increasingly argued precisely for an awareness of genital sexuality to be restored to the image of the Virgin Mary and for the abandonment of the legend of a non-vaginal delivery. I am reminded of Steinberg's observation that medieval theologians drifted away from the full implications of the Incarnation and it was the artists who pulled them back. Modern theologians' calls for the "vaginality" of the Virgin to be recognized, or for "female divinity" to be associated with female sexuality,[65] are anticipated, even if only in the margins of discourse, by well over five hundred years by the dramatists of the late medieval religious plays.

---

[64] Mills, "Some Precise Cittizins," 219, 225; Ryan, "Playing the Midwifes Part," 446.

[65] Ribas, "Liberating Mary, Liberating the Poor," 135; Caputi, "Naked Goddess," 186–7.

CHAPTER 4

Walsingham or Falsingham, Woolpit or Foulpit? Marian shrines and pilgrimage before 1538

In the *Court of Venus,* a mid-sixteenth-century miscellany, mainly consisting of poems and anecdotes, occurs a poem, attributed to Chaucer but clearly written in the 1530s, entitled *The Pilgrim's Tale.* It was likely written by Robert Singleton, at one time chaplain to Anne Boleyn and a convert to the reformist cause. In enthusiastic ballad stanzas that occasionally rise above doggerel, it expresses a common reformist attitude to pilgrimages. The pilgrim of the poem's title is setting out from Lincolnshire – the origins of one of the strongest protests against the process of dissolution of the religious houses in the late 1530s – "toward Walsingham apon my pelgrymage." On the way, he undergoes a conversion experience and realizes that pilgrimages are "sprong owt of Antichrist" and in the past have deceived many pilgrims who "have put trust in suche fablis vayn."[1] Whereas the reformers scorned all "feign'd miracles," a phrase repeated throughout the period so often as to become a cliché, pre-Reformation Christians had expected what Ethan Shagan terms "frequent spontaneous eruptions of the divine," and to reap earthly, heavenly (or at least purgatorial) rewards for completing their pilgrimages "for religion's sake," as Erasmus put it.[2] In 1455, to take merely two instances, the pope confirmed the awarding of indulgences offered by the Archbishops of Canterbury and York "having regard to the devotion of people who flock" to a Marian shrine in Liverpool; at Stainar, and Hemingbrough, near Selby Abbey, indulgences were granted by the pope for the feast of the Assumption of the Virgin for the miracles worked there "by the merits of the said Virgin."[3] The indulgence industry

---

[1] Fraser, *Court of Venus,* 82, 92, 98.
[2] Shagan, *Popular Politics,* 64. For "feigned miracles," see e.g. Frere, *Visitation Articles,* II, 67.
[3] Webb, *Pilgrimage in Medieval England,* 103–4, 105.

had developed slowly from around 1200 and then expanded rapidly in succeeding centuries. Indulgences could be given for multiple reasons – from rewards for arduous pilgimages to shrines to road repair crews for preventing travelers en route from swearing when their pilgrimage carts overturned. Initially sought after for an individual's own benefit, gradually – "when and by whom . . . is unclear," R. N. Swanson notes – indulgences became transferrable to the afterlife, their availability to pass on to the dead in Purgatory first officially approved in 1476. The advent of printing meant that pilgrimage sites could advertise the availability of indulgences more aggressively. Many developed what Swanson terms "almost package-tour" pilgrimages, with the indulgence documents that were earned becoming more elaborate and "more consciously a marketing device."[4]

Yet although pilgrimages – whether for a day or two to a local shrine or for weeks or months to a far-off one – were a commonplace part of late medieval everyday life, they had long drawn attacks from those miscella-neous groups of heretics that were labeled "Wycliffites" or "Lollards." Pilgrims, complained a typical attack, grovel, touch, kiss, or lick the relics, "strokande and kyssand these olde stones and stokkis, laying doun hore grete offryngis, and maken avowis right there to thes dede ymagis to come the nexst yeer again."[5] Our Lady of Woolpit's shrine, in the church of St. Mary at Woolpit, in Suffolk, was jeered at by Lollards as "Our lady of Foulpit."[6] As the most prominent of all Marian objects of pilgrimage, the "wyche of Walsingham" and her supposed miracles, which are celebrated so enthusiastically in the Pynson Ballad, was the special target of scorn. Lollards often sneered at "Falsingham" or "the wych of Walsingham." A typical Lollard exhortation was to "not adore an image, the blessed Mary of Walsingham, nor the blood of Christ at Hailes," thus linking two pilgrimage sites centered on physical relics, milk and blood, against which reformers expressed particularly outraged scorn.[7]

A recurring criticism of pilgrimages was that they encouraged sexual immorality. Like the reformers after them, Lollards often tinged their dis-approval with scatological remarks about whores, venereal disease, and pro-miscuity. But the conservative Thomas More made a not dissimilar remark, that "our lady was a vyrgyn and yet at her pylgrymages be made many a foule metynge." In his *Dialogue concerning Heresies*, in which he defended "the

---

[4] Swanson, *Promissory Notes*, 18; *Indulgences in Late Medieval England*, 14, 53, 172.
[5] *Ibid.*, 99, 100; Bernard, "Vitality and Vulnerability," 231; Duffy, *Stripping of the Altars*, 382, 387.
[6] Paine, "Our Lady of Woolpit," 8–12.
[7] Peters, *Patterns of Piety*, 215; Shagan, *Popular Politics*, 167. For Lollards, see Aston, *Lollards and Reformers*.

veneration & worship of images & relics, praying to saints & going on pilgrimage," he warns "you men of London" to make sure they accompany their wives on pilgrimage to Our Lady of Willesdon, just outside London, "or keep them at home with you! Else you'll be sorry." He was especially scornful of women's devotion, commenting sarcastically on the London wives praying before a image of the Virgin near the Tower, imagining that it smiled upon them, and mocking a discussion about which of the various "ladies" they preferred to visit. Yet More himself made a pilgrimage to Our Lady of Willesden the week before he was arrested, in April 1534, staying at a relative's house and, anticipating his possible arraignment, taking time there to put some affairs in order. Willesden was a typical local pre-Reformation shrine to the Virgin, with pilgrims regularly visiting its dark Madonna, probably blackened by candles, a spring of clear water said to cure the plague, and, like many other pilgrimage sites, subject to regular criticism for the unruliness of pilgrims. Along with its "sisters," Our Lady of Willesden was taken to London in 1538 to be burned, despite the Suffolk priest Robert Creukehorne's maintaining (before Latimer and Cranmer, no less) that the Virgin had appeared to him to urge him to preach that "she wold be honored at Eppiswhiche and at Willesden as she hath bee in olde tymes." [8]

Like Erasmus and other exponents of the "new learning," More was concerned that images, pilgrimage, and miracles be neither abused nor rejected. A common Wycliffite or Lollard assertion was that pilgrims all too easily believed that images themselves brought about miracles. Despite recurring criticism of pilgrimages, few ordinary medieval pilgrims would have worried about such niceties – and there was undoubtedly widespread encouragement to identify the Virgin with her various images. A powerful Madonna, her relics, and the highly charged Mariocentric atmosphere of a pilgrimage to a place such as Ipswich or Walsingham did not merely memorialize the past; each of the "images" burnt in 1538 in some sense *was* the Virgin, literally an embodiment of pilgrims' sense of the divine. Holiness was also directly apprehended in specific sensory details that pilgrims encountered both at and en route to the shrine – sights, sounds, tastes, sensations, feelings stimulated by bells, lights, prayer, music, water, incense, relics, processions, rituals, souvenirs, and badges – all of which helped make the Virgin present to the pilgrims and spilt over into the supposedly non-sacred world around. A pilgrimage, whether to a nationally famous shrine such as Walsingham or a local shrine such as Woolpit or

---

[8] More, *Dialogue concerning Heresies, Works,* VI, 100; Stewart, *The Life and Letters of Sir Thomas More,* 29; Vail, *Shrines of Our Lady,* 223; Mitjans, "Thomas More's Veneration of Images," 67–8.

Willesden, proclaimed the possibility of personal intimacy with the Virgin, not merely as a distant historical figure but there, in the details of a particular place. It was, of course, this overall aura of materialistic holiness, divinity expressed through observable realities and experienced by the senses, to which Lollards and, eventually, the reformers objected.

The English Madonnas of the late Middle Ages included not only those that were burned in 1538, but those representations in local shrines found in and near every cathedral and religious house, in every county, every parish. The number of pilgrimage sites in England in the late Middle Ages that were dedicated to the Virgin – or more strictly speaking, as Carroll points out, were "maddonnine" shrines, dedicated to different Madonnas – runs into the hundreds, and if we were to count all public pictorial representations, it would have been difficult to walk a few yards, at least in towns and villages, without some reminder of the Virgin's presence. The nineteenth-century compiler of Mariological legends and trivia Joseph Waterton comments that "images of our Ladye . . . must have been as commonly placed in house-corners and in walls, as they are yet to be seen in Catholic countries."[9] Eighteenth- and nineteenth-century antiquarians assiduously tracked down hundreds of local shrines which had been reputedly places of great pilgrimage. Every parish church, of course, had one or more statues of the Virgin; Stanley Smith, the historian of Our Lady of Ipswich, calculated there were at least sixteen shrines in Suffolk alone that were subjects of special devotion.[10] The effects of the century of iconoclasm have blurred the fact that no less than in, say, Italy, multiple and at least in the popular mind relatively distinct "metacults"[11] of the Virgin existed. More rather testily pointed out to his adversary Tyndale that each different Madonna was, of course, associated with the "official" Virgin Mary; nevertheless, each "Lady," to use the common English term, maintained a separate identity.

The most famous Marian shrine in England was undoubtedly that at Walsingham. Around the middle of the fifteenth century, probably about 1465, a four-page poem that tells the story of Walsingham's supposed origins was written. It is conventionally named the "Pynson Ballad," for its printer, Thomas Pynson. First printed about thirty years later, it is a combination devotional manual and guidebook, an example, in Diarmaid MacCulloch's phrase, of "hagiographical tourist literature . . . worthy of a modern popular novelist, and with about as much historical content."[12] As Dominic Janes

---

[9] Carroll, *Veiled Threats*, 23; Waterton, *Pietas Mariana Britannica*, 1, 183.
[10] Smith, *The Madonna of Ipswich*, 12. [11] Carroll, *Madonnas that Maim*, 59, 62.
[12] MacCulloch, *Reformation*, 414, 456.

and I have summarized in the history of Walsingham, the Pynson Ballad was designed as part of an aggressive "invention of tradition," designed to establish and parade the antiquity and prestige of the Walsingham shrine.[13] It tells "howe by myraccle it was founded," allegedly in 1061, when a "noble wydowe" in Walsingham Parva, Richeldis de Faverche, had three visions in which the Virgin told her to build a replica of the Holy House of Nazareth. Mary Beth Moser notes that in the Virgin's miraculous appearances, she typically "appears to someone and makes very specific requests or demands that sacred space (a chapel or church) be built to honor her"; she "does not leave it to chance or someone else's idea of where a church should be," but makes it clear that she "is in control of the situation."[14] Richeldis was, according to the ballad, given the choice of two sites. She chose one, but next day was amazed to find that the house had been miraculously assembled on the other, over two hundred feet away.[15]

As with most "invented traditions," there are some vaguely connected historical events behind the story of Walsingham's miraculous origins.[16] The name Richeldis is indeed recorded in Walsingham, although almost a century after the date claimed in the ballad, so most modern historians (as opposed to pious readers of the ballad eager to accept its tale as historically accurate) date the beginnings of a private chapel that became an Augustinian priory in the mid twelfth century rather than Pynson's date of 1061. By the mid fifteenth century, however, it may have seemed politically important to date the story of the Virgin's appearance to Richeldis back to a year before the Norman Conquest, and so affirm Walsingham's native English origins, but it was also important, as Carroll has argued, to preempt another invented tradition which was also taking shape in the mid fifteenth century, that of the miraculous transportation (by angels) to Loreto, Italy of the "original" Holy House of Bethlehem.[17] The Pynson Ballad is the only "source" for Walsingham's supposed origin. No other account that is even remotely similar exists, and even Erasmus, in his detailed description of Walsingham, published in 1524, does not mention it – though he does recount a story of the origin of the shrine's two wells as springing out from under the Virgin's feet, presumably on the occasion of her initial visit.

[13] Janes and Waller, *Walsingham*, 1–20.
[14] Moser, "Blood Relics"; Chidgey, *Our Lady of Penrhys*, 5.   [15] Dickinson, *Shrine*, 125.
[16] The phrase "invented tradition" is, famously, that of Hobsbaum and Ranger, *Invention of Tradition*. For its application to Walsingham, see Coleman and Elsner, "Tradition as Play," and Janes and Waller, *Walsingham*, 1–20.
[17] Carroll, "Pilgrimage at Walsingham," 39–40.

Whether the Virgin appeared in a dream or vision or in an actual apparition, Walsingham's founding legend is by no means unique. Coleman observes that all pilgrimage shrines have such originary stories, including many in which the Virgin appears and orders a church or chapel to be built. Carroll notes that typically "the most powerful Madonnas are not only those whose images are kept in distant rural sanctuaries," often in existing dedicated sacred spaces, or else near some other "natural healing site."[18] As well as their origins in such an event, such sites are often located in an obscure place that is difficult to access; they come to be associated with or possess a famous and powerful devotional object, image, or statue to which pilgrims make often arduous pilgrimages; there is usually some ongoing material connection with natural forces such as water, and there is always evidence of a continuing divine presence in the form of a succession of miracles. Such a story of origins is attributed to the image of Our Lady of the Taper at Cardigan, in modern times revived as the national Catholic Marian shrine of Wales. A medieval sacred space was typically established, James Bugslag explains, in a "position between the 'human' space" of a settlement, such as a town, and the "'savage' space of the open land": in this case, a statue of the Virgin carrying the Christ Child, and with a burning taper in her hand, was found at a remote spot near the mouth of the river Teifi. It was taken to the parish church but refused to remain there, miraculously returning three or four times to its original isolated spot until it was realized that the Virgin's wish was that a chapel was to be built precisely where it had been found.[19]

In addition to his celebrated ballad on Walsingham, in 1520, at the instigation of Abbot Richard Beere of Glastonbury, who had recently visited Loreto, Pynson also printed a poetical account of the origins of the shrine of Our Lady of Glastonbury. It occurs in a life of Joseph of Arimathea who, according to one of the many versions of the Grail legend, visited England and was instructed by an angel "Of our Ladye's Assumpcyon to bylde a chapel":

> So Joseph dyd as the aungell hym bad
>   And wrought there an ymage of our Lady
> For to serve her gret devocion he had,
>   And that same ymage is yet at Glastenbury
> In the same churche: there ye may it se.[20]

---

[18] Coleman and Elsner, "Tradition as Play," 274–79; Coleman, "Pilgrimage to 'England's Nazareth'," 54–5; Carroll, *Madonnas that Maim*, 26.

[19] Bugslag, "Local Pilgrimages"; Williams, *Welsh Cistercians*, 149; Waterton, *Pietas Mariana Britannica*, II, 10–1, 284; For the modern shrine at Cardigan, see www.ourladyofthetaper.org.uk.

[20] Luxford, *English Benedictine Monasteries*, 61–2. For the Penrhys poem, see Waterton, *Pietas Mariana Britannica*, II, 280.

As at Walsingham, the lesson of the Virgin's insistent wishes had to be learned. Evesham Abbey's story of origins includes a double apparition of the Virgin, first to a shepherd, Eof (or Eoves), and then to St. Egwin, who was "blessed with a golden cross" which the Virgin "carried in her hand," after which he commenced the building of the abbey. In the case of Our Lady of Penrhys, one of the companion sisters burnt with the Walsingham image in 1538, the originary story tells of a statue of the Virgin that came miraculously from Heaven and was lodged in a tree until a chapel was built at the top of a mountain near a holy well, which (as at Walsingham and Woolpit) also sprang up at the Virgin's command.[21] Penrhys also has its equivalents to the ballads Pynson printed for Walsingham and Glastonbury. Gwilym Tew, a poet who flourished in the late fifteenth century, wrote an "Ode to Our Lady of Penrhys," setting out her powers and miracles. Another poet, Rhisiart ap Rhys, likewise praised the allegedly immovable statue for healing "the diseases of the multitude who wait upon thee, and are healed the second night." Reformers scorned such stories. A few years after the Penrhys poems were written, one of Cromwell's agents wrote of the pilgrims "gadding, with a few clothes" to worship what was revealed to be "but an image of wax, for the lame and the blynde," and which proved not to be as unmovable as the pious had asserted and was one of the "sisters" taken to London for burning in 1538.[22]

Appearances of the Virgin to demand the building of a chapel or shrine, however, would often come with a warning. There are also legends in which she punishes those who refuse to obey her command to build a church or chapel. Such events suggest that she has independent powers and can readily use threats of punishment or retribution for refusal, skepticism or ingratitude. In the title of Carroll's celebrated study, the multiple Madonnas under whose protection the shrines were could easily become "Madonnas that maim," both a "source of danger and a source of protection from that danger."[23] Benedetta Ward instances a number of occasions in England when the Virgin's predilection for punitive powers is demonstrated: she notes the commonplace phrase *vindicta Mariae* to describe such instances of punishment, which might even include the offender's death. Erasmus, in a typically gleeful sideswipe, amusedly criticizing yet at the same time expressing a degree of indulgence for such foolishness, has one of his interlocutors

---

[21] Sayers, *Evesham Abbey*; Waterton, *Pietas Mariana Brittania*, II, 33–4.

[22] For the fifteenth-century Welsh poets who praise Our Lady of Penrhys, see Lord, *The Visual Culture of Wales*, 220.

[23] Carroll, *Madonnas that Maim*, 77. For a further example in which a refusal to build is punished, see Waterton, *Pietas Mariana Britannica*, II, 147–8.

comment, not dissimilarly, that "the sayntes haue theyr weapones or myschefues, whiche they send apon whome they liste."[24]

When pilgrims set out for Penrhys or Willesden, Ipswich or Walsingham, what drew them most? It was the particular "Image" of the Virgin. Most share similar characteristics. At Warwick there was "a feire ymage of gold of our ladi goddess mother"; Our Lady of Lincoln, in Lincoln Cathedral, sat in a four-posted chair, with a crown of silver and gilt, decorated in stones and pearls, with the Child on her knee, also with a crown with pearls and stones. At Walsingham the statue of the Virgin and Child burned in 1538 was made of wood; she too sat in a chair, with the Christ Child across her knee; the statue had a gold crown paid for by Henry III, a gold circlet given by Henry VIII, and, when visited by pilgrims, would also have been decorated in jewels and trinkets, surrounded by *ex votos* and other tributes, including, after Erasmus's visit, a poem he wrote in praise of the Virgin.[25] The Woolpit shrine probably had no special ballad, nor many visits from Erasmus or other poets, but like them it had an "image," with a striking set of silver beads with three gold rings, given on condition "that the parson of the said town let them abide about Our ladyes neck continually." Woolpit's image dated at least from the early thirteenth century, when the monks at nearby Bury St. Edmunds – Lydgate's monastery, it will be recalled from Chapter 3 – were ordered to be the recipients of its pilgrims' offerings. The statue was likely housed, as at Walsingham, in a side chapel which was wrecked in the late 1530s and most likely finally destroyed in 1551 when Suffolk authorities were sent to "the chappell . . . called Our Lady of Wulpit" with the order that "the leade therof in sembable wise to take down . . . and to make sale of all the tymber, stones iron and glasse cuming of the said chappell to the Kings said highness most advantage." No less than Walsingham, though on a local rather than a national level, Our Lady of Woolpit had played an important place in local life. By the fourteenth century, the village had been granted a fair, to be held on the feast of the Virgin's nativity. By the fifteenth century, there are records of bequests of jewels, rings, wax, "a stained cloth," girdles, beads, candles, and a scepter for the image of Our Lady.[26] Pilgrimages on behalf of the deceased are recorded in the late fifteenth century from nearby villages, and in 1501 there is even a record of a pilgrimage on behalf of Henry VII's queen,

---

[24] Carroll, *Veiled Threats*, 158; Ward, *Miracles and the Medieval Mind*, 141; Erasmus, *Pilgrimage*, 26.

[25] Waterton, *Pietas Mariana Britannica*, II, 63, 221; Dickinson, *Shrine*, 19, 43, 65; see also Kamerick, *Popular Piety*.

[26] Paine, "Our Lady of Woolpit," 8.

Elizabeth. There was a well dedicated to the Virgin, although in a typical episode of how holy wells are "re-invented," no mention of it occurs before the 1550s, and all the lore about it – healing, miraculous properties, visitors, the curing of weak eyes – dates from no earlier than the eighteenth, and thereafter is increasingly elaborated in the outbreak of nostalgic medievalism in the nineteenth and twentieth centuries, until in 1957 it becomes labeled the Woolpit Holy Well and (in yet another invented tradition) described as "a favourite resort of pilgrims during the Middle Ages,"[27] thus firming up what is only very vaguely based on historical records.

As England's premier Marian site, one of Walsingham's distinctive names was "England's Nazareth," pointing to the palimpsestic presence of the Holy Land in England. It was therefore both local and exotic, with domestic and patriotic associations, and yet connected to a wider spiritual universe, a reminder that religious power could be experienced in a local landscape far more practicable to reach than its original. For any medieval Christian, Jerusalem and the Holy Land were the quintessential medieval pilgrim sites, the places where Christ's divinity had been made concrete, where the Virgin had actually been present, and where relics of her could be seen, touched, and venerated, and whence (along with Ephesus, where, according to some stories, she had spent her last years and whence she ascended to Heaven) most of those distributed around European shrines had come. Chaucer's parson reminds his fellow pilgrims to Canterbury that Jerusalem should be their ultimate pilgrimage goal, but few people were able to make such a long journey; Margery Kempe, from Lynn, was one laywomen who did so for whom we have detailed records.

Relics of the Virgin were a prominent part of any shrine's drawing power. As Leigh Ann Craig comments, "the belief that a saint's physical remains, tomb, or personal possessions formed a bridge between the earthly and the divine lay at the very heart of the veneration of saints."[28] Parts of a saint's body – blood, bones, hair, or (with the Virgin) milk – would dramatically increase connectedness with the holy personage in Heaven. In the case of the Virgin since, according to the widespread belief, although not yet dogma, her body was assumed into Heaven, secondary or tertiary relics,

---

[27] *Ibid.*," 8–12. In a charming "invented tradition" seeking to emphasize the reformers' iconoclasm, the website of St. Mary's, Willesden – where a new statue of Our Lady of Willesden has been erected – quotes what is admitted to be, "unfortunately," a nineteenth-century fabrication of a letter from one of Cromwell's agents reporting "they have an image of Our Ladye in robes sarcenet and with stones with a vaile of lace embroidered with pearles." "The image," claims the letter, "is most certynly abused with moche superstition": see www.stmarywillesden.org.uk/Virgin5-2.html.

[28] Craig, *Wandering Women and Holy Matrons*, 234–5.

objects that had touched her, or had been attached to her body, or on which she had sat, rested or leaned and therefore which retained some of her aura and power, overwhelmingly predominated. Bourne, Lincolnshire, had a "piece of that stone on which the Archangel Gabriel descended when he saluted the Blessed Virgin Mary"; Walsingham, at least according to Erasmus's narrative, had a piece of wood on which the Virgin had rested.[29] One common example found all over England and Europe was what Waterton terms her "*Zona* or girdle."[30] Woolpit's records list a number of girdles. They were especially recommended as aids to childbirth and were found plentifully in churches along the Walsingham Way, en route to the shrine.[31] Originating in stories of the Virgin's Assumption during which she hands or drops a girdle to St. Thomas (as in the play discussed in Chapter 3), the original sacred girdle (*Ostensione della Sacra Cintola*) is claimed by the Tuscan city of Prato, but examples were multiplied across Europe. The reformers were especially sarcastic about the use of "girdles, purses, measures of our Lady, or other superstitious things, to be occupied about the woman while she laboureth, to make her believe to have the better speed by it."[32]

A widespread Marian relic was a sample of the Virgin's milk. As the reformers repeatedly pointed out, often with enormous sarcasm and obvious distaste, there were multiple samples right across Europe. Surveying Marian relics in Coventry and Lichfield, Rubin comments that "few people in the diocese lived far from a pain-relieving girdle or a life-giving drop of Mary's milk." Erasmus's interlocutor Menedemus comments that it is certainly a devout act on a pilgrim's part to revere "such an excedynge precious relyque" which is appropriate "to be worshipyd," especially since he is assured at Walsingham that their milk was not merely scraped from a cave floor in the Holy Land but "came out of the virgynes brest" and was transported circuitously through Europe via Paris.[33] Erasmus's tone in his depiction of the Walsingham milk is one of slightly superior amusement rather than dogmatic hostility, and, we might sense, given his consistent though usually understated reverence toward Mary, conveys a yearning for something which the milk, as an image of the Virgin's motherhood, represents rather than his belief that the relic was

[29] Maniura, "Our Lady of Prato," 211–12; Waterton, *Pietas Mariana Britannia*, II, 4; Erasmus, *Pilgrimage*, 42.

[30] Waterton, *Pietas Mariana Britannica*, I, 88. Waterton mentions the Virgin's chemise, I, 42–3, and cloths that had "touched the original" and thus become "sanctified relics," 90. Rubin, *Mother of God*, 376, mentions a number of other English examples.

[31] For girdles on the way to Walsingham, see Morrison, *Women Pilgrims*, 27–35.

[32] Frere, *Visitation Articles*, II, 59.   [33] Rubin, *Mother of God*, 377; Erasmus, *Pilgrimage*, 42–4.

literally pressed from the Virgin's breast. What is more objectionable to him than dubious relics was the exploitation that might accompany them. We should contrast Erasmus's amused tone with Calvin's raw indignation at the same phenomenon. Calvin viciously attacks those for whom the dogma of the assumption of Mary's body to Heaven "has deprived them of all pretext for manufacturing any relics of her remains, which otherwise might have been sufficiently abundant to fill a whole churchyard," leaving only clothing, hair, and milk. "With regard to the milk," he goes on, there is not perhaps a town, a convent, or nunnery where it is not "shown in either large or small quantities." Indeed, he concludes, "had the Virgin been a wet-nurse all her life, or a dairy, she could not have produced more than is shown as hers in various parts. How they obtained all this milk they do not say, and it is superfluous here to remark that there is no Foundation in the Gospels for these foolish and blasphemous extravagances."[34]

Images, relics – and miracles. Pilgrimage sites built their reputation in part upon the miracles that were attributed to the saint. In the face of growing reformist scorn, Thomas More affirmed that there were indeed "miracles done in our dayes at divers images." The poets of Penrhys compiled lists of the Virgin's miracles, which include her curing pain, sickness, and dumbness. Curiously, Walsingham's list of miracles is small. The most prominent recorded examples are Edward I's escape from death from falling masonry, which he attributed to Our Lady of Walsingham and which motivated his annual pilgrimages, and the rescue of a boy from one of the wells; and – a little closer to what we might expect from an active Virgin's repertoire – the Virgin miracle story mentioned in Chapter 3 of the mounted knight, Sir Ralph Boutefort, who in 1314 was reputedly pursued by an enemy and, calling on her to rescue him, was given miraculous entry to the shrine through a seemingly impassable gate. The Pynson Ballad tells us, however, that Our Lady of Walsingham has "dayly" displayed her power in the "many miracles," including the "many sek ben here cured by Our Ladys myghte," the "Lame made hole and blynde rest forred to syghte," along with the deaf and lepers cured, and even the "dede agayne revuyed." Carroll comments that such miracles, especially raising from the dead, look suspiciously like those of Christ in the Gospels, and attributes the list to growing Christocentrism in the fifteenth century. But it is important to note that in the ballad these miracles do not reflect the new Christocentric humanist learning: they are directly attributed to the power of the Virgin, not to God or even Christ. They are brought about by the Virgin herself. At Penrhys,

[34] Calvin, *Treatise on Relics*, 249.

it is even stressed that "the image of Mary is no less efficacious / than Mary of Heaven to heal."[35]

Feigned miracles, what Hugh Latimer termed "fooleries," were one of the reformers' favorite targets. For them, miracles were found only in the Gospels: William Tyndale's defiant view was that "God hath made an everlasting testament with us in Christ's Blood against which we may receive no miracles." It is not surprising that Catholic polemicists typically responded by naming the continuation of miracles as one of the "apostoli-call markes" of the true faith and one most "wanting in Protestants." When the Irish Abbey of Muckross was devastated, the image of Our Lady was rescued and hidden in the foot of a dead tree, which immediately there-after – "Lo, immediately the dead tree revived," exclaims its historian – bloomed in response for the protection of Our Lady.[36]

As the number of his remarks I have quoted make clear, about a decade before the crises of the 1530s were reached, a distinguished and articulate observer offered some detailed comments on pilgrimages, relics, miracles, and the place of the Virgin in a time of transition. That figure is Erasmus, who visited Walsingham around 1512, probably making the trip from Cambridge. Despite his later reputation as the herald of the Reformation, not least in England, where translations of his biblical paraphrases would become required reading in Edwardian churches, throughout his career Erasmus repeatedly affirmed that he was deeply devoted to the Virgin, affirming his belief in her intercessory powers, and assuring the faithful that Christ would be sure to be "easily moved" by her, since he would be "so loving of you, so compliant, so reverent that he denies nothing to the supplicant." Around 1504, he wrote what his modern translator Craig Thompson calls "an unusually fervent and rhetorical supplication" to Mary, calling her "the true Diana," and in his colloquy *Naufragium* (*The Shipwreck*) celebrates her triumphantly taking over the roles once occupied by pagan goddesses: "formerly," he quips, "Venus was protectress of sailors," but "since she gave up guarding them, the Virgin Mother has succeeded this other who was not a virgin."[37]

---

[35] Carroll, "Pilgrimage at Walsingham," 41; Waterton, *Pietas Mariana Britannia*, II, 48; Chandlery, *Mary's Praise on Every Tongue*, 90; Chidgey, *Our Lady of Penrhys*, 7–8. The Walsingham knight's story is set out in Whatmore, *Highway to Walsingham*, 90–2, and Dickinson, *Shrine*, 57, 92.
[36] Latimer, *Sermons*, 51; Tyndale and Frith, *The Works of the English Reformers*, 362; Fulke and Gibbings, *Stapleton's Fortress Overthrown*, 76; Waterton, *Pietas Mariana Britannia*, II, 309.
[37] For Thompson's remark, see Erasmus, "Pean Virgini Matri," 33; Erasmus, *Pilgrimage*, 16–17. For a survey of Erasmus's statements about Mary, and other women saints, see O'Donnell, "Mary and Other Women Saints," 105–21.

As a leading exponent of the "new learning," however, Erasmus's devotion to Mary was firmly Christocentric; he consistently insists on the Virgin's subservience to Christ, often preferring to call her "mother of Jesus" rather than "Mother of God," and even on occasions leaving as an indifferent matter the question of her perpetual virginity. In his account of Walsingham, his interlocutor Menenius asks about the Virgin, "How wold she be worshipyd?" and his friend Ogygius simply replies: "The most acceptable honor, that thou canste doo to her is to folowe her lyuynge."[38] In assessing the cultural and psychological dynamics of Marian pilgrimages before 1538, Erasmus's *Peregrinatio* therefore provides us with a fascinating contrast with the popular Mariology of Pynson Ballads celebrating Walsingham or Glastonbury. The years between the Pynson Walsingham Ballad (written around 1465) and the *Peregrinatio* (written in the early 1520s) reflect some of the major changes that are occurring in popular religion and the broader society in the crucial pre-Reformation period. The ballad focuses on its shrine's miraculous origins, the Virgin's miracles, and her continuing interventions in history and individual lives. It is distinctly Mariocentric. Christ is not explicitly mentioned. The Virgin's miracles are her own, even if their details are kept vague. Erasmus, however, comes down to examining particulars and he does so in a tone very different from the Pynson Ballad's rapturous affirmation of the Virgin's interventions. By presenting his account semi-fictionally, he can accompany each story he is told with a degree of amused skepticism derived from the "new learning," while continuing to allow the comforting pleasure of the old magical world to shine through. He repeats the legend that the wells or "fowntayne" did "sodenly sprynge owte of the erthe at the commaundement of our lady"; he recounts the "miracle" of the knight's rescue by Our Lady, with his skeptical interlocutor Menedemus asking whether he really took "so maruylous a myrakle for a trewthe."[39] These matters are not chosen innocently by Erasmus, but his tone overall is gently mocking, occasionally a little elitist and self-indulgent, as if he trusts his learned audience to share his good-humored enjoyment of the superstitions of popular religion so long as they are not taken too seriously.

It was a stance that has led him to be criticized by both Catholics and Protestants over the centuries. The pilgrimage colloquy was written at a time when humor combined with sound learning rather than destruction might still have seemed a plausible weapon of reform; in the mid 1530s, as the relics and miraculous statues, girdles, and smocks were shown

---

[38] Erasmus, *Pilgrimage*, 64.   [39] *Ibid.*, 38, 35.

(or asserted) one after another to be fraudulent, Erasmus's remarks could more easily be taken as supporting a more radical brand of reform. In the preface to the first English translation of the *Peregrinatio*, the anonymous translator, likely one of Cromwell's stable of ambitious young humanists, praises Erasmus for setting forth "the supersticyouse worshippe and false honor gyvyn to bones, heddes, iawes, armes, stockes, stones, shyrtes, smokes, cotes, cappes, hattes, shoes, mytres, slyppers, sadles, rynges, bedes, girdles, bolles, belles, bokes, gloves, ropes, taperes, candelles, bootes, sporres" and other "soche dampnable allusyones of the deuyle" that are contrary to scripture and constitute not only heresy but sedition. Most of the items in this remarkable sentence are, in fact, nowhere mentioned in Erasmus's colloquy, although such lists are a common rhetorical effusion in reformist bishops' injunctions.[40]

Not surprisingly, this first translation of his colloquy, published in the crucial years of 1536 or 1537, also highlights the sexually scandalous side of the veneration of the Virgin that so appalled the reformers. Erasmus himself is certainly not above making slightly lascivious jokes about Mary. He has his two fictional friends joke about the (in)famous vision of St. Bernard receiving the milk directly from the Virgin's breast. He comments that the Walsingham canons are forbidden to sit too close to the Virgin's milk to prevent them having lascivious thoughts. It is also kept apart lest the milk of the Virgin should be "defowlyd by the kyssynge of men." Kissing milk is deliberately incongruous; Erasmus choice of "kissing" is clearly directed at eroticizing the Virgin's breasts, the source of the milk. And then, towards the end of the visit, his guide asks Ogygius whether he would like to view the "our ladyes secretes" or her "pryvytes," phrasing in which in the English translation (though less explicitly in the Latin) Erasmus takes some particular coy pleasure, and which clearly inflamed those among Cromwell's inspectors who were looking for some scandal.[41]

Stories of feigned relics and superstitious practices are easy to mount up. It was equally easy to point to ecclesiastical corruption and fraudulence. But the surge of destruction that erupted in the late 1530s as part of what was presented as the reform of religious institutions, even as early as Wolsey in the 1520s, points to something deeper. When Kristeva speaks of the "power" of the Virgin, and when we consider the multiple ways by which that power was expressed within late medieval culture, we may start to understand the

---

[40] *Ibid.*, 6–7; see also Bishop Nicholas Shaxton's Injunctions to the Salisbury diocese in 1538, Frere, *Visitation Articles*, II, 59–60.

[41] *Ibid.*, 42, 57, 64–5.

distinctive level of hostility directed against her. There is, comments
Beattie, "at times" throughout the history of the Christian Church, "an
overwhelming masculine fear of . . . the female body and the generative
power of the mother."[42] Any shrine dedicated to the Virgin, whether
Walsingham or Woolpit, Penrhys or Ipswich or Willesden, had this special
distinction: it was a place of immanent female power, centered on an event
in which a woman's body was revered as the vehicle of salvation, which
encouraged devotees to revere, and even worship, that body. So we should
therefore ask – as I did in Chapter 2, concerning the sexual dynamics in
which the Virgin was depicted and venerated in the late Middle Ages – what
of women's understanding of the Virgin? And in particular women pilgrims'? What were the likely or possible interactions between women and
their sense of journeying to revere a fellow woman?

Here we can draw on a number of studies, mainly in the past decade, of
medieval women's experiences on pilgrimage, notably by Susan Morrison
and Leigh Ann Craig. Morrison's pioneering work on women pilgrims in
England showed that women were most likely the majority of pilgrims to
Marian shrines. Most likely, she argues, women went on pilgrimages with
specifically women-oriented experiences in mind: to heal or make fruitful
their bodies, to enhance their fertility, to protect unborn and living children, to ensure safe deliveries, avoid birth pains, increase lactation, and
generally affirm their roles in procreation. The experiences of being moth-
ered or the yearning for a protecting and healing relationship to compensate
for real or imagined anxieties and losses may well have been a powerful
aspect of men's dedication to the Virgin, but actual or prospective motherhood was overwhelmingly at the center of the experience of a Marian shrine
for women, and no experience, observes Craig, of "motherly intervention,
breastfeeding, and caregiving could fail to recall" the Virgin. Craig's survey
of over 700 miracles stories – accounts, partly fictional, of pilgrimages to
miraculous shrines across Europe – likewise show that the normative roles
for women on pilgrimage simply continued their expected roles as wives,
mothers, and caregivers. Women tended to act as intercessors more than
men, petitioning the saint on behalf of others, and were also more likely to
bring petitions of relief for gynocological problems and mental stress.[43]

Motherhood is, of course, hardly a gender-neutral phenomenon. It is an
ideological construct as well as a complex physical and emotional experience. Historically, it has by no means been free of male control (and not just
in the late Middle Ages) and it has been at the core, as Theweleit notes, of

---

[42] Beattie, *God's Mother*, 52.   [43] Craig, *Wandering Women and Holy Matrons*, 126, 90–1, 96.

male fantasies regarding the possession and control of women's bodies. Kristeva argues that the Church constructed the image of the Virgin in part to direct and control women's embodied maternal power: the possible subversion of the power of the father by women's autonomy is contained, masculinist ideology thereby "gratified," and women seemingly "satisfied."[44] Women pilgrims, especially pregnant, would-be or recently pregnant women, would have the contrast between Mary, the immaculate Virgin Mother, and their own lives and bodies, repeatedly reinforced.[45] As Morrison shows, women traveling to Walsingham were carefully directed through a network of churches, chapels, and resting places that stressed the dominant, essentially masculinist, understanding of motherhood, pulling women into a pre-prepared fantasy structure that would reinforce their social inferiority, psychological dependence, and subservience to a de-sexualized ideal of women which did not necessarily coincide with their own bodily experiences. Kristeva also argues, however, that the pregnant female body may assert itself as outside the law of the father, and therefore is potentially a threat to patriarchy: for a woman, pregnancy and childbirth can be experienced as something of a bond that escapes the rule of the father, perhaps even as a reunion with the body of her own mother, thereby bringing back a primal homosocial bond. As Grace Jantzen comments, "the desires of the unconscious are desires of and for the body, focused initially on the body of the mother, and subsequently on all the others who stand in for the (m)other."[46] That fear of women's independence of the male authority of God would emerge viciously in the reformers but it was also present in orthodox thinking about women, women's bodies, motherhood, and sexuality in the Middle Ages.

But there is another dimension to the bodily experiences of pilgrimage for women other than motherhood, whether experienced as controlling or potentially liberating. We are dealing here, of course, with speculation, with one of the situations where Miri Rubin acknowledges we must infer the emotions associated with the Virgin indirectly, from tone, intensity, and passion, all difficult to clarify, even detect, from the seeming rigidity of the documentary culture.[47] Throughout the experience, and in multiple ways, motherhood involves matters of sexuality. Morrison notes that women pilgrims clearly generated "an anxiety on the part of post-plague English

---

[44] Kristeva, *Tales of Love*, 310.
[45] For Kristeva's discussion of maternity, see "Motherhood according to Giovanni Bellini," in *Desire in Language*, 237–70, and "Stabat Mater," *Tales of Love*, 234–66.
[46] Morrison, *Women Pilgrims*, 26–9; Jantzen, "What's the Difference?" 32.
[47] Rubin, *Emotion and Devotion*, 79, 81–2.

society of movement and hierarchical disruption," and that anxiety centered on their sexuality.[48] Both Church authorities and Lollards attacked what they saw as the corruption and immorality often displayed by pilgrims, from the playing of bagpipes and jangling of bells to the sales of charms and badges and sexual improprieties. Yet, for women, such opportunities for deviant behavior on pilgrimage may well have opened up experiences and roles that called into question the restrictions on their expected behavior and thus expanded a woman's sense of self. The high level of female participation in pilgrimages and the anxiety that surrounded women pilgrims suggests where alternate expressions of self-discovery and liberation may have resided. Beattie remarks that a more women-centered consideration of sexuality within medieval religion could expose "the internal contradictions and inconsistencies" of traditional Mariology and so "a creative space of new symbolic meanings" for women and for Christian experience might well be "opened up from within."[49]

We may get some help on how this "creative space" of women's possibilities may have occurred from studies of women pilgrims' experiences at two post-Reformation Marian shrines, Lourdes and Fatima, for which there is (unlike late medieval pilgrimage) a detailed archival culture available to study. Writing about women pilgrims to Lourdes, Fiona Bowie observes that the ecclesiastical authorities try, with only limited success, to "move pilgrims from an individual, ecstatic, female-focused experience to one based on the Church and its sacraments, highly structured and male in orientation." Likewise, in her study of women pilgrims at Fatima, Lena Genzoe points to a tension between women's perceptions of the sacred "in contrast to the interpretations offered by the male hierarchy." The "female link to Mary" of the mothers, healers, and caretakers of families coming together are seen as "marginal or deviant," but for the women themselves, the experiences of the pilgrimage provide a more "direct and personal relationship" with the Virgin. In both cases, Mary is felt to offer direct guidance to the women pilgrims outside roles designated by the Church, and Mary herself is widely seen by the women as a "divine figure in her own right."[50]

These are examples from Marian shrines founded four hundred years later, and so are subject to different historical pressures. Yet the continuities are intriguing. Althaus-Reid suggests that for hundreds of years, women may well have experienced their own sexuality in relation to the Virgin far more positively than the ecclesiastical authorities wanted, and that "hidden in the closet" there has always been a level of unacknowledgable sexuality that the authorities tried to render "hidden and forgotten."[51] As Carroll repeatedly points out, we should be careful not to identify the official pronouncements of the Church with people's actual practices, especially in such a highly charged experience as sexuality. Elena Vuola gives the example of over four hundred years of popular Mariology in South America where, she argues, "there is a living tradition of devotion to Mary with a very human [feminine] face, coming close to women in their most intimate and real experiences," one that "is sometimes in open contradiction with the 'official' Mary ... especially when it comes to her bodiliness, sexuality and motherhood." It is, needless to say, difficult to get more specific. Carroll's suggestion from some of his early Freudian studies that the fantasy of an "earthly woman impregnated by God the father" allows a "daughter to gratify an oedipal desire vicariously" is a tempting partial explanation – though those sensitive to Steinberg's "modern reticence" might simply prefer to say, with Beattie, that women's sense of the divine has characteristically "focused more on immanence than transcendence,"[52] and that the bodiliness of Christianity is more easily located in women's experiences.

Complaints about pilgrims' riotous behavior do not always imply sexual activity, but certainly sexual experience seems to be a recurring phenomenon in remarks about pilgrimages.[53] Chaucer's Wife of Bath was notorious for "wanderynge by the weye."[54] Particularly aggressively directed toward Marian pilgrimages, the London Lollard Elizabeth Sampson accused Our Lady of Willesden of being a "burnt arse elf," while the "men and women which go to her of pilgrimage" are in danger of having their "tails ... burnt." For good measure, the outspoken Lollard called Our Lady of Crome, near Greenwich, "but a puppet." As Malcolm Jones notes, the reformers "had it in for Our Lady of Willesden": for one, she was a "stewed whore," for another, the Virgin was "the chefe lady mastres" of "whordom and letcherousness."[55] Morrison also points to the recurring hints of sexuality in the margins or interstices of the pilgrimage experience in the overtly erotic badges that were often carried by pilgrims. In addition to

---

[51] Althaus-Reid, *Indecent Theology*, 27.

[52] Vuola, "Seriously Harmful for your Health," 152, 148; Carroll, *Catholic Cults*, 7, 73, 159; Beattie, *Eve's Pilgrimage*, 23.

[53] For connections between pilgrimage and sexuality, see Mathieu, *Sex Pots*; Pastoetter, "Tourism and Sex," 107–10. Finucane, *Miracles and Pilgrims*, 40, observes that "casual sexual opportunities were no doubt more likely on pilgrimage."

[54] Chaucer, "General Prologue," l. 467, *Riverside Chaucer*, 31.   [55] Jones, *Secret Middle Ages*, 32–3.

solemn representations of such sacred moments as the Annunciation that would be found on ordinary, pious pilgrim badges, there were, Morrison shows, many parody badges: a walking vulva dressed in pilgrim garb with staff and hat, two pilgrim vulvas hand in hand, are just two examples. Who would wear such badges? Were they worn to signify sexual availability? Were they worn secretly? Would a badge showing a pilgrim vulva signal some message of erotic openness to another woman or, simply, her identification with the Virgin's (hidden) sexuality? [56]

We do not know definite answers to these questions. Nor do we know, at least directly, the fantasies by which ordinary women expressed or explored their own desires while on pilgrimage to any shrine that was so obviously connected to their own experiences. But they do suggest the place of sexuality on pilgrimage and by extension the relationship between women's sense of their own sexuality and the Virgin. Mary's bodily nature may well have been decoded very differently from the ways in which the authorities insisted, and provided a model of independence – whether of sexual freedom or simply space and temporary independence – outside or at least not fully under the control of authorities, whether ecclesiastical or familial, and also perhaps opened the possibility of greater community among women. There would been many options in the pilgrimage experience that would have been unusual for most women. While authorities would have stressed the obedience and duty in Mary's own behavior, the manner by which late medieval women lived out their experience of a Marian pilgrimage may well have emphasized more their sense of newness and adventure based on their sense of dislocation or slippage between what Liz McAvoy terms "what women were *told* about their own bodily experiences and their own intimate experiences of them."[57]

We get some singular evidence from one person who would presumably have strongly disapproved of the erotic badges, even while she might have been fascinated by their explicitness. That is Margery Kempe. Kempe's remarkable account of herself has been hailed for its (perhaps unwitting) "recourse to the experiences of her own body and its female specificity in order to forge an alternative – and feminine – route to religious experience." Her classic account of her own journeys, even as far as the Holy Land, presents a particular woman's experience of pilgrimage.[58] It understandably involved her constant fear of robbery or physical attack. We are told that

[56] Jones, *Secret Middle Ages*, 249; Morrison, "Ophelia, Waste, Memory," 57–61.
[57] McAvoy, *Authority and the Female Body*, 24.
[58] McAvoy, *Margery Kempe*, 15; Staley, *Margery Kempe*, 73, 224.

"che was evyr aferd to be ravischyd or defilyd." But a particular affront to the pious matron from Lynn were threats from what she saw as irresponsible and pleasure-loving fellow pilgrims, and she sometimes chose not to continue with groups apparently more bent on pleasures than piety. At times, some fellow pilgrims refused to travel with her: "thei wold not gowyth wyth hir for an hundryd pownd." Women, as Morrison notes, frequently "suffered crimes . . . peculiar to their gender" – she instances a woman who was kidnapped and made to spend several days in the municipal brothel – but Margery sees herself as the "weak creature" who might easily succumb not just to surprise attacks but to the temptations offered by fellow pilgrims and encounters on route and even to her own lascivious fantasies, as in the celebrated occasion when she records that she was tempted by the sight of a man's penis. Her account of her experiences is a remarkable source for understanding women's roles in the fifteenth century, but as Craig points out, the treatment she received for her fastidiousness was not, in fact, unusual for women pilgrims, who were frequently abandoned by fellow pilgrims for their behavior, devotional extremity, or what one pilgrim termed "inquisitive prying into unprofitable matters."[59] Reading in the gaps of Kempe's narrative, it may be that the alternate pathways were being created not by the celebrated matron from Lynn, but rather by those fellow pilgrims of whom she disapproved. Perhaps the results of such behavior gave the women unexpected relaxation and pleasures that would prove positively therapeutic – and would then add to the feeling of well-being when they journeyed to a shrine. As Julia Holloway comments, women on pilgrimages were given access to unaccustomed power and might discover a voice they would otherwise have had silenced and suppressed and they may well, she speculates, been dramatically gratified by that experience of independence.[60]

It is this pivotal position in a world about to be changed that makes Erasmus all the more important as a commentator on both Marian shrines such as Walsingham and other places of pilgrimage such as Canterbury, where the action of the second half of the *Peregrinatio* moves. The primary focus at Canterbury is on the tomb and relics of Becket, but there is still the opportunity to glance at the Virgin's place in the cathedral: "There standythe forthe a certayne aultre whiche is dedycate to our lady, it is but a lytle one, and I suppose set there for no other purpose, but to be a olde monumêt or sygne, that in thos dayes there was no great superfluyte. There thay saye

[59] Morrison, *Women Pilgrims*, 58; Craig, *Wandering Women*, 162.
[60] Holloway, *Saint Bride and Her Book*, 168; Craig, *Wandering Women*, 126.

that thys blessyd martyr sayd his last good nyght to our lady." In this section of his colloquy, Erasmus inserts the name of his friend Colet who, he tells us, is "a man bothe vertuouse and well learnyd, but he had lesse affectyon toward pylgremages than," Ogygius regrets, "I wold that he shuld haue." Menedemus then asks whether that makes Colet "one of Wyclyffes scoleres I warrante you?" to which Ogygius assures him "I thynke nat, althoghe he had redde hys bokes." But (one can almost hear Erasmus laughing quietly in the background since the possession of heretical books was a serious matter in the 1520s, one which Erasmus's friend Thomas More for one took very seriously) "how he came by thaym I cannat tell."[61]

As Erasmus published his colloquies, the "new learning" was contributing to a major revaluation of all pilgrimages. The roots of the new humanism, however, go back at least a century or more, and therefore that revaluation had been gradually developing for over a century. Barbara Newman points to Jean Gerson's early fifteenth-century nervousness before the "sheer goddess-like grandeur and autonomy" accorded to the Virgin in such representations as the *Vierge Ouvrante* (statues in which the persons of the Trinity are revealed within her womb) or the highly erotic ecstasies of female mystics. Gerson's concern that such devotions might be seen as "embarrassing, scandalous, or even blasphemous" anticipates the reformers' concerns a century later. He encouraged the development of the cults of St. Joseph and the Holy Family partly in response to what he perceived as heretical Mariological tendencies. Like Erasmus after him, Gerson did not oppose the cult of Mary as such, but his actions, Newman comments, amount to a "campaign to replace the Marian trinity," which he perceived emerging in popular devotion, by the cult of the Holy Family in order to "bring the Virgin safely back to earth, when she could be tamed and domesticated by her husband." A century later, in the hands of the reformers, the new Christocentrism became, MacCulloch claims, "a wedge to split apart the edifice of intercession by Mary to her Son which had become so all-pervasive in Western popular devotion." [62] Those contradictions emerge in open controversy and eventually violence in the 1530s.

Like his friend More, a central figure of humanist reform, Erasmus could acknowledge with tolerant humor that most accounts of saints' lives and their shrines might well be only legend, and that maintaining pilgrimage sites involved a certain amount of skullduggery, without calling for their

---

[61] Erasmus, *Pilgrimage*, 70, 72.
[62] *Ibid.*, 19; Newman, *God and the Goddesses*, 284, 287, 290, 317; MacCulloch, "Mary and Sixteenth-Century Protestants," 193.

destruction. Into the *Pelegrinatio* Erasmus inserts a gentle parody of a Marian miracle story. Menedemus recounts a (presumably fictional!) letter from the Virgin to one Glaucoplutus (the Swiss reformer Zwingli). The letter's main point is to warn against the extremities of iconoclasm which Erasmus saw developing among the reformers. Mary complains about being overworked by the triviality and even immorality of petitions addressed to her. She thanks the reformer for discouraging irresponsible pilgrims from making shameful bargaining petitions to her, including those "a shamfast yongman dare scantly aske of a Bawde, yee they be suche thynges as I am ashamyd to put in wrytynge." But she cautions him (and the reformers generally) that if he rejects her, he is dangerously close to rejecting Christ himself. Observing in passing – in a typically Erasmian gleeful sideswipe, amusedly criticizing yet expressing a degree of fondness – "the sayntes haue theyr weapones or myschefues, whiche they send apon whome they liste," he characterizes the Virgin's moderation (indeed, one can imagine Erasmus's quiet conviction that he could speak for her, and that her views would be, shall we say, Erasmian): "But as for me thou canst not cast owt, except thou cast owt my sone, whiche I hold in myne armes. I wyll nat be seperat frome hym, other thou shalt cast hym owt with me or els thou shalt let vs bothe be, except that you wold haue a temple withowt a Christe."[63]

The letter from the Virgin – which must assuredly have been delivered to her, the pious pilgrim tells us, by angelic messenger – warns against what Erasmus saw as the extremity of increasing evangelical iconoclasm. It is jocular in tone but ends on a firm note, and Erasmus himself asserted that the colloquy on pilgrimages was written to oppose, not support, the increasingly outspoken radicals. In an apologia appended to the 1524 edition of the *Colloquies*, he reassured readers who saw only his mocking that he was indeed serious and was ridiculing only "charlatanism": "In *A Pilgrimage for Religion's Sake*, I reproach those who with much ado have thrown all images out of the churches . . . those who exhibit doubtful relics for authentic ones, who attribute to them more than is proper, and basely make money by them." He acknowledges that while he wants to draw attention to those who "exhibit doubtful relics," to criticize those who "are crazy about pilgrimages undertaken in the name of religion," especially those who "attribute to them more than is proper, and basely make money by them," nonetheless he emphatically censures "those who have thrown all images out of the churches."[64] The conservative Ten Articles of 1536, issued around the same time as the publication of the English translation of

---

[63] Erasmus, *Pilgrimage*, 21–7.   [64] Erasmus, "The Usefulness of the Colloquies," 626–31.

Erasmus's colloquy, likewise acknowledged that "images be suffered only as books, by which our hearts may be kindled to follow the holy steps and examples of the saints represented by the saint." Erasmus's views also turned out to be in large part in line with those of the Council of Trent: "since the nature of man is such that he cannot without external means be raised easily to meditation on divine things ... certain rites [and] ceremonies" are permitted whereby "the minds of the faithful [are] excited by those visible signs of religion and piety." Therefore, "images of Christ, of the Virgin Mother of God, and of the other saints" should be retained, with "due honour and veneration" accorded them.[65]

What Erasmus did not anticipate was the uses to which his critique of pilgrimages in the *Peregrinatio* would be put by Cromwell's propagandists, preachers, inspectors, prosecutors, and, eventually, by his wrecking crews, as the reformers looked for justification for their attacks on religious houses, pilgrimages, relics, and what they saw as idolatry. The Erasmian tone of tolerant moderation was ignored or distorted. But however politically useful his views proved to Cromwell and the reformers in their build-up to the dissolution of all religious houses in the late 1530s, his moderation finally did not persuade the followers of Calvin and Zwingli, whose influence in England, even by the time the *Peregrinatio* appeared in English, was growing and would emerge strongly under Edward VI and to some extent under Elizabeth, as the wave of image-removal and destruction continued and the churches across England were whitewashed, stripped, and vandalized over the next century.[66]

The material in Erasmus's colloquy was extremely useful to Henry's and Cromwell's attack on religious foundations not just to eliminate pilgrimages (for which the king had developed a particular antagonism) or "feigned relics," but very specifically to transfer their wealth to the Crown. In 1534, Cromwell ordered a survey of wealth held by monastic property, the *Valor Ecclesiasticus*.[67] Predictably, given the not too hidden agenda, the commissioners gave special attention to finances of shrines such as Walsingham. As well as the income of the shrine as a whole, they requested separate information for the "Holy Milk," the chapel of St. Laurence, and the Holy House itself. They also made an unusual special report on Walsingham in a separate list of Articles of Enquiry. It consisted of detailed

[65] Trent's pronouncement is in Noll, *Confessions and Catechisms*, 199–200, 210. For an alternative, Catholic but more critical, view of Trent's pronouncements on idolatry and the material representation of the Virgin, see Beattie, *Eve's Pilgrimage*, 111–13.

[66] For Calvin on "anthropomorphizing" see Michalski, *Reformation and the Visual Arts*, 64.

[67] See *Valar Ecclesiasticus*.

questions that were clearly drafted by someone who had read the *Peregrinatio*, though with far more hostile intentions than Erasmus. Predictably, the commissioners' decision was that the priory was corrupted by "notorious incontinency" and "great superstition." One of Cromwell's agents, Richard Southwell – whose grandson, the Catholic martyr Robert, will make appearances in the following two chapters – wrote to Cromwell that during their inspection they had found "a secret privy place within the house . . . in which there are instruments, pots, bellows, flies of such strange colours as the like none of us had ever seen." It was surmised (or hoped) to be alchemical equipment, but in fact, any "art of multiplying" involved was likely the "multiplying" of pilgrims' badges or tokens – and presumably not the erotic ones.[68]

The Walsingham Commissioners' questions have the same critical, almost predatory tone as the preface to the translation of the *Peregrinatio*. It is possible that the translator was even one of those drawing up the questions: mixed into the matters requiring responses by the shrine were some that, by detail and phrase, could only have been taken from Erasmus. The questions turn Erasmian amusement into scorn, probing not just particular miracles which supposedly "Our Lady performed," and asking on what basis the claims were examined, but whether any of the so-called miracles could not rather "have proceeded directly from God" – that in itself a distinctive reformed emphasis – and, further, why any should be attributed to Our Lady or, if so, why to the particular image of Our Lady at Walsingham, which reflects another pressing issue for reformers. Such questions imply a wholesale rejection of the medieval world's magical universe in which miracles could be a daily occurrence. But even more radical is one particular question Cromwell's eager empiricists pose: "what proof is there that [the supposed miracle] could not have been worked by natural means?" It was one thing to wonder about corruption in the priory and ask cynically whether "Our Lady perform as many miracles now as she did when there were greater offerings made to her"; it was quite another to question of the existence of miracles themselves.[69]

Across England, a similar pattern of events occurred in accordance with an Injunction of 1538 which labeled as "men's phantasies" and "things tending to idolatry and superstition" the "wandering to pilgrimages, offering of money, candles, or tapers to images or relics, or kissing or licking the

---

[68] Stephenson, *Walsingham Way*, 62; see also the account of Walsingham in Marshall, *Religious Identities*, 133–7.

[69] For the text of the Commissioners' Articles, see Stephenson, *Walsingham Way*, 62; Gillett, *Walsingham*, 61–3.

same."[70] At Caversham, near Reading, a statue of the Virgin (and a well named for St. Anne) had attracted pilgrims since the twelfth century and had acquired a gold crown and silver plating. In 1532, Catherine of Aragon had come there to pray during the height of the Anne Boleyn crisis. One of Cromwell's agents reported that "I have pullyd down the image . . . where-unto wasse great pilgremage" and that during the inspection "there com in" pilgrims "with images of wax." The ex-votos, lights, and other appurtenan-ces were destroyed and "defacyd . . . thorowly in exchuyng of any farther resort thedyr."[71] By the late 1530s, it was as if the sources of power on which the old magical universe had been based had suddenly vanished. Keith Thomas famously pointed to the blurring of magic and religion in the later Middle Ages: many of all the comforting stories, the rituals and practices of the world that was dying, relied on that blurred distinction that certified miracles of the Virgin and the saints as legitimized magic.[72] Ideology consists, after all, of what is made to appear as common sense. But for the new "stories" of the new emerging world to achieve the matter-of-fact-ness of the residual ideology, it was a process of getting the old stories of the efficacy of pilgrimages to the shrine, the Image, the Virgin's milk, and the way of life they embodied, "out of their heads."[73] "Men's minds," a number of the reformist bishops' injunctions asserted, could be "stirred and kindled," and the idols needed to be made to "vanish away."[74] Looking back a decade later, in his catechismical *An Instruction into the Christian Religion*, Cranmer told the faithful to consult "your owne fathers," who "wer greatly seduced by certayne famouse and notoriouse ymages, as by oure ladye of Ippeswiche," and others "whom many of your parents visitide yerely, leauing their owne houses and families. To them they made vowes and pilgrimages."[75]

Pilgrimages were forbidden and gradually ceased. By 1539, acts of volun-tary surrender by those remaining religious establishments were permitted – but by then most had been dissolved, and their "feign'd relics" removed and destroyed, including the Blood of Hailes, the Virgin's milk at Walsingham, the "images" of Walsingham, Ipswich, Penrhys, Willesden, Woolpit, and hundreds of other places of pilgrimage. Thousands of girdles, hairs, bones,

---

[70] Frere, *Visitation Articles*, II, 37.
[71] Waterton, *Pietas Mariana Britannia*, II, 10–11. See also the revived shrine's website: www.ourladyand-stanne.org.uk/shrine.htm.
[72] See the classic study, much in need of qualification, but still powerful in its thesis, Thomas, *Religion and the Decline of Magic*.
[73] Stephenson, *Walsingham Way*, 48, 49, 64, 66; Gillett, *Walsingham*, 65.
[74] Frere, *Visitation Articles*, II, 57, 115.　[75] Cranmer, *Short Instruction*, 23.

heads, shoes – even Erasmus's beam of wood on which Mary had reputedly sat – would, the reformers hoped, be destroyed or simply become the empty souvenirs of a vanishing age. Catholics over the next few centuries would bewail the systematic sacrilege and, like Edmund Waterton, look back to the death of Henry VIII as God's judgment upon "one whom Englishmen have cause to execrate" for having "desecrated the sanctuaries of the Blessed Mother of God, and caused her venerated images of Walsingham and other places to be burnt . . . So died by the just judgment of God the despoiler of ENGLAND THE DOWER OF MARY."[76]

So we return to the events of the long summer of 1538. The magical universe of the Middle Ages was one in which the world of nature, and special places and objects within it, were invested, not with merely memorial significance, but by the real presence of divinity – a sacred spot, a well, a statue, a relic, an apparition. Even if he was only partially conscious of it, or expressed it with a degree of reluctance, Erasmus's gentle critique of the cult of the Virgin was a precursor of a new world.

[76] Waterton, *Pietas Mariana Britannica*, I, 218–20.

*Fades, traces: transformations of the Virgin
in early modern England*

CHAPTER 5

Fades: Elizabethan ruins, tunes, ballads, poems

In the course of a "perambulation" through Kent around 1570, the Protestant chronicler William Lambarde wrote:

> I must needs take cause, highly to prayse God, that hath thus mercifully in our age delivered us, disclosed Satan, unmasked these Idoles ... and raced to the grounde all Monumentes of building, erected to superstition and ungodlyenesse: And therefore let very godly man ceasse with me from henceforth to marvaile, why Canterbury, Walsingham, and sundry such like, are nowe in these our days become in manner waste, since God in times paste was in them blasphemed most.

On the opposite side of the country, in a survey of Wales in the early 1540s, the antiquarian John Leland had similarly found the remains of a ruined village "wher the pilgrimage was," that had served the needs of pilgrims to Our Lady of Penrhys, also destroyed in the Dissolution.[1] Such holy places dedicated to the Virgin as Walsingham and Penrhys fared especially bleakly in the first wave of iconoclastic cleansing, as well as in the first concerted consolidation of iconoclastic laws after Henry's death, under Edward VI, when, for instance, the destruction of Woolpit, initiated in 1538, was completed in 1551. In an era when the Virgin's presence in approved liturgy and devotion was drastically reduced, images torn down or burnt, rood screens – Mary and John flanking the crucified Christ – torn away, desecrated, painted over – though (in a few cases) hidden away by the faithful – the number, and even the accessibility of places dedicated to the Virgin faded. The bonfire of the "sisters" in London in 1538 was both a material and a symbolic reality that had echoes across the country.

But if pilgrimages winding across the landscape, with their accoutrements of pious devotees and hucksters, religious badges and their erotic parodies, had represented popular religious culture before the Dissolution, where do we turn for its equivalent afterwards? With a few marginal or

---

[1] Lambarde, *Perambulation of Kent*, 235–6. For Leland, see *The Itinerary in Wales*; Williams, *Welsh Cistercians*, 149.

spasmodic exceptions, pilgrimages stopped. But we cannot ignore their reminders, the remnants of the destinations of the pilgrims, the ruins of shrines, priories, abbeys, nunneries, wayside chapels, and parish churches, that continued to (and to a surprising extent, still) dot the rural and even many urban landscapes of England. The search for what from now on I term the "fades" and "traces" of the presence of the Virgin in post-Dissolution England starts with the ruins themselves.

By the end of the sixteenth century, wrecked or abandoned religious buildings had become a striking presence in the English landscape. The destruction of shrines, abbeys, priories, and chapels in the 1530s and over the following century created a landscape of devastation and ruin, not unlike the aftermath of a war. It was a vista that would be viewed either as idolatry overcome and superstition abolished, or else as the ruins of a once proud and nurturing way of life. All across the country, Cromwell's agents, who had been preparing for five or more years as he increasingly took charge of England's internal affairs, were dispatched to hire local workers – who may well have previously maintained the buildings – to carry out his policy. It had originated with his master, Wolsey, to reform monastic living and where necessary close or consolidate some smaller religious institutions, and as the policy firmed up under Cromwell, retained some of its less radical aspects. Some monastic churches were adapted to local parish use. Many outbuildings were turned into granaries or other farm buildings. Some resources were diverted to educational or charitable ends. But the overwhelming number were destroyed.

The first phase of destruction did not occur overnight, but a few weeks would have been enough to render their targeted sites inoperable, without their being able to completely remove all traces. Desecration and partial wrecking would do: as one of Cromwell's agents reported to him: "I pullyd down no Howse thorowly . . . butt so defacyd them as they shuld nott lyghtly be made Fryerys agen."[2] Over the next generation, with the window glass and leaded roofs removed, the buildings were often incorporated into new structures or fell into further ruin, reminders to all of a passing era. Stone would be used for building elsewhere or left as piles of rubble. Lead and metal were sold along with ransacked jewels and trinkets; doors, windows, and glass were carted away; altars, fonts, and other religious paraphernalia put to other more profane uses. A small local Marian shrine such as Woolpit's chapel would have been made unusable quickly and left for its destruction to be completed a decade later. William Barlow, once an

[2] Shagan, *Popular Politics*, 162; Schwyzer, *Archaeologies*, 73.

Augustinian prior and, in 1536, reformist Bishop of St. David's, reported to Cromwell, in a grim phrase, that he "had done refourmation," not only destroying the celebrated image of the Virgin with a taper in her hand, but also removing the lead from the bishop's palace, an act he repeated when translated to a new bishopric at Bath and Wells.[3] At Walsingham, the Holy House and the vial of the Virgin's milk would have been immediately destroyed, no doubt with a mixture of glee and guilt. The site of the Holy House is visible today as a slightly raised rectangle grassed over and, eerily, according to an archeological investigation in 1961, just a few inches of soil and grass cover the ashes of the Virgin's chapel beneath.[4] Ethan Shagan quotes from an extensive interrogation of those still plundering the ruins of the Abbey of Hailes two years after it was demolished. The record shows that the local people seized doors, pipes, windows, lead, and "small items of every conceivable description," from roofs to floor paving. One man who looked back to his father's participation in the event recalled him saying: "might I not as well as others have some profit of the spoil of the abbey? For I did see all would away; and therefore I did as others did."[5]

Surveying in 1539 the previous year's work, one of Henry VIII's supporters, Sir Robert Wingfield, proclaimed that "sorceries and enchantments that have been set forth by such as long have continued the usurpation of Gods authority" had been providentially abolished. The reformers' goal was that the familiar and comforting magical world – the apotropaic powers of relics, the aura of the pilgrimages, holy wells, therapeutic anchoresses, the hotels, baths, wayside chapels, hermits, and chantries – would disappear. Much in the way that, in Shakespeare's *The Tempest*, Prospero's magical world must, he at least partly regrets, disappear into "air, into thin air," the new men of Protestantism were forcing a (perhaps not so) "brave new world" upon what at least in part was a bewildered populace.[6] Along with doctrinal and liturgical changes, such as forbidding the singing of the *Regina Coeli* (Queen of Heaven) and *Salve Regina* (Hail [Holy] Queen) as "untrue or superstitious" anthems, guilds were abolished (and therefore the remaining community religious plays were put under more pressure) and, as Duffy points out (though with some exaggeration as to the extent), "the entire repertoire of sacred music from late antiquity to the recent past [was] swept aside in a matter of months."[7] An even more drastic long-term change in

---

[3] Harris, *Our Lady of Cardigan*, 7.　　[4] Green and Whittingham, "Excavations at Walsingham Priory."
[5] Shagan, *Popular Politics*, 162–3.
[6] Bernard, *King's Reformation*, 596; Shakespeare, *The Tempest*, IV. i. 148, v. i. 183.
[7] Frere, *Visitation Articles*, II, 151; Duffy, *Fires of Faith*, 3.

sixteenth-century popular culture was what Steven Kaplan terms "the Protestant refusal to attend to the magical needs of the people," rites and customs which had been part of local habits and beliefs, which were often inseparably connected with religious practices. The result was often that traditional beliefs – which the authorities tried to repress or else confined to quaint superstition (such as fairies), legends (such as Robin Hood) or leisure or health-related activities (visiting wells and spas) – were maintained only on the margins of English society, by small communities, families or individuals.[8] In outposts of Catholic resistance such as rural Lancashire, many customs retained their adherents. In the north-west, there were repeated complaints well into the next century that holy water, surreptitious pilgrimages (for instance, to St. Winifred's shrine at Holywell), prayers for the dead and other devotional customs continued. Even in Protestant writers, such as Spenser, a number of medieval folk practices remained, even if (at least explicitly) shorn of their former religious associations.[9] Early in the next century, the Laudian Bishop Richard Corbet would memorably sum up this confluence of nostalgia for Catholic and folk magic in his poem, "The Faeries Farewell," wistfully dismissing the world of "rewards and fairies" as the world of bygone superstitions that have died out or fled from Protestant England

> By which we note the fairies
> Were of the old profession,
> Their songs were *Ave Maries*,
> Their dances were procession;
> But now alas they all are dead
> Or gone beyond the seas,
> Or further from religion fled
> Or else they take their ease.[10]

The reformers' "brave new world" had broader ramifications, and it is the dismissal of the magical world of fairies, aves, and the "old abbeys" Corbet calls upon his readers to "lament." In the transition from "late medieval" to "early modern" we are seeing a gradual shift from a sacramental understanding of the universe to what we loosely call the modern "secular" world. My study of the Mariological dimension of this transition will, I hope, be read as calling into question the clarity of such a break, and blurring the

---

[8] Kaplan, *Understanding Popular Culture*, 179; Walsham, "Recording Superstition in Early Modern Britain."

[9] Reay, *Popular Culture*, 109–10: Shell, "St Winifred's Well." For a suggestive treatment of popular culture in Shakespeare, Spenser, and Jonson, see Lamb, *Popular Culture*.

[10] Corbet, *Poems*, 49–50.

absolute distinction between the "world we have lost" and its "brave new" successor. In her recent study, Regina Mara Schwartz argues that the challenges to the traditional world are epitomized by the transition from a transubstantialist world, one that infused all material creation and human signification with the presence of God in the way the doctrine of transubstantiation in the Catholic Mass did with the sacramental elements. Like me, she sees the longings apparently lost by the desacralization of the universe as displaced onto other cultural forms, in what she terms a movement from the "sacrament" to the "sacramental" in the arts and in the development of a "sacramental poetics." It is an appealing concept, but it needs to be qualified: many of the elements of the emerging secular world's "sacramental poetics" were present long before the transition, and many remnants – what I term "fades" and "traces" – were present long after.[11]

In the zigzagging of religious change in the middle of the century, the upholders of papal power and those who believed in England's obligation to remain part of the universal Church were undoubtedly convinced that they would eventually be able to resume their habitual practices and that the old world had not been permanently overthrown. For them, the reformers' goal of destroying "the old memories" in order to "make us new"[12] was an audacious and futile process perpetrated by upstart radicals who had temporarily seized political power and taken advantage of Henry VIII's unfortunate marital and dynastic anxieties. When Mary Tudor took the throne in 1553, conservatives assumed all would return to the traditional ways, or at least to some semblance of them, and her accession was compared with the Virgin's own role in salvation history, returning to intercede for and rescue her people. Duffy has argued that the re-Catholicization of England under Mary was both efficient and provided Tridentine Catholicism with a model of reform, led by Cardinal Pole, who had nearly become what would have likely to have been a reformist pope.[13]

In 1563, the Council of Trent affirmed what appeared to be a commonsensical viewpoint (and ironically one not far from Erasmus's views), acknowledging that images and representations of divine personages were certainly legitimate ways of venerating the saints, but that abuses of idols might occur, and decreeing that superstition, lasciviousness, profiteering should be avoided, and all claims of miracles require approval by proper authorities. But in England, as William Wizeman comments, "it would have taken longer than Mary's reign to renew the quest for saintly aid in

---

[11] Schwartz, *Sacramental Poetics*.   [12] Peters, *Patterns of Piety*, 208.   [13] Duffy, *Fires of Faith*, 206.

holy places."[14] The demolition of buildings and the redistribution of land had been done sufficiently thoroughly by Cromwell and those who followed him that the fate of the religious houses or traditional shrines could not be reversed. Norman Jones states that "Property was the great sweetener of the Reformation,"[15] guaranteeing not just support for establishing royal supremacy over the Church in the 1530s, but reinforcing the longer-term hegemony of the nationalistic Protestantism embraced by the newly enriched landed gentry. Habitable buildings and the attached estates could also be used to reward Protestant supporters – in the case of Walsingham, a minor branch of the Sidney family, for example – and therefore the remnants did not entirely disappear. Sketches and photographs from later centuries show that the process of demolition at Walsingham was never completed. A manor house for respectable Protestant gentry gradually emerged, with wishing wells, pleasure gardens, and quaint outcrops of ruins.[16] This redistribution of land as a consequence of the politicization of religion in the 1530s was arguably, in the long run, the most important material change in the period. Power was transferred to those loyal to the new regime and the few years of Mary's reign did not materially affect that deep-rooted revolution.

With the accession of Elizabeth in 1559, however, the reformers were back in power, many fired with a new vehemence born of persecution and exile. As part of the Elizabethan opposition to Trent, in his *Godly and Necessarye Admonitions of the Decrees and Canons of the Council of Trent* (1563), the preacher John Day reiterated the Protestant attack on Rome's "idolatry, superstitions, and abuses," its "horrible impiety [and] idolatry," which all good Protestants should abhor – and destroy. Elizabeth may have allowed for a modicum of ordered ceremony and a limited number of commemorative saints' days, and even tolerated images in her private chapel, and a few Catholics in her court and entourage, but her regime continued the attacks on the sacramental, in both essentials and incidentals. With the important exception of Catholic exiles, recusants, and conforming "church papists," Duffy is not exaggerating when he asserts that by around 1570 England's religious and geographical landscapes had been dramatically changed.[17]

But as the sixteenth century lengthened, and the abandoned religious houses fell further into disrepair or simply degenerated into crumbling piles, they started to acquire complicated memories and associations. Aston

---

[14] Wizeman, *Theology and Spirituality of Mary Tudor's Church*, 239.
[15] Jones, *English Reformation*, 4.   [16] Waller, "Protestantization of Walsingham," 67–82.
[17] Duffy, *Stripping of the Altars*, 382, 387; Aston, *England's Iconoclasts*, 46.

argues that, even by mid century, a new generation of Protestant historians and antiquarians was becoming deeply affected by the presence of ruins: "the landscape held a series of signposts to the destroyed monastic era, and they led to nostalgia and poetry, as well as to antiquarianism and history."[18] Ironically, it was John Bale – fervent Protestant, dramatist, bibiliophile, and, most famously, the antiquarian who provided Foxe with material for the *Book of Martyrs* – who was among the first to lament the destructiveness. He was particularly disturbed by the random vandalization of historical records, lamenting that "in turning over of ye superstycyouse monasteryes ... this would I have wyshed (and I scaresely utter it without teares) that the profitable corne had not so unadvisedly and ungodly perished with the unprofitable chaffe." Even a convinced Protestant such as Bale could look back to the first generation of iconoclasts and say it was "a wicked age ... muche geven to the destruccyon of thynges memorable." Fifty years after the Dissolution, "many do lament the pulling downe of abbayes," lamented Francis Trigge in 1589; while "superstitious uses" and "laysy lubbers and poppyshe bellygoddes" needed to be abolished, wrote the Norfolk antiquarian Henry Spelman early in the next century, the presence of the wasted ruins suggested that they might better have been put "to some godly purposes."[19] This new nostalgia – a word, Schwyzer points out, not recorded in England before 1549 and its usage closely tied to the huge transformation of the English countryside caused by the sight of ruined remnants of the Old Religion – became especially noticeable by the 1580s.[20] For a minority of Elizabethans the "golden age" proclaimed by the regime's propaganda was not their own insecure, debt-ridden, economically depressed one, with its ageing queen and nervous theological polarizations, but a time that lay before Henry VIII turned upon the monasteries.

"But we wretches here in the world, what should we doe without the glorious Virgin?" wrote the sixteenth-century Spanish historian Alonso de Villegas.[21] Where was the Virgin in this generation of transformation in England? Did she disappear? What evidence can we find in the poetry, drama, and popular culture over the century of iconoclasm? We can trace a complex mixture of acceptance, regret, and nostalgia in the age's poetry – along with transformations of the Virgin's presence which are emergent in the wider culture. Traditional poems on the Virgin continue to be written by Catholic loyalists in the transitional generation, after the revolutionary changes of the late 1530s and under Edward until around 1570, the year in

---

[18] Aston, "English Ruins," 232.   [19] *Ibid.*, 237, 246.
[20] Schwyzer, *Archaeologies*, 97.   [21] Villegas, *Lives of Saints*, II, 524.

which Rome officially declared Elizabeth excommunicate and the legitimate target of Catholic rebellion, and remain largely within the medieval devotional tradition. Around that date, however, we can see a change in both Catholic and Protestant imaginings of the Virgin as the religious atmosphere, both within England and outside, becomes more confrontational. We also see the emergence of an interesting phenomenon – the presence not only of what I term "fades" as older traditions die out, but a miscellany of "traces" in which the Virgin makes remarkable reappearances and transformations, even within the seemingly most hostile contexts. It is as if something she represented (or misrepresented) would not disappear but insisted on speaking through the emergent discursive structures of early modern England.

A quaint holdover of the old ways is a long poem on the Virgin written by a Catholic priest, William Forest, whose brother was the John Forest who was burnt as a papist heretic around the date that the images of the "sisters" were burnt in London and referred to by Latimer in his boast that the images would not last so long in their bonfire as the papist heretic. Forest most likely commenced the poem under Mary, but it was largely written under Elizabeth. Historically as well as poetically anachronistic, Forest's nearly 4,000 lines of Lydgatean fourteeners reflect an earnest prayer, as his sole editor in the past nearly five hundred years puts it, to reverse England's "dead or dying desire" for Mary. He begs the Virgin to reclaim her rights in the alien land that England had become, bitterly blaming one woman for England's plight – not Elizabeth herself, but Anne Boleyn, her mother. The theology of the poem takes us back to the decades before Henry's divorce and the Dissolution. Forest defends not just the Virgin Birth and Mary's perpetual virginity (matters on which most Protestants would have agreed), but strongly affirms the Virgin's intercessory role, her Immaculate Conception, and Assumption. The poem includes a lively if somewhat unconsciously amusing blazon of the Virgin, as Forest, seemingly unaware of poetical or moral improprieties which the Council of Trent was already considering, let alone any idolatrous sexualization, celebrates her bodily charms. He praises her "maydenlye feete," "most chaste pure wombe," "innocent harte," "fruitefull Breasts," her hands and "maydenlye Mowthe," her "blessed" tongue, lips, even her "nostrelles," ears, arms, and eyes. It is all slightly ridiculous, continually punctuated by Aves, but it is an echoing remnant of an older world which was, for most English men and women, gradually being replaced.[22]

---

[22] Forest's poem remained in the Harleian Mss until it was printed in the early eighteenth century. The only modern edition, still unpublished, is the dissertation ed. Keena, *Forest*.

In the last quarter of the century, however, a new generation of Catholic poets, some living and writing in England itself, others in exile, and some moving in and out of England, many as missionary priests, started to emerge. The key figure is Robert Southwell. Born of Norfolk gentry in a family enriched by property from the Dissolution, his grandfather had been one of Cromwell's agents of demolition in Norfolk, and ruins recur in his poetry as metaphors for the dereliction suffered by Catholic England. He grew up closely in contact with recusant families and by the late 1570s was in Jesuit training in Rome, eventually to return to England in 1586 to minister to the increasingly isolated and frequently persecuted Catholics. Sweeney comments that the "country house circuit" became "the center of the Jesuit support network in England," which at least for a while held the Catholic Church intact in England.[23] For five years Southwell managed to escape significant attention from Walsingham's spies, moving around London and country society, usually in disguise, sometimes protected by the great Catholic rural families.

Southwell was part of a group which saw as its firm goal not just support for faithful Catholics but active preparation for the return of England to its former faith. Southwell even warned Elizabeth that the ecclesiastical leaders of the past would be appalled to "see their Reliques burned, their Memories defaced," and all "Monasteries" either "burned" or "profaned." In Rome he was therefore intensely trained in opposing what his superior William Allen termed the "impieties, blasphemies, absurdities, cheats, and trickeries of the English heretics."[24] Southwell was also an accomplished poet, aspiring to be a national literary figure no less than Protestant poets such as Sidney or Spenser. He was determined to bring a very different aesthetic into English poetry at a time when the impact of Petrarchism was belatedly but powerfully entering the English court, both as a poetic mode and as part of the political chicanery built up around the cult of the queen. Southwell's critique of Petrarchism will be focused on in Chapter 6. He brings to both his Latin and English poetry – two significant volumes published in 1595, after his capture in 1592 and execution in 1595 – early signs of the focus on the dramatic and sensual and intense visualization that is associated with the "Baroque," but which also reaches back to late medieval devotion. Jesuit meditation techniques intensify the emotionality of the believer's sight: Sweeney writes of the "new foregrounding of sensual apprehension" which allowed for a highly emotional relationship with the object of veneration,

---

[23] Sweeney, *Snow in Arcadia,* 105.
[24] Southwell, *Humble Supplication,* 29–30; Sweeney, *Snow in Arcadia,* 5.

whether God, Christ or the Virgin.[25] It is a poetic that stresses the unworthiness of the poet, lover (or devotee), and looks for consolation for the sufferings of perpetual exile – both spiritually and, given Southwell's situation, materially. To the repentance and self-abasement of the traditional devotional lyric, Southwell adds political alienation, exile, and an apprehension of perpetual danger.

Southwell's training in Rome involved a highly focused "Mariality," an intense devotion to Mary that emphasized her central role in salvation in ways that were anathema to Protestants. He supervised a local chapter of the Sodality of the Virgin Mary, a feature of all Jesuit training, in which addressing "Most Holy Mary," the "most unworthy" devotee yet "longing to serve thee" vows to "choose thee this day to be my Queen, my Advocate, and my Mother," a dedication created as a deliberate challenge to Protestant denigration of the Virgin.[26] A similar obsessive, self-abasing devotion to Mary imbues his poetry, especially a long sequence of poems in which the lives of Christ and the Virgin are intertwined and paralleled, much like (though not exactly following) the decades of the rosary or other sequences of meditative prayer in which the life of the Virgin is highlighted as central to salvation history. Sweeney suggests that Southwell brings specific memories of the Madonna chapel in the Gesù, the Jesuit Church in Rome, and that when he describes the Immaculate Conception, the Virgin's nativity, and other traditional Marian moments, he has the paintings clearly in his mind. Regardless of whether there was such a specific meditational focus, Southwell attempts to create a detailed visualization of the Annunciation (which he terms "The Virgin's Salutation"), the Assumption of the Virgin, and the poem with which the sequence begins, "The Conception of our Ladie," in which the reader is directed to see, as if looking at the details of a painting, and through sight, to feel:

> Our second Eve putts on her mortall shrowde,
> Earth breedes a heaven for gods new dwelling place
> Nowe ryseth up Elias little cloude
> That growing shall distill the shoure of grace

Mary is hailed as the "second Eve," immaculately conceived and eventually ascended to Heaven as the triumphant embodiment of a redeemed material world. She is "proclaymed Queene and mother of a god" and – in phrases that would certainly not have endeared him to Protestant Englishmen in the 1590s – "a prince she is and mightier prince doth beare" (Visitation),

---

[25] *Ibid.*, 44.   [26] Pilarz, *Robert Southwell and the Mission of Literature*, 220.

and when she dies, she remains "queen of Earth" and as well, "empresse of the skies":

> Gemm to her worth spouse to her love ascendes
> Prince to her throne Queene to her heavenly kinge,
> Whose court with solemne pompe on her attends
> And Quires of Saintes with greeting notes do singe.[27]   (Assumption)

The Assumption of the Blessed Virgin, it will be recalled from Chapter 3, was one of the episodes that came under early suspicion in medieval plays, and to Protestants it remained an objectionable unscriptural and idolatrous expression of papistry. Southwell is deliberately confronting the Protestant universe that had, in the reformers' eyes, been emptied of superstition, and stressing, defiantly, how the body of the Virgin stands for the redemption of the whole created world. It is intriguing, for example, to contrast Southwell's celebratory tone with that of Fulke Greville's powerful, grim verse, much of which was also written in the last years of Elizabeth's reign. Greville repeatedly stresses the abandoned, predestined sinfulness of a restless individual in a lonely, desacralized universe in which, at best, mankind's lot is deserved pain, reflective of inherent sinfulness. For Southwell, observing what Sweeney terms a "Calvinised Albion,"[28] the universe envisaged by Protestants such as Greville or even (less extremely but still, underneath, a de-feminized cosmos) that of Philip Sidney, was always teetering on the verge of despair; and such cosmic negativity as a Protestant poetic envisaged was incompatible with what would have been perceived as a superstitious, magical world giving a central place to transformative stories centered on the body of a mere woman. How that comparison holds when we set Greville, Sidney, and Southwell within the Petrarchan tradition, which drew heavily on the rhetoric of Marian devotion, will be a subject of Chapter 6.

To patriotic Protestants, then, Southwell was properly captured, tortured, and executed as one of the instigators of terrorism in the dangerous 1580s and 1590s. His Marian poetry would be seen as blasphemous superstition, the verbal manifestations of his life of subversion and idolatry. Around the time of Southwell's death – for Catholics, his martyrdom – in *The Faerie Queene,* the Protestant poet Edmund Spenser is drawing on the long tradition of scatological rhetoric in order to undermine such views and to affirm a belief in Elizabeth as the Reformed Virgin and true Queen of England.[29] Spenser's blatant and sometimes brutal Protestant side has been

---

[27] Southwell, *Collected Poems*, 3, 6, 12.   [28] Sweeney, *Snow in Arcadia*, 128.
[29] Quotations are taken from Spenser, *Faerie Queene*, ed. Hamilton.

played down in the extraordinary revival of his work as quintessentially "English" in the past fifty years and more, notwithstanding some of his – perhaps genuine, perhaps simply confused – vacillations about the value of the material world, including poetry itself. In Book One of *The Faerie Queene*, the magician Archimago creates a witch, the "false Duessa," who stands for both the Church of Rome and what, as a loyal Protestant, Spenser saw as papist exaggeration of the role of the Virgin Mary (i. viii. 35); she is also associated with the biblical Whore of Babylon, another slur conventionally directed at Catholics in Protestant propaganda. Her inner corruption is covered over with gaudy robes, and when she is stripped and her body displayed, she is revealed as false and ugly. Spenser's poem is fully in line with the most commonplace of Protestant propaganda. In fairness to him, we need to observe an important inconsistency over his whole career about his treatment if not of Catholicism (represented near at hand by the Irish) but of the papist view of images. In the same first Book, Spenser attacks corrupt clergy and church robbers in the figure of Kirkrapine, who are not only "Wonte to robbe Churches of their ornaments / And poore mens boxes of their due reliefe," but also to steal the "rich vestiments" of "the holy saints" (i. iii. 17).

Kirkrapine's activities seem to recall the destruction of churches and holy places by Protestant iconoclasts. Did Spenser perceive the irony? Or in his mind was there "good" and "bad" iconoclasm? Over the twenty years in which he wrote his poem, it seems that he felt increasingly ambivalent about the destruction of ancient monuments and the violence and corruption that accompanied the purging of images. One of the reasons *The Faerie Queene* was unfinished – quite apart from Spenser's own death – was that it had become so ideologically self-contradictory that it was perhaps unfinishable. When his Knight of Temperance, Guyon, destroys the Bower of Bliss at the end of Book Two, it is with the intemperance of the Protestant iconoclasts:

> But all those pleasant bowres and Pallace braue,
>   *Guyon* broke downe, with rigour pittilesse;
>   Ne ought their goodly workmanship might saue
>   Them from the tempest of his wrathfulnesse,
>   But that their blisse he turn'd to balefulnesse:
>   Their groues he feld, their gardins did deface,
>   Their arbers spoyle, their Cabinets suppresse,
>   Their banket houses burne, their buildings race,
> And of the fairest late, now made the fowlest place.   (ii. xii. 83)

Such contradictions are found throughout. At the end of Book Six, we are told of monks' cells where "what filth and ordure did appeare, / Were

Yrkesome to report," and yet in the next stanza they are described as containing "Images" of "goodly hew" which the poem's final great enemy, the Blatant Beast, who shares some of the characteristics of Kirkrapine, randomly destroys, much in the manner of the iconoclasts who vandalized Ely's Lady Chapel (VI. xii. 24–5). At the book's end, the Blatant Beast is recaptured, but breaks his bonds and escapes to roam the world, destructive, anarchic, and uncontrolled. As Schwyzer notes, at the end of this, the final completed book of Spenser's poem, there appears to be a "sudden wavering in allegiance to the historical Reformation." On the one hand, the Beast is the enemy of Courtesy; on the other, Sir Calidore, the Knight of Courtesy, has to use some blatantly discourteous means to overcome the Beast. Unusually sensitive to the swirling winds of ideological change in the late Elizabethan period, and perhaps without its author's awareness, Spenser's poem records not merely his own but his generation's anxieties about what England had done fifty years earlier to its religious heritage. "Was Spenser," asks Schwyzer, following in the long tradition of Spenser scholars who have puzzled over the ending of Book Six, "at last giving vent, perhaps unconsciously, to long-repressed traditionalist yearnings"?[30] What Sir Calidore finds as an alternative to the random violence of the world in which he has to defend Courtesy is, intriguingly, an idealized woman, whose name, Pastorella, perhaps suggests the natural beauty and mystery of the country and the healing powers of the female. Intriguingly, however, what is missing from Spenser's treatment of the virgin Queen of England is any positive view of motherhood. Just as Protestant theologians downplayed the cosmic significance of Mary's maternal role, so motherhood in *The Faerie Queene* is a positive only when it contributes to the genealogy of the English monarchy. Spenser often constructs the lineage of his heroes and heroines but whenever the physicality of mothering appears in the poem, it is in the form of monstrosity, ugliness, and deformity.

Spenser may have at times been an iconophobe, but was he (as perhaps many reformers were, in different ways) an idealist consciously believing that the Queen of England, "th' Idole of her makers great magnificence" (II. ii. 41), provided her subjects with a Reformed alternative to the Virgin? It is an assertion frequently made: after the accession of Elizabeth, it is often alleged, many of the characteristics of the Queen of Heaven were transferred into a nationalistic cult centered on Queen Elizabeth herself. Just as symbols of nationhood often replaced religious iconography in religious ceremonies and churches, so the argument goes, part of the Elizabethan regime's drive to achieve national unity invested the Queen of England with some of the aura of the Queen of Heaven. Helen Hackett has argued, however, that there was not a direct and deliberate transfer of qualities and epithets from the Virgin Mary to the Virgin Queen, and that the elaborate iconography that surrounded Elizabeth had classical and political origins as much as religious ones. "Transfer," therefore, may be an exaggeration. It is, nevertheless, hard to read patriotic encomia to Elizabeth without seeing them within the historical context of the Reformation and the crusade carried out by the Protestant regime against the cult of Mary. Steven May quotes Sir Henry Lee's saying that at court it was important to say "*Vivat Eliza*" instead of "an *ave mari*."[31] Spenser, not totally consistently, tried to avoid inviting idolatry in the case of Elizabeth. As Helen Cooper notes, "there is an increasing tendency in panegyrics of Elizabeth to elide the earthly and heavenly Virgin Queens," but Spenser generally "holds back from suggesting that his faerie queen might be an object of worship."[32] In the exuberant praises of Belphoebe in Book Two, however – her face is "so faire as flesh it seemed not, / But heauenly pourtraict of bright Angels hew" – the vocabulary recalls the Pynson Ballad's praise of the Virgin who was "able to heale the sicke, and to reuiue the ded." Belphoebe's eyes were "Kindled aboue at th'heauenly makers light"; she overcomes sin and "quenched base desire"; and despite her chastity, uncannily echoing the language by which the Virgin had been eroticized, we are invited to admire:

> her snowy brest, [which] did diuide
> Her daintie paps; which like young fruit in May
> Now little gan to swell, and being tide,
> Through her thin weed their places only signifide.   (II. iii. 29)

It is against such descriptions that, in the early seventeenth century, Catholics understandably directed their indignation when they accused Protestants of idolizing mere mortal women in ways they themselves had been criticized for describing the Virgin herself.[33]

In *The Faerie Queene*, Spenser is drawing on medieval romance material, properly (though not entirely) purged of its Catholic associations. By the 1580s, despite their rejection by humanist educators, the taste for pre-Reformation romances – stories of Robin Hood, tales drawn from "old and ancient antiquaries"[34] – returned in poetry and prose fiction; Sidney's *Arcadia*, written in the early 1580s, first published in 1590, adds a level of

---

[31] May, *Elizabethan Courtier Poets*, 356; Hackett, *Virgin Mother, Maiden Queen*, 3–7. See also Pugh, "Sidney Spenser, and Political Petrarchism."
[32] Cooper, *English Romance in Time*, 183.   [33] Dolan, *Whores of Babylon*, 118.   [34] Lodge, *Works*, II, 4.

Protestant theologizing to the medieval setting he gets in part from Ariosto. As Deanne Williams observes on its remarkable revival, what is primary in "the fortunes of medieval romance in the Tudor period" is its faith not in miraculous interventions by the Virgin (or any lesser saintly presence) but the "redemptive capacity of sin."[35] I return to the remarkable Mariological affinities with romance when I consider Shakespeare's last plays in Chapter 7.

Within the poetry that grew from the confrontational ideological landscape of the late sixteenth century, a special place is occupied by a curiously large number of poems and ballads written about Walsingham. The Virgin's greatest shrine maintains a powerful presence in Elizabethan and popular culture well after its "image" was burned in 1538. If the traditional ascription in Bodleian Manuscript Rawlinson Poet. 219 is correct, Philip Howard, Duke of Arundel, wrote an angry poem expressing revulsion for precisely what, in this chapter's opening quotation, William Lambarde was celebrating: that "nowe in these our days" such seats of "superstition and ungodlyenesse" had become "in manner waste, since God in times paste was in them blasphemed most." Arundel was one of the leaders of the Catholics in and around the court: Southwell was in effect his family's private chaplain, especially active when Arundel was imprisoned, and he may have helped get Southwell's poems published in 1595.[36] His poem, usually labeled "[In] The Wracke of Walsingham," is definitely a specifically "Catholic text," to use Shell's useful distinction, "not simply a religious one."[37] It is an outright rejection of the Reformation, the Elizabethan settlement, and looks straight back to the Dissolution as the start of the outrage. Fifty or more years after it was destroyed, England's greatest Marian shrine has become the symbol of both the destruction of traditional religion and the poet's defiance of the Protestant revolution.[38]

The speaker in the poem is presented vividly as if right there, "in the wrackes of walsingam." His Muse is the heavenly "Queene of Walsingam," but the earthly alternative who now rules England is a false queen. As May points out, in one of Arundel's other poems, a long "Fourfold Meditation," there are some stanzas on the Virgin Mary which were omitted from the 1606 published edition, with similar sentiments in which he "developed a telling contrast with that earthly virgin he had formerly adored" and the

[35] Williams, "Medievalism," 222.
[36] Shell, *Catholicism, Controversy*, 11; Sweeney, *Snow in Arcadia*, 115.
[37] Lambarde, *Perambulation of Kent*, 236; Shell, *Catholicism, Controversy*, 17.
[38] The poem is quoted from Norbrook and Woudhuysen, *Renaissance Verse*, 531–2.

neglected Mother of God.[39] The sheep grazing in Walsingham's ruins remind him of faithful Christians who have been destroyed by the Protestant "raveninge wolves." What was once a "holy land" is now "Levell with the ground," the "waies" of Walsingham – a reference to the many routes, the "Walsingham waies" that led to the shrine – are now empty, and where Walsingham's fame was proudly trumpeted, "blowen," now the only sound is the melancholy cry of owls. The final stanza turns from mournful plaint to direct invective, as absolute in its views as the reformers themselves:

> Weepe, weepe o Walsingham,
> > Whose dayes are nightes,
> Blessinges turned to blasphemies
> > Holy deedes to dispites,

cries the indignant poet, who ends with a denunciatory couplet:

> Sinne is wher our Ladie sate
> Heaven turned is to Hell.
> Sathan sittes wher our Lord did swaye
> Walsingam oh farewell.

What to Lambarde, surveying with some satisfaction the destruction of Walsingham, Canterbury, and other shrines, is a sign of the triumph of the Gospel, to the author of this poem was a sign of blasphemy and an inconsolable loss.

The poem speaks to the continuing presence of the Virgin in Elizabethan culture despite her exile from Elizabethan official religious life. It is, of course, not perhaps surprising that memories, however fading or (in this case) indignant and defiant, would be manifest in the remnants of the Catholic community. What is more intriguing is Walsingham's continuing presence in the popular culture of poem and ballad – and right in the heart of the Elizabethan Protestant establishment. By the last decades of the century, by then a generation or two after the Dissolution, the name Walsingham had come to refer less to the site of the shrine (now a country gentleman's home which becomes known as Walsingham "Abbey") than to the title of both the tune and the words of a popular folk ballad. References to it are sufficient in number to suggest that it was a well-known part of Elizabethan popular culture – as both the words of a ballad that could be sung to a distinctive tune, also termed "Walsingham," and a lyric poem in its own right. This is the famous "Walsingham Ballad."

---

[39] May, *Elizabethan Courtier Poets*, 347, 215.

There are over thirty extant musical variants from the period by over twenty composers who worked with the Walsingham tune. They are found in many collections, published and unpublished, including the century's premier collection of keyboard songs, the *Fitzwilliam Virginal Book*.[40] William Byrd's "Walsingham Variations" is the first composition in the book; John Bull's variations, likely written to compete with Byrd's, are also included in the Fitzwilliam Book. Both composers take over a melody that had become part of Elizabethan folklore and elaborately and lovingly enhance it. There are also lute settings by Francis Cutting, John Dowland, Edward Collard, and John Marchant.[41] It was, it is often asserted, the most popular tune of the period. Such popularity makes what Bradley Brookshire terms the "covert speech" of Byrd's "*roman à clef*" of his Walsingham composition all the more significant for our understanding of the continuing presence of the Virgin in late sixteenth-century England. Byrd, the premier Elizabethan keyboard composer, maintained his Catholicism unwaveringly. He was employed in Elizabeth's chapel, and as Master of the Queen's Music, he dutifully composed for the Anglican liturgy. His Norfolk patron, Edward Paston, a poet and musician himself as well as a collector and patron of music, provided a refuge for Byrd and allowed his association with East Anglian recusants.[42] Most of Byrd's music, as Brookshire shows, retains a fierce allegiance to the more militant recusant forces, and is especially forceful in the Walsingham variations and other similar non-liturgical compositions, where he is not tied down by his duties to the Protestant queen. He clearly works to sacralize a common folk tune and, employing a structure that has identifiable connections with his religious works, gives his audience an expression of their shared sense of the Virgin's loss from Elizabethan England. The result is a composition in which memory of the Virgin's presence is made to interrogate the Reformation and the spiritual impoverishment of Elizabethan England, as well as to comfort those who hoped for a renewed, Catholic England. Bull's variations of the Walsingham tune, also in the *Fitzwilliam Virginal Book*, likewise go far beyond what an ordinary musical setting of a ballad would

---

[40] Maitland and Squire, *Fitzwilliam Virginal Book*. The Fitzwilliam Book is traditionally attributed to the Catholic collector Sir Thomas Tregean, but see Thompson, "Francis Tregean the Younger," 1–31. See also for detailed musicological discussion Brookshire, "Bare ruin'd quiers," 199–216.

[41] For variations by Cutting (7), Corkine (4), and Collard, see Morrongiello, "Roads to Ralegh's *Walsingham*," 17–36. Byrd, Bull, Dowland, and Cutting all had or were suspected of Catholic sympathies, while Bull lived in Catholic Europe for some time.

[42] For Byrd's role as, in Brookshire's phrase, the "house composer" of Appleton Hall, see Brett, "Edward Paston," 51–69.

demand. By virtue of choosing the Walsingham tune, both composers are making passionate expressions of loss and defiance, no doubt all the more able to be articulated because, as music, their work would escape the verbal scrutiny or censure that a poem might attract. The Walsingham Ballad's continuing presence and popularity in late Elizabethan and Jacobean England constituted both a memory of the Virgin's power and an affirmation of the need for an alternative, even if only through poetry and music, to the seemingly irresistible dominance of the Protestant Reformation.

But the Walsingham Ballad was more than a popular and nostalgic tune that appealed to the Catholic remnant. Its words also echo through late Elizabethan literature and well into the seventeenth century in a number of closely related versions that suggest a widespread fascination with its suggestive story. All the extant versions of the poem and its many incidental echoes refer back to a basic situation: an abandoned lover encountering a pilgrim on a road – presumably since it is somewhere on a road to Walsingham, it is an echo of the "Walsingham Way," still in the 1580s listed as a major highway across England[43] – who is returning from the shrine. The bereft lover bewails that his beloved has also gone on pilgrimage there but has not returned. He enquires whether the pilgrim has seen her. Asked how she would be recognized, the lover describes her. Bishop Percy's eighteenth-century collection of ballads, in which the Walsingham Ballad, along with the ruins themselves, become increasing objects of nostalgic curiosity, includes another quite distinct narrative, a dialogue between a pilgrim and a herdsman. The pilgrim, who turns out to be a woman, is wanting to learn the way to Walsingham so she may repent and die – she has treated her lover so cruelly that he has died and she wishes to join him.[44]

The most famous "stand-alone" version of the ballad is not attached, even indirectly, to the Catholic remnant. It is the one attributed to that most flamboyant of Elizabeth's Protestant courtiers, Sir Walter Ralegh.[45] While, as I have suggested, it is somewhat over-simple to say that Elizabethans transferred their feelings for the Virgin Mary to Elizabeth the Virgin Queen, there is no doubt that Elizabethan propaganda did exploit the connection. When Elizabeth was entertained at Kenilworth in 1576, a Savage Man proclaimed:

---

[43] Harrison, *Description of England*, 399.
[44] I am indebted for insights into the Walsingham Ballad and its many variations to Alison Chapman: see "Ophelia's 'Old Lauds'" and "Met I with an old bald Mare."
[45] For a more extensive reading of "As You Came from the Holy Land," see Waller, "Ralegh's 'As You Came from the Holy Land.'"

> Queene? What the Queene of Heaven
> They knew her long agone
> No, sure, some Queene on earth,
> Whose like was never none.

Many of Ralegh's poems likewise consistently invest the aging queen with the epithets of the Virgin. He is the worshiper; she is powerful and unapproachable (at least so it must have especially appeared to the egocentric Ralegh as he languished in the Tower or during other periods of disgrace); but he affirms that she is able, if only she turns back to him, to bring solace and forgiveness.

Ralegh's Walsingham poem starts with a note of puzzlement.[46] It follows the common outline of the ballad – an abandoned lover asking a pilgrim if he has been to the "holy land" of Walsingham and whether he has seen his lover who has abandoned him:

> As you came from the holy land
> Of Walsingham,
> Met you not with my true love
> By the way as you came?

After setting out the initial situation, however, Ralegh's version takes a very distinctive turn. The initial dialogue between the sympathetic but puzzled pilgrim and the abandoned lover, and the conclusion, with its ambiguous narrative voices, not only shows Ralegh brilliantly giving his readers the opportunity to enter into different roles in the discovery of love's disillusions in a bleak universe, but also adapting the ballad to his own personal and political agendas in what Leonard Forster termed the "political Petrarchism" of the Elizabethan court.[47] The "holy land" becomes an idealization of the court; the "way" to Walsingham becomes the pathway courtiers take to the queen's presence and from which he is now, like the lover of the poem, excluded. The original Lady of Walsingham was of course the Virgin Mary. The lady of this poem may be powerful but, unlike the Queen of Heaven, she is clearly mortal. And knowing Ralegh's ambition and his view of his own merit, it would be perfectly in character for the pilgrim to blame the lady and to attribute his fall from favor as her falling away from her "old" lover:

> I have loved her all my youth,
> But now old, as you see,
> Love likes not the falling fruit
> From the withered tree.

---

[46] Ralegh, *Poems*, ed. Latham, 120–2.　　[47] Forster, *Icy Fire,* 122–47.

The angel-like figure may be, in appearance, "by her gait, by her grace," a queen, but she is fickle, misled, ungrateful – and yet it is vital at the same time that she is praised and remains wise, all-powerful, eternal.

Most of Ralegh's poems written around the time when, in the early 1590s he was in disgrace with the queen, are similarly self-advertising, expressing adoration of Elizabeth and deeply hurt by her rejection, and always with his own political agenda in mind. We may usefully contrast Ralegh with Southwell here: on the one hand, the flamboyant Protestant devoted to the Virgin Queen, living dangerously, and primarily for himself and his reputation; on the other, the committed Catholic living even more dangerously for the cause of the Queen of Heaven. In satiric attacks in both poems and sermons, Southwell attacks what he sees as the false Virgin. Ralegh might at times have felt negatively about Elizabeth, but largely repressed those feelings. For a Catholic such as Southwell, however, the false queen is an obscene parody of the true queen. As Sweeney comments, looking back to Southwell's family origins not far from Walsingham, which his own uncle had helped demolish in the 1530s, "had Walsingham been ruined only to be set up again by courtly poets as the shrine of an earthly queen?"[48] At war for men's souls, the aggressive Catholic priest cannot look to the past, not even to his own boyhood in Norfolk – he must look to the future. The Shrine of the Virgin to which Southwell now looks is that of Loreto, a living pilgrimage site with its authenticated Holy House transported miraculously from the Holy Land; ironically, it will also become the refuge of early modern England's last great Marian poet, Richard Crashaw, who will play a major part in Chapter 8.

In Ralegh's poem and in other versions of the Walsingham Ballad, there are still traces of that earlier, now abandoned, world. Indeed, it is hard to account for Ralegh's using the Walsingham Ballad if he knew of its associations. Was it just "in the air"? Two conflicting discourses centered on the two queens are certainly present in the poem, even if Ralegh acknowledges (and even perhaps knows) only one of them. Because it is derived from and carries echoes of the lost Walsingham, it is as if the poem nevertheless knows the other: it carries the remnants of an earlier discourse that disrupts and fissures Ralegh's adaptation of the ballad without his being conscious of it.

At the end of the magnificent evocation of loss, disillusion, and nostalgia of "As You Came from the Holy Land," one could imagine in the hands of a Catholic such as Arundel or Southwell that the poem might take an emphatic movement back to the Shrine of Walsingham, and end with a

---

[48] Sweeney, *Snow in Arcadia*, 215.

re-dedication to the Queen of Heaven. But not with Ralegh – nor with Protestant England by the last decade of the century. We are in a world that has abandoned the Virgin – but it is a world which, as it were, she herself has not quite abandoned, or at least it is one where her stories continue to make themselves heard. In Ralegh's hands, the ballad becomes a refrain of protest, certainly not for the return of Catholicism, but rather for something he cannot name that is lost and irrecoverable, something indefinable (at least by him) that has been destroyed in Elizabethan life. Given the visibility of the ruins (not only of Walsingham but right across the landscape), "destroyed" is perhaps too extreme, but the traces of Walsingham that continue have undoubtedly been transformed, and in Ralegh's hands into undifferentiated despair. Protestants saw the cult of the Virgin as delusion and sinfulness, with the only ultimate reality what Ralegh pleaded for in his last poetic fragment, probably written before his execution in 1617: "And from the earth, the grave, and dust, / The Lord shall raise me up, I trust."[49] In such a world, there is no place for the Virgin. At least in his mind, she is not beside him, not there to appeal for intercession, and at the end what she represents is not embodied in any human being.

Another poem, also written in the 1590s, shows powerful traces of Walsingham in the late Elizabethan transformation of the shrine from religious icon to ambiguous repository of loss and nostalgia. It is the Sixth Song ("Lady: Pilgrim") by Sir Robert Sidney in which the Virgin, and specifically Our Lady of Walsingham, makes another typically disruptive comeback. The Sidneys were also closely bound to the fortunes and largesse of the Elizabethan regime. Consequently, as with Ralegh, when the Virgin or "Virgin Queen" is mentioned in the context of the Elizabethan Sidneys, a reasonable assumption has always seemed to be that the reference is to Elizabeth Regina, by the Grace of God Queen of England. But there was, as in Ralegh's version of the Walsingham Ballad, still lurking in the cultural and psychological hinterlands, the other Virgin Queen, even (however marginal her presence may have been) in late sixteenth-century England, even in the ultra-Protestant Leicester circle. This other Virgin Queen does not feature much in biographical or critical studies of Philip Sidney or, indeed, the other Sidneys. Even before his early death in 1586, Philip became (and remains) a Protestant culture hero, and in English literary history, so powerful has been his iconic status that his connections with Catholic intellectual and religious circles have been marginalized or repressed. Recent revisionist historians of the Reformation have long

---

[49] Ralegh to Cecil, July 1592, *Works*, 655.

pointed to the centuries-long protestantization of scholarly discourse on the Elizabethan period, whereby Catholic issues and Catholic culture were systematically marginalized for hundreds of years.[50] It is further understandable, given the Sidneys' own anxiety to prove their loyalty to the new Protestant regime: like all *nouveau* Elizabethan politicians, they had at once to acknowledge and repudiate their Catholic ancestors; and of course Philip himself had been born in the reign of the Catholic Queen Mary, and even named after her husband, Philip II of Spain.

That the "real" Virgin Queen should return to haunt one of the most evocative poems written by a member of the Sidney family is not just ironic, but opens a startling perspective on the second generation of early modern England's protestantization. Robert's Sixth Song takes as its starting point the Walsingham Ballad and, in fact, as Croft noted in his edition, the first stanza is "set to the tune of Walsingham." Sidney, Croft observes, "must have had the tune in his head when composing song 6 for his words can be sung to it, and the haunting ballad air repeated throughout the poem's thirty-four stanzas imparts a compelling sadness to the alternating speeches of Lady and Pilgrim." Although not in ballad form, the poem's situation is yet another variant of the basic starting point of the Walsingham Ballad, a faithful woman asking in the lilting tones of the ballad tune whether the pilgrim has met her absent lover: "Yonder comes a sad pilgrim, / From the east he returns, / I will ask if he saw him / Who for me absent mourns." Like Ralegh, Sidney adapts the ballad's starting point to his own situation. Unlike Arundel and Ralegh, Robert Sidney was never imprisoned in the Tower, but no doubt he considered his stint of military duty in the Low Countries and consequent exile from the Court and his home at Penshurst as imprisonment enough. He composed his poems (identified as his only in the 1970s) in the Netherlands, whence Robert certainly looked across the sea, not to the Virgin in Walsingham but – dutiful Protestant and (largely) constant husband that he was – a little further south, toward Kent, to Penshurst, and his wife. The "Lady" is a projection of his wife, who "doth rest / Near Medway's sandy bed." Sidney's absences were frequent and extensive, and in his poem are contrasted with journeys he wishes to be making, not to a distant shrine, but to her. The poem's pilgrim has been sent, we learn, by the exiled "knight" of whom the lady asks for news, to affirm his devotion to her. The pilgrim, a strikingly papist-sounding "aged father," in itself a nostalgic trace of an older world evoked by the ballad no

---

[50]   Shell, *Catholicism, Controversy*, 250; Duncan-Jones, "Sir Philip Sidney's Debt to Edmund Campion," 97–113.

longer current in Protestant England, asks her (in the lilting movement of
the ballad's lines) by what "tokens" he might recognize her knight:

> Many one see we lady,
> As we come, as we go:
> By what tokens, how should I
> Your knight from others know?

The lady replies that he can be known for his steadfastly wearing "griefs
livery," and the fact that he undoubtedly "turns his eyes" westward, back
toward Kent and Penshurst itself, "where love holds fast his heart." The
pilgrim acknowledges to the lady that he "once saw such a one," but tells her
that the knight now has died "near to the sea ... on a sandhill," looking
westward toward where he knows she waits, and vows his love for her with
his last breath. The lady's response takes the poem into the conventional
world of Petrarchan paradox: how could he die since she is his life? The
pilgrim's philosophy is, by contrast, stark and stoical: the universe he
invokes is hostile to any such idealization, nor does it seem to provide any
religious consolation. It is the lonely universe of Protestant masculinity,
ruled by the stern God of the Reformers, from which the original Lady of
Walsingham has been exorcized.[51]

Why did the Walsingham poem, and the tune, appeal to Sidney?
Perhaps, as I suggested with Ralegh, it was just "in the air"? Did a level of
unidentifiable melancholy appeal to his sense of exile and loss? And why is
the figure of a woman so insistently powerful? What is missing is any
woman figure beyond what Sidney in one of his letters to his wife terms
the "world and the actions of it,"[52] the world over which Queen Elizabeth
ruled. As in Ralegh's Walsingham poem, there is certainly no alternative
Virgin Queen, no replacement of one Virgin Queen by another. But there is
one difference from Ralegh's poem: in the poem's devotional world, it is the
grieving lady of Penshurst who replaces the heavenly Lady of Walsingham.
His lady can be recognized, the knight says, because she alone represents
"what worth of all else men faign / Is all proved true in her." She embodies
what is good, rare and fair; her breath is "Life-nursing"; she has a "heav'n-
opening face," epithets that recall those traditionally accorded the Queen of
Heaven. Where she is not is a "dark cave / Where her lights do not shine,"
and her knight's last wish is to be buried near her.

---

[51] Sidney, *Poems of Robert Sidney*, 185–95. For a more extensive analysis of Robert Sidney's poems, see
Waller, "The Other Virgin."
[52] Sidney, *Domestic Politics and Family Absence*, 36.

Sidney's poem uses the traditional metaphor of pilgrimage. Pilgrimages had now been forbidden for over fifty years. But here pilgrimage is neither a journey of dedication to a special, holy place nor even a journey undertaken for the sake of discoveries made on the way. Grace Tiffany has shown how in the Reformation period the idea of pilgrimage underwent a transformation. For medieval pilgrims, those who so irritated Latimer for their "wanderings," at the end of their journey was a place made holy by its association with a material object, a relic or reminder of an event or mystery. For Protestants, by contrast, "pilgrimage" was a metaphor justified by the fallen nature of man, not ending in a sacred place or person, but finally only, for the elect, in God: "To the Protestant mind there are ... no sacred places, only redeemed souls."[53] The sacred site is replaced by the journey itself and the pilgrimage is in the mind. So in Philip's *Astrophil and Stella* 5, the Protestant Petrarchan lover knows that he should not deify the beloved, since "on earth we are but pilgrims made, / And should in soul up to our countrey move." In the revision of his *Arcadia*, as Helen Moore has argued, pilgrimage is similarly transformed from the desire for a sacred place to seeing the journey itself as a spiritual testing ground for the elect, tolerating suffering and deprivation for the sake of virtue and as a reflection of election.[54]

In a sense, Robert Sidney's poem *is* about the Virgin Mary, just as Ralegh's is – she is the powerful absence that haunts without fully entering the poem. The "original" Walsingham is present in the rhythms and the sentiments, in the deep yearning and affirmation of spiritual transcendence, but it has become detached from the Virgin. Ironically, even if in accordance with good Protestant belief about the spirituality of marriage, the fetishization of unqualified devotion to an inaccessible distant beloved has now been transferred onto a dutiful waiting wife and the mortality of her arms, hair, lips, and breasts. As Tiffany correctly notes, there is an implied transference of religious devotion to mortal lovers by the "mystical joining that renders them worthy of sainthood, including pilgrimage to their shrines."[55] It is that affirmation – one hesitates to call it awareness since it is spoken by the poem rather than the poet – to which Sidney's poem points. As with Ralegh's, the "original" Walsingham discourse speaks through his poem even though Sidney is barely aware that it lurks there, let alone of its wider power.

---

[53] Tiffany, *Love's Pilgrimage*, 30.
[54] Sidney, *The Poetry of Sir Philip Sidney*, 167; Moore, "The Pilgrimage of Passion in Sidney's *Arcadia*," 62–3.
[55] Tiffany, *Love's Pilgrimage*, 118.

For what is notable about the mortal "lady" of Sidney's poem is not just that she replaces the lady who inspired the original Walsingham Ballad, but that the attitude of the pilgrim named in the poem's subtitle is so similar to those devotees who would have come to Walsingham to venerate the Lady of the Shrine. We are therefore witnessing in the knight's devotion a radical transference in the object of worship from the divine to the human. She is idealized as the bearer of divinity:

> To find her will be small pain—
>   See, and thou canst not err:
> What worth of all else men feign
>   Is al proved true in her.
> What is good from her mind grows,
>   What rare is, is her grace;
> Nothing fair is that not flows
>   In her heaven-opening face.[56]

The "lady" is evoked as real flesh and blood despite her absence; he longs to lie in her arms, and the final thirty-one lines of the poem are in fact a remarkable blazon in which the poet fantasizes that she will give voice to a display of precisely those physical and emotional features which she knows draw him to her and the absence of which has led to his pining away. His "Lifes delights" are to be found in her arms where he will finally be "laid." Her hair will be wound around him; her eyes will light him to his rest; her lips will serenade him; and in her heart his epitaph will be written: "The most loving, most beloved / To death by absence pressed, By no time to be removed / At full joys here doth rest."[57] The rhetoric of such compliments is commonplace enough in the late Petrarchan love poem, as I will suggest in Chapter 6, but as Ben Jonson remarked sardonically on John Donne's praise of Ann Drury, such lines on a mere woman were "profane and full of Blasphemies [and] he told Mr. Donne, if it had been written of ye Virgin Marie it had been something."[58] That is precisely the point. Philip's Astrophil knows, with some unease, of the perils of erotic idolatry, and his sonnet of renunciation, "Leave me, ô Love,"[59] voices the approved Protestant rejection of idealizing human love – just as the cardinal sin in the papist veneration of Our Lady of Walsingham was, in the reformers' minds, idolatry. The idolatrous comparison of mortal beloved to the Queen of Heaven is derived from yet another medieval tradition that overlaps with Marian devotion, Petrarchism, which will be the subject of Chapter 6.

---

[56] Sidney, *Poems of Robert Sidney*, 191.   [57] *Ibid.*, 193–5.
[58] Jonson, *Timber*, 4.   [59] Sidney, The *Poetry of Sir Philip Sidney*, 161.

The final example of the traces of the Virgin in her manifestation in the Walsingham Ballad is undoubtedly the most famous, even if it is, in some senses, hidden. In the opening lines of *Hamlet,* Act 4, scene 5, the bereaved and distracted Ophelia sings yet another version, without the characteristic introduction but with the unmistakable melody in the background:

> How should I your true love know
> From another one?
> By his cockle hat and staff,
> And his sandal shoon . . .
> He is dead and gone, lady,
> He is dead and gone;
> At his head a grass-green turf,
> At his heels a stone . . .
> White his shroud as the mountain snow . . .
> Larded with sweet flowers
> Which bewept to the grave did not go
> With true love showers.   (IV. v. 23–6, 29–32, 34, 36–8)

These lines reverberate well beyond their immediate context of Ophelia's madness. They may be seen as referring not just to the anguish of broken love, but to England's loss of religious innocence, its break with the Catholic Church and its entrance into the darker world of modernity. Throughout the play Ophelia has been surrounded by the Catholic trappings that Elizabethan authorities had tried to eliminate. Isolated and alienated in a society that traps and exploits her, she can be taken as representing the alienation suffered by Catholics within the new, harsh world of Protestantism, with its empty fallen, material universe and its transcendent, masculine God. Her lover, like the Walsingham pilgrim, has gone, apparently never to return, and she waits for him in vain. Ophelia is, in Susan Morrison's striking metaphor, part of the "waste" of Reformation England. Morrison suggests that Ophelia's snatches of song are the trash of cultural memory from the past. The traces of the Walsingham song evoke the great shrine's wasted past and, acted out in Ophelia's madness, is a protest against the destruction not only of an individual life but a whole cultural nexus. Like the memory of Walsingham in the iconoclastic Protestant imagination, Ophelia's sexuality has become associated with decay and corruption: Laertes warns her against the "canker" of sexuality and "contagious blastments"; Polonius refers to Hamlet's affections for her as "unholy suit / Breathing like sanctified and pious bawds" (I. iii. 39, 42, 129–30), and Hamlet himself is revolted by female sexuality in what he fantasizes as his mother's "rank sweat of an enseamed bed / Stew'd in corruption and making love / Over the nasty sty" (III. iv. 92–4). The Golden World of the Protestant Virgin Queen is not so golden after all.[60]

The traces of the Walsingham Ballad – as Chapman has shown, there is a host of incidental references throughout the early seventeenth century[61] – scattered across the cultural landscape are not individual lyric outbursts. All have a specific point of origin – the existence, perhaps in the past, perhaps only in legend, of the Shrine at Walsingham, the "holy land," as many of the versions, including Ralegh's, describe it. The ballad likely grew as yet one more reaction to the loss of a specifically Catholic, Mariological dimension to English post-Reformation life. It records the transformation of England's greatest Marian shrine into a rich symbol of human loss, tragedy, and nostalgia, a shift from the world view before the Dissolution to the world which Shakespeare's Ophelia evokes, in her echoes of the ballad, two generations later. The Virgin may indeed have faded from the emotional and spiritual life of Protestant England but traces of her liminal suggestiveness have remained.

---

[60] Morrison, "Waste Space," 61–2.   [61] Chapman, "Met I with an old bald Mare," 217–31.

CHAPTER 6

Traces: English Petrarchism and the veneration of the Virgin

Although they are written from the heart of the Elizabethan Protestant court, the Walsingham poems by Walter Ralegh and Robert Sidney provide evidence of the fading but still intense, even paradoxical, presence of the Virgin in Protestant England. Not merely behind the poems but also in some sense inhabiting them is the medieval tradition of veneration of the Virgin. However, they are also, along with hundreds, probably thousands, of poems written in early modern England, deeply influenced by another medieval tradition intimately connected with the Virgin. For three centuries much of what Foucault termed "confessing" and writing "the truth" of human sexuality had been mediated through a multi-leveled discourse, at once a rhetoric and a psychology, derived from (or foisted upon) the poetry of Petrarch – what became known as Petrarch(an)ism.[1] It was a fashion that came to England late. Furthermore, it came laden with deeply embedded Catholic associations, and a rhetoric that borrowed heavily from Mariology. The common rhetoric shared by religious devotees and love poets alike had been fully acceptable in Italy, France, Spain, and elsewhere in Catholic Europe. But it entered the English court in the 1520s and 1530s, around the same time as the impetus to reform gathered momentum and, most germanely, when "idolatry" had become a matter of enormous controversy. For the rest of the sixteenth century it was the most fashionable poetical rhetoric for court lyrics and, following Philip Sidney's *Astrophil and Stella* (1581–2, published 1591), became a dominant mode not merely of poetry in English court circles but, as it had across Europe, of understanding desire and its interactions with the self and the wider social world.

Petrarchan poetry provides more than a rhetoric for declaring passionate but frustrated love though sonnets and related songs. It is a psychology and a philosophy – and aspires at times to be a substitute or supplementary

---

[1] Trinkaus, *Poet as Philosopher*, 2; Foucault, *History of Sexuality*, 1, 61. For the English translation of Petrarch's lyrics used here, see the bilingual edition translated by Armi, Petrarch, *Sonnets and Songs.*

religion. It is predominantly written in the subject position of a suffering, usually (though not exclusively) male, lover contemplating a beloved's, usually a woman's, effects on him. Erotic idealization, as has often been pointed out, is a form of "oppression through exaltation,"[2] in which the object of idealization rarely exists in a relationship of mutuality or as the subject of her own desire. On a superficial level of apparent praise, the poet could focus on the beloved's external beauties – eyes, hair, complexion, speech – or on her actions, possessions, surroundings, even on other objects, associated with her – a room, a favorite pet, her handkerchief or other accouterments, as well as on more apparently spiritual qualities such as her chastity, wisdom, virtue. "She" (to adopt for convenience the conventionally gendered role) is overvalued in order that she can be, the lover narcissistically hopes, exclusively the subject of "his" desires. But the real focus is on her effects on the poet himself, which leads him to continually question why the experience of love is so dislocating, and his broodings are typically described in contradictions, particularly the ubiquitous Petrarchan paradoxes such as fire and ice, peace and war, blindness and vision, clarity and uncertainty. Despite such continual dislocation, he is inevitably and helplessly drawn to her. Both her characteristics and the events of their relationship put him in a state of delicious anxiety, forcing him to search out and adopt some trustworthy discourse that seems to describe his plight and thereby allow him to construct a self, even temporarily, one that will give him momentary reassurance in a world that is unpredictable, uncertain, threatening and in which the outcome of his love is never certain and entirely dependent on her.

The self – the sense of being a self-conscious "subject"– that emerges from such poetry is consequently an especially insecure one, and the poem is only an attempt to achieve some momentary stability, even at the cost of perpetual anxiety and pain. Petrarchism is therefore typically expressed as masochism, with the beloved depicted as the cause of her lover's feeling cruelty, disease, sleeplessness, and distress, and the lover rejoicing in receiving such continual pain and loss, the persistence of which at least gives him a sense of continuing identity. That impasse between the joy of love and its miseries defines the mental and emotional understanding of the Petrarchan experience: delight countermanded by anguish, excitement by disappointment, achievement by loss, frustration by hope, the love of God by the love of the world, obscurity by fame, passivity by restlessness, public by private, icy coldness by the fire of passion. Sexual consummation – indeed, even

[2] Theweleit, *Male Fantasies*, I, 283–4.

sometimes, presence – is rare in this poetry. Indeed, there would be no need often to write if presence or consummation were attained: the hope for presence is always countermanded by the fear or actuality of absence, even death.

In the *Canzoniere*, Petrarch himself does not merely express an intensely evocative picture of his sufferings, let alone portray Laura as a human, even if idealized, woman. Very explicitly she and her effects on the devout worshiper are compared with the Virgin. But the comparison is not designed to stress Laura's humility and inferiority alongside Mary. Much of the vocabulary for his admiration of Laura is in fact drawn from the stock medieval veneration of the Virgin and applied without reservation to Laura and his worship of her. Petrarch does not want to have to choose between Laura and Mary. He sometimes identifies Laura with the Madonna, seeking her as his own personal revelation of the divine and intercessor with God, as if the two were one. At other times Laura is presented in a competing relationship with Mary, especially in the poems purportedly written after Laura's death. Her eyes have lit his way through life, and now she rules him from heaven. Indeed, when she enters heaven, all the saints and angels surround her and proclaim her uniqueness in creation. After her death, Laura becomes further identifiable with the Virgin. He sees her apparition, prays to her, praises her for being among the saints, has a vision of meeting her in heaven where her beauty still captures him, envisages her telling him she wishes he enjoyed immortality with her, and repeatedly places her in an intercessory role for him. Laura becomes his personal guide toward heaven, and at times, like Dante before him in his invocation of Beatrice, the way in itself. Both Mary and Laura stand for all the beauty we can perceive in the material world and beyond, and yet – before her death, which paradoxically gives him the relief of no longer having the temptation of physical consummation – because Laura is at least potentially a real body, she threatens to become the more alluring. In a poem supposedly written on the eleventh anniversary of his meeting with her, Petrarch confesses to "the nights spent in a raving mind / With that cruel desire" and asks God to forgive him his eleven years of idolatry under the "*dispietato giogo*," the pitiless burden – which he knows will nevertheless continue (*Rime* 62).[3]

That tension gives energy to one of the poems' most powerful contradictions, between his split loves, what Petrarch quite explicitly terms his "idolatry." Mary may be the woman of the Apocalypse who is clothed in the sun, but throughout it is Laura who has been associated with the sun: "*tra le*

---

[3] Petrarch, *Songs and Sonnets*, 98–9.

donne un sole," "she who among women is a sun" (9). Only in the final poem of the collection (366) does he renounce his love for Laura, and then he turns not to God or Christ but to the Virgin herself, to that other woman with whom Laura has always been merged or been, in a sense, a rival. In that final poem, Petrarch does dutifully try to separate the two female figures, yet the way to heaven (as well as his poetical inspiration) has been the mortal woman. As Anita Obermeier puts it, for Petrarch, "in the end, Laura's inspirational power still supersedes Mary's."[4]

What happened when this rhetoric and its rich associations came to England, and especially when it entered Reformation England? *Tottel's Miscellany* (1557) – its full title is *Songes and Sonettes Written By the Ryght Honorable Lord Henry Howard, late Earle of Surrey, and other* – has often been seen as not only introducing the Petrarchan style to England, but also as combining the Petrarchan manner with specifically Protestant themes and thereby setting the distinctive contradictory tone of English Petrarchism. Its most important poems are those by Wyatt and Surrey, who were the first poets seriously to introduce the Petrarchan manner into England. Wyatt's alleged associations with Anne Boleyn have contributed to building a somewhat sentimentalized picture of him as a reformist sympathizer, and the conventional reading of Elizabethan court poetry is that the emphasis in Wyatt's or, a generation later, Philip Sidney's, poems, becomes focused on the moral dilemmas of erotic experience, and that this English development is a distinctive protestantization of Petrarch.

Petrarchism was certainly adapted to political purposes in Elizabethan England, by means of the propaganda machine behind the cult of the Virgin Queen. As we saw in Chapter 5, in the case of Ralegh, Elizabeth systematically encouraged her (male) courtiers to relate to her in the role of Petrarchan lovers, always in hope, caught between desire for advancement and fear of losing their places, singlemindedly devoted to the hopeless attainment of her favor, and grateful for any token. Elizabeth had herself, after all, translated Petrarch, dabbled in writing Petrarchan verse, and clearly saw in the Petrarchan manner a way of accessing its Mariological subtext for political ends. The Elizabethan court used Petrarch's poems as a rhetorical master-text, where display and self-aggrandizement were, paradoxically, expressed with appropriate humility, and thus became the means of acquiring place and the possibility of power. The Italian philosopher Giordano Bruno, when introducing himself to Philip Sidney, playfully reprimanded him that in *Astrophil and Stella* Sidney was following Petrarch's idolatrous

---

[4] *Ibid.*, 10–11, 514–21; Obermeier, *Auctorial Self-Criticism*, 155.

celebration of a mere woman instead of employing such praise for the English Madonna-Queen.[5] So Petrarchism was not simply a charming and sophisticated fashion for court entertainment. Especially in the last twenty years of the century, it was part of public policy.

But Tottel did not only popularize the rhetoric of the *canzoniere* and help make it politically acceptable to a reformed Elizabethan court. In an important corrective to the traditional view of English Petrarchism, Stephen Hamrick shows that Tottel (who was engaged in finalizing his collection of poems during Queen Mary's reign) also introduced a "religious vocabulary and the representations of ritual practice" in delineating the idealized beloved that should have alerted the iconoclastic religious authorities, and which was in part removed in subsequent printings. Augmented by epithets from medieval moralizing and classical references, the beloved's divinity is continually stressed. She is a paradise, a goddess, a divine bringer of bliss with gifts divine.[6] There are a number of translations and many imitations of Petrarch in the colection: Wyatt, Surrey, Grimald, and the other poets collected by Tottel are using Petrarch's poems as a workshop, teaching themselves a rhetoric which, whether they were aware of it or not, still carried a heavily charged ideology which was touching on a particularly sensitive issue in Elizabethan England. The rhetoric of idolatry – that as a poem attributed to Wyatt exclaims in helpless disbelief, "And for a woman haue I set at nought / All other thoughts" – is echoed throughout, and carries over to most of the English *petrarchisti*, even those with obvious Protestant affiliations. Spenser protests about what he sees as the exaggerated idealism of the beloved and relates her beauties to their Maker: she is "My soverayn saynt, the Idoll of my thought," but also, he insists, she is "the glorious image of the makers beautie" (*Amoretti*, 61).[7] Shakespeare's mock protest in Sonnet 105 reflects the tension brought about by the introduction of Petrarchan rhetoric in a protestantized society:

> Let not my love be called idolatry,
> Nor my beloved as an idol show,
> Since all alike my songs and praises be
> To one, of one, still such, and ever so

[5] Pugh, "Sidney, Spenser, and Political Petrarch," 243; Gatti, "Petrarch, Sidney, Bruno," 154.
[6] Hamrick, "Tottel's Miscellany and the English Reformation," 329–61.
[7] "Waites complaint vpon Loue," *Tottel's Miscellany*, 45; Spenser, *Amoretti and Epithalamion*, 93.

In Sonnet 110, the fair youth is "a god in love, to whom I am confined," and as an early annotator of Shakespeare's sonnets remarked at the end of his copy of the 1609 collection: "What a heap of wretched Infidel Stuff."[8]

The English Protestant poet traditionally singled out as simultaneously most aware of, and yet exploiting the dangers of what Calvin called "this matching of contraries,"[9] the rhetoric of religious idolatry implicit in Petrarchism, is Philip Sidney. From about 1581 or 1582, when Sidney wrote *Astrophil and Stella,* and especially after 1591, when it was first published, readers sighed over its tragi-comic enactment of what Sidney calls "poor *Petrarch's* long deceased woes" (Sonnet 15). Praised by Ralegh as the English "Petrarch," a phrase echoed by generations of commentators ever since, Sidney's *Astrophil and Stella* is conventionally seen as the triumphant maturity of Elizabethan poetry and the first full, belated but spectacular, adaptation of Petrarchism to English Protestant aristocratic culture.[10] Highly dramatic in its mode of self-presentation, the sequence shows its hero as sensitive to the danger of worshiping "an image which we ourselves do carve" (5), the verb itself even suggesting the three-dimensional statues of which Sidney's fellow-Protestants were so suspicious. Astrophil confesses, like Petrarch, that against his reason and knowledge he will continue to "adore" Stella's image in the "temple" of his heart, and a sonnet outside the *Astrophil and Stella* sequence, "Leave me, ô Love which reachest but to dust," can easily be read as the Protestant equivalent to Petrarch's renunciatory final poem: "Then farewell world, thy uttermost I see / Eternal Love, maintaine thy life in me."[11]

But where Petrarch turns to the Virgin, the earnest Protestant Philip Sidney turns directly to God. Intriguingly, his brother Robert, at least in the Walsingham poem, as we saw, turns to his wife. Robert's Song 6 is typical in its use of the idealizing (or idolatrous) vocabulary of the Petrarchan tradition. Croft describes the "Religion of Love" in his poems as the "medieval cult of the Virgin ... blended with Neoplatonism"[12] to which one needs to add strong elements of Ovid, whose earthy rhetoric bubbles continually under (and frequently above) the surface of early modern love poetry. But the idealizing vocabulary is paramount. The lover's soul exists in "purest fyre" (Song 4); he accepts both the joys and the griefs of love because he is bound by his devotion to his beloved, and is in "bonds of service without

[8] Wyatt, "Mine old dear Enemy, my froward master," *Collected Poems,* 7; Groves, "Shakespeare's Sonnets and the Genevan Marginalia," 115.
[9] Waller, "This Matching of Contraries," 331–43.
[10] Sidney, *Poetry of Sir Philip Sidney,* 172; Klein, *The Exemplary Sidney,* 26.
[11] Sidney, *Poetry of Sir Philip Sidney,* 163.   [12] Sidney, *Poems of Robert Sidney,* 68.

ende" (Sonnet 13). He looks to see his beloved as if awaiting an apparition: "I wait t'adore, in rays as sweet as bright, / The sun lodg'd in your eyes, heavens in your breast," and he hopes that through her love he may say that "through a veil" he "saw glory" (Sonnet 22). This is the familiar syncretic Petrarchan vocabulary of plaint and paradox with a idealized female figure in the distance: on the one hand, the poems express the high idealism of the lover who affirms the beauty of "those fair eyes" which still "shine in their clear former light" (Song 12); on the other hand, he experiences the "pains" which, as the devoted and unworthy lover, "I unceasingly sustain" (Sonnet 2). The beloved's beauties are "born of the heavens, my sowles delight" (Sonnet 3), while inspiring the lover's passions are "purest flames kindled by beauties rare" (Sonnet 4). As he contemplates in pleasurable agony how she takes "pleasure" in her "cruelty" (Sonnet 25), he asks her why she "nour-ishes" poisonous weeds of cold despair in love's garden instead, given his unfailing devotion, of the plants and trees of love's true faith and zeal (Song 22). The dominant mood is that of frustration and melancholy; it focuses to an unusual degree on the lover's helplessness. He suffers incessantly from "griefs sent from her whom in my soul I bless" (Song 23). The world is a dark cave where love's lights never shine except through the beloved's eyes, the "purest stars, whose never dying fires" (Sonnet 1) constantly burn a path between the heavens and the lover's soul.[13]

We have here, then, a fascinating phenomenon of interweaving dis-courses: the rhetorics of the veneration of the Virgin and Petrarchism are not identical, but the underlying connections between the two are startling. And in the history of Petrarchan poetry, there were indeed poets, including Petrarch himself, who saw the connection. Some, both Catholic and Protestant, saw it and were, from quite different viewpoints, wary of it.

Some of the parallels and differences are clear: central to both is a transcendent woman figure, a worshiper, and a relationship involving complex dynamics that were central to our understanding of desire, sex-uality, and identity in the early modern period. We can see shared patterns of worship, characterized by fetishism and masochism, the beloved's sup-posedly causing of her lover to feel cruelty, disease, distress, and pain just as separation from the Virgin caused anguish in the worshiper. The Petrarchan lover asserts the beloved to be – and in some sense needs her to be – beyond his reach, as more pure, more perfect, forbidden, unattain-able, unapproachable, absent, belonging to someone else. In the language of the seemingly endless Petrarchan paradoxes, she has a cold heart that denies

---

[13] *Ibid.*, 129, 135, 137, 139, 167, 177, 219, 225, 249, 301.

her fair outside; he himself has no peace and yet is continually at war; he burns and freezes; he is simultaneously loved and hated; he is totally dependent on her nurturance, yet he must break away if he is to achieve any individuation. She often seems especially arbitrary and cruel, but she is a projection of his own narcissism, a fantasy or – as the reformers would say about the idolization of the Virgin – a superstition, a blasphemy, an "image," that torments him, even when he sleeps:

> I, seeing better sights in sight's decay,
> Cald it anew, and wooed sleepe again:
> But him her host that unkind guest had slain.[14]

As the worshiper of an image, often the lover knows that, like Petrarch, he is open to the charge of idolatry. Many poems face and explore that charge. The titillation of flirting with idolatry is here evoked by Michael Drayton:

> Some misbelieving and profane in love
> When I do speak of miracles by thee,
> May say that thou art flattered by me.

In language eerily reminiscent of Marian miracle tales, such as in Pynson's ballads dedicated to the Madonnas of Walsingham and Glastonbury, Drayton's lover goes on to deny that his love is idolatrous and also to assert the efficacy of her miracles. The "unbelieving" are exhorted to "see" the revival of the dumb, cripples, blind, and deaf:

> A dumb-born muse made to express the mind,
> A cripple hand to write, yet lame by kind,
> One by thy name, the other touching thee;
> Blind were mine eyes till they were seen of thine.
> And mine ears deaf by thy fame healed be,
> My vices cured by virtues sprung from thee.

Drayton urges his "misbelievers" to look at his mistress and see the miracles she performs.[15]

As in Marian devotion, the primary sense involved in Petrarchan discourse is sight. The male gaze in Petrarchism is directed obsessively at the beloved's body – usually not as a whole but as the sum of separable parts, as if the lover is possessing her body and then turning it into multiple relics. In a seminal article in 1980, Nancy Vickers pointed out that the distinction between a woman's "beauty" and her "beauties" is a consistent feature of the whole Petrarchan tradition. When Renaissance theorists, poets, or painters

---

[14] Sidney, *Poems of Robert Sidney*, 161.   [15] *Elizabethan Sonnet Sequences*, 44,

wished to represent a woman's body, she argued, Petrarch's verse could be used to justify their aesthetic choices, making her "available to be partitioned, with each of her features accorded object status separate from the totality." The "whole body" of Petrarch's Laura appears to him at times "less than some of its parts," and the technique of describing the mistress through the isolation of those parts became universal within the Petrarchan tradition.[16] The classic Petrarchan trope is the lover's devotion to the beloved's picture; the lover's admiring eye attempts to fix the mistress not just as a beautiful object that he wishes to possess, but often as a guarantee against the threat she represents.

What happens, however, if "she" looks back at "him"? Or actively watches herself being watched and instead of feeling positioned as an object, attempts to defy the gaze and assumes "gazing back" as a viable subject position? Whenever she does act in relation to her own wishes – predominantly by rejecting him – she is castigated by him as cruel, a beauteous outside framing a heart of stone, the punishing mother figure from whom he is expelled and yet whom he continues to desire. Within these compulsively repeated patterns, the Petrarchan lyric presented itself as an appeal for mercy based on an acknowledgment of fear of discontinuity and helplessness before (or even in the absence of) the cruel, hard-hearted, alluringly yet frustratingly chaste mistress. Psychologically, her effects on him are like those the child feels in the birth, weaning, and separation/individuation process, or whenever the child must leave the comfort of the mother and is thrown alone into the world, yet being inevitably drawn, in reality or fantasy, back to her, puzzled yet reassured by familiar tortures and afraid that her look or even the slightest glance will be a rejection. That combination of desire and fear was, as we saw in Chapter 1, what the iconoclasts may well have feared as they confiscated, mutilated, and burnt the images and statues of the Virgin: the once all-nurturing mother from whom we must break and are desecrating may still be watching us and have power over us.

In an uncanny, if distorted, echo of Marian devotion, the Petrarchan lover indulges himself in intense self-abasement. The essence of masochism is the pleasure taken in delayed gratification, in the pain of denial and waiting. It assigns to the other the absolute power of forbidding pleasure, giving the all-powerful beloved the power to rule absolutely, at least within a script he has laid down, over his life and death. It is a stance most common in the "serious," less so among the "witty," Petrarchists; it is ubiquitous in Petrarch, in Sidney, in Shakespeare, and, belatedly, in Wroth. It is found

[16] Vickers, "Diana Described," 265–79.

less in Donne, and by the time Petrarchism has reached the Cavalier poets, it has virtually been eliminated and replaced by a masculinist bravado of scorn.

The anxiety of the Petrarchan situation, like Marian devotion, is intimately and inextricably bound up with the premier male perversion that seeks to come to terms with the fear of the beloved's overwhelming power, fetishization, which entails a displacement of sexual desire away from the identity of a woman to a lesser substitute for her. It can be some accessory or garment, but it provides both comfort and a guarantee against the threat that her wholeness represents. He therefore depicts her as the "possessor of selected parts or qualities only. He anatomizes them. And if even that is too intimate," he turns from human to "inanimate objects, such as garments, granting them a certain amount of humanness." A sexual fetish, notes Kaplan, "is significantly more reliable than a living person . . . when the full sexual identity of the woman is alive, threatening, dangerous, unpredictable, the desire she arouses must be invested in the fetish . . . fetish objects are relatively safe, easily available, undemanding of reciprocity."[17]

Unlike a real woman, who may (presumably!) have desires of her own and therefore, in patriarchal society, be even more threatening to the supposedly autonomous male, the fetish can be commanded and controlled. The lover's move, from the real to the fetish, is precisely the reverse of Orlando's determination in Shakespeare's *As You Like It* to move from the world of fantasy to the world of the real: "I can live no longer by thinking" (v. ii. 50). The Petrarchan lover, by contrast, is more comfortable meditating on his beloved's qualities one by one, not least because the delicious agony can be extended indefinitely. The classic fetishistic move assumes that it is easier to deal with and "miss" the overwhelming power of the beloved when one is alone to "think," when the lover has the beloved in fantasy rather than in the flesh. However much the beloved's absence may be bewailed, it is paradoxically welcome. The Petrarchan poem itself, as many commentators have pointed out, cannot be written in the beloved's presence, and so absence becomes a precondition for writing of the miseries of her absence. That works as a clever and recurrent trope: "sometimes all a man needs is his fetish, for embedded in the fetish is the drama, the characters, the stage set, and an entire history of the lost desires and confused imaginings of childhood." The clinical literature is full of stories of the bizarre, banal, outrageous, and ordinary in this most widespread of predominantly, though not exclusively, male paraphilia, as, indeed, is the Petrarchan tradition, from Petrarch's (or Laura's) glove (*Rime* 199) to Stella's glove, let alone her "face . . . hand . . . lips . . . skin" and "the best" part, about

---

[17] Stoller, *Perversion*, 59; Kaplan, *Female Perversions*, 35.

which Astrophil "blush[es] to tell" (*Astrophil and Stella*, 69, 77).[18] As the aptly (and possibly, really) named Jane Anger put it, "as they may but see the lyning of our outermost garment, they straight think that Apollo honours them . . . if we will not suffer them to smel on our smockes, they will snatch at our petticotes . . . At the end of mens faire promises is a *Laberinth*."[19]

In Chapter 3, following Michael Carroll's "sidling up" to popular Catholicism in the light of psychoanalysis, I suggested that in trying to understand the psychological dynamics of devotion to the Virgin, we should investigate its relations to characteristic (and predominantly male) "perversions," trying to use the term clinically rather than moralistically. To develop a parallel argument, here is an account of the "inner life" of Petrarchism, which extends some of the points with which I have started my discussion of it in relation to Mariology:

> Petrarchism is theater, the production of a scenario, for which characters – in the form of people, parts of people, and nonhuman (including inanimate) objects – are cast. The performance is played before an audience, a crucial member of which is the Petrarchan lover himself viewing [himself or herself] performing . . . Petrarchism is a detour that, at best, leads asymptotically to intimacy: it never arrives . . . Petrarchism is centered not upon the partner, but upon [the lover] . . . The pain and frustration of earlier times live on unresolved, carried within, always a potential threatening force motivating one to resolutions that never quite work, to an undoing never quite done.

This probably would be accepted as an accurate, if incomplete, account of the major dynamics of Petrarchism. It is, however, as it stands, a misquotation, adapted from one of the clinician and theorist Robert Stoller's studies of erotic behavior. Instead of "Petrarchan" and "Petrarchan lover," the words Stoller uses are actually "perversion" and "perverse person." He goes on to draw conclusions that would also be acceptable (were we not now alerted) as a description of other aspects of Petrarchism. The perverse situation (I restore Stoller's terms, though the reader is invited to substitute for it as we move along) is scripted to help the lover deal with the overwhelming power of the object of his desire. The careful scripting of these erotic scenarios is seen as an "aesthetic" task: the perverse scene is "most pleasing when it is seamless, when it does not give hints that it was constructed, when it looks as if it sprang full-blown from unconscious depths. If not created spontaneously . . . then it should look as if it was."[20]

---

[18] Sidney, *Poetry of Sir Philip Sidney*, 200, 205.
[19] Kaplan, *Female Perversions*, 34, 116; Anger, "Protection for Women," 59, 60, 70.
[20] Stoller, *Observing the Erotic Imagination*, 31–2. I draw here on my earlier discussion of "Petrarchism as Perversion" in *Sixteenth Century Poetry*, chapter 4 and *Sidney Family Romance*, chapter 4.

A major literary device in Petrarchan poetry – and sufficiently fashionable, especially in the sixteenth-century French court poetry, to constitute itself as an identifiable genre – is the blazon, or *blason*. Derived from heraldry, a display of a coat of arms or allegiance, the blazoning poem displayed not just the beauties of a mistress, but signaled the possession of her by the poet-lover. On the surface, it displays confidence and competitiveness, but there is, as Jonathan Sawday points out, "an interior anxiety" born of the blazon's use as "a ready means of asserting male prowess through the commodification of the female body." Sawday draws parallels with the emergence of anatomical dissection, by which the interior of the body – the mystery beneath the alluring surface of the beloved – was increasingly open to inspection. Like erotic scopophilia, anatomy evolved into a way of seeing into the mysteries of the female, involving a "male science" which sees and a "female subject who was observed." It is, he argues, parallel to the blazon, considered either as a poetic form or in incidental details within a poem – or, as I shall suggest in the following chapter, within a poetic "anatomy," most notably John Donne's "Anniversary" poems on the young girl Elizabeth Drury. Sawday's brilliant thesis needs to be qualified somewhat when we consider women Petrarchan poets (just as women devotees of the Virgin force us to qualify or propose an alternate mode of Marian experience). But he is right when he points to "a European artistic tradition which located within the female body the source of a disturbing and dislocating power."[21] The missing discursive structure which Sawday largely ignores, except to comment briefly on the medieval feminization of Christ and parallels between poetic blazons and Baroque art, is that of Marian devotion, which focused intensely – indeed, if one takes Stoller's analysis of perversion seriously even obsessively – on the Virgin's body.[22]

The absorption of "idolatrous" rhetoric into English Petrarchism attracted critiques from both Catholics and Protestants. For the Calvinist Fulke Greville, for instance, both Petrarchan idealization and Marian devotion share the same idolatrous self-deception. They both involve projections of delusion and superstition upon fallen nature by an irredeemably depraved human imagination – never a capacity to be trusted. For Greville, who supported the execution of Mary Queen of Scots with the virulence of a crusader, and repeatedly and savagely attacked the Catholic Church in his political treatises, the only virgin queen to be even mentioned in his writing was she who sat in England, "the red, and white Rose quarter'd in her

---

[21] Sawday, *The Body Emblazoned*, 204–5, 211, 208, 219, 222, 197, 198.   [22] *Ibid.*, 193, 198.

face."²³ Most of his poems, which may have started in a friendly competition with Philip Sidney, are certainly imbued with the patriarchal paraphernalia of Petrarchism – the idealization of the beloved (3, 8), the insistent dynamic of attraction and repulsion (38, 43), love as a battle (9), the paradoxes of the lover's "joy" and "woe" (69), the "seeing blindenesse" (12) of the lover.²⁴ But Greville was never at ease with the Petrarchan insights into selfhood or the evocative nature of poetry that so attracted Sidney. He is especially skeptical of the idolization of the beloved, the self-deluding patterns of attraction and repulsion, and even the playfulness and calculated vacillation between pain and pleasure that characterize the Petrarchan lover.

Often this negative reaction emerges in the numerous, and commonplace, metaphors of strain, violence, disease, aging, or appeals for death. *Caelica* 22 displays the frustration and pain of surveying relics of the beloved as he surveys the trinkets, the "true knots," rings and colors by which he disguises the hollowness of love. His memory of them produces in him a self-mockery and a self-castigating hopelessness: "Must I lose ring, flowers, blush, theft and go naked, / Watching with sighs, till dead love be awaked?" The disillusion of the last lines here – "Mad girles must safely love, as they may leave, / No man can print a kisse, lines may deceive" – is a projection upon women by the insecure and grasping male imaginary, of change which always is "a hatefull power" (60).²⁵ It is as if the lover can deal with a woman only when he can aestheticize her, when her beauty and desirability are a complement only to him, and the power of her unpredictability and even her physical presence is no longer a threat. But she is inevitably, fatally, identified with changeableness. The conclusion of *Caelica* 70 exclaims: "Let me no longer follow Womenkinde / Where change doth use shapes of tyranny." In his "Letter to an Honorable Lady," Greville dismisses the hypocritical idealism by which a man praises a woman as his "mistres," by which "reverend name men commonly call those, whom they meane, by corrupting, to make their servants." Greville is suspicious of "the Woman growing mannish, the Man womanish" (26). There are, he asserts, "distinct . . . Lawes of each Estate," proper by nature to each: "our [i.e. Men's] fame lying in hazard, armes, bloud; theirs [i.e. women's] in silence, modestie, restraint."²⁶ For Greville, nothing female – no mistress, certainly not the idolatrous Catholic Virgin – plays a part in salvation.

The absence trope is a favorite one for Greville. The magnificent *Caelica* 45, "Absence, the noble truce / Of Cupid's war," is one of the age's most powerful poetic manifestations of protest against the idealization of the

---

²³ Greville, *Selected Poems*, 113.   ²⁴ *Ibid.*, 46, 49, 52, 70–1, 96.
²⁵ *Ibid.*, 61, 88.   ²⁶ *Ibid.*, 97, 61; Greville, *Prose Works*, 78, 82.

beloved's non-presence, with its sober, concrete acknowledgment in the final stanza, which is, in its brevity and directness, a brilliant dismantling of the whole Petrarchan tradition and by implication any beliefs in the fetishization of relics and substitutes for reality:

> But thoughts be not so brave,
> With absent joy;
> For you with that you have
> Yourself destroy:
> The absence which you glory,
> And burn in vaine:
> For thought is not the weapon,
> Wherewith thought's ease men cheapen
> Absence is paine.

Another long-acknowledged characteristic of Petrarchism critiqued in *Caelica* is the power afforded to the "curious knowledge" (38) gained by sight by means of the voyeuristic male gaze. "Fear," states *Caelica* 7, keeps us "long at gaze." Our eyes, as characterized in Greville's taxonomy, are ever "curious" (43); we continually visualize our desires in pictorial terms, holding them in our self-deceiving minds, "dreaming," as he puts it in *Caelica* 88, of "curious mysteries." The ultimate mystery which we can never achieve is knowledge by means of the beloved. *Caelica* 56, "All my senses, like beacons' flame," is a ruthless dismantling of this aspect of the Petrarchan (and Sidneian) world. With a combination of parody, derision, and cynicism, the poem lays bare the pretentiousness and the real loss of fulfillment involved in idealization and overvaluation, and in the movement from presence to absence, the body to the spirit:

> He that lets his Cynthia lie,
> Naked on a bed of play,
> To say prayers ere she die,
> Teacheth time to run away:
> Let no love-desiring heart,
> In the stars goe seek his fate,
> Love is only Natures art,
> Wonder hinders love and hate.
> > None can well behold with eyes,
> > But what underneath him lies.

I will return shortly to Greville's word "wonder," which he uses here with bitter irony to cover any delusory idealization of absent beauty embodying or even pointing to any spiritual reality.[27]

---

[27] Greville, *Selected Poems*, 76–7, 71, 74, 119, 84–5.

To contrast with Greville's critique of the common ground between Petrarchism and Marian devotion, I turn from the Protestant Sidney and the Calvinist Greville back to the Catholic Southwell. For Catholics, it is the true "knowledge" represented in the Virgin that makes the rhetoric of Petrarchan adoration a deceptive parody – or, at best, a deviation from the recognition of where female power in the scheme of salvation lies. Southwell's poems on the Virgin combine the traditional praise of Mary with the obsessive idealization and self-effacement of Petrarchism, but in Southwell's case in order to re-direct, not negate, the Petrarchan rhetoric. He reprimands the "misdeeming eye" of "lew'd love" ("Lew'd Love is Losse"), and when he turns to the Virgin, the Petrarchan epithets seem to be literalized, not used as hyperbole:

> Her face a heaven two planettes were her eyes
> Whose gracious light did make our clearest day
> But one such heaven there was and loe it dyes,
> Deathes darke Eclipse hath dymmed every ray.
> Sunne hide thy light, thy beames untymely shine
> Trew light sith wee have lost we crave not thine.
>
> ("The Death of our Ladie")

These lines, with their Petrarchan vocabulary, suggest, as Scott Pilarz argues, that we have "found an object worthy of the lavish adulation that secular poets waste on the women they love."[28]

Another Catholic poet who fled England the year Southwell was executed was Henry Constable, who also enthusiastically celebrated the Virgin in devotional rhetoric by flaunting her identity as a real queen as opposed to the earthly, destructive queen of England:

> Cease then, O Queens who earthly crowns do wear
> To glory in the pomp of worldly things:
> If men such high respect unto you bear
> Which daughters, wives, & mothers are of kings;
> What honour should unto that Queen be done
> Who had your God for father, spouse, & so.[29]

As Alison Shell comments, pointing to one of the major confrontations in late sixteenth-century poetry and religion, in Constable's poems, as opposed to what Protestant poets such as Spenser and Ralegh were doing, "the love-language which Elizabeth encouraged from her admirers is transferred to another object, the Virgin Mary."[30]

---

[28] Southwell, *Collected Poems*, 54, 11; Pilarz, *Robert Southwell*, 227.   [29] Constable, *Poems*, 185.
[30] Shell, *Catholicism, Controversy*, 126.

For yet another perspective on the relationship between these two powerful discourses – between Mary and Laura, as it were – from late in the
Petrarchan tradition I turn back to Chapter 2 in which, after reviewing the
characteristic patterns of predominantly male devotion to the Virgin,
I posed the question of how women might have positioned themselves in
relation to the predominantly male encoding of the Virgin. I want now to
link my argument there to my consideration of Petrarchism. Women
Petrarchan poets have been the subject of a number of important studies
in recent years; in early modern England the most detailed connection is
with Robert Sidney's daughter (and Philip's niece), Lady Mary Wroth
(1586?–1652?), whose *Pamphilia to Amphilanthus* (published 1621) is the
first collection of Petrarchan verse in English by a woman. It is a major
document at the very end of the tradition and a prime source for our
attempting to read, today, what it was to be gendered as a woman in early
modern England and how the female poetic (and erotic) subject might be
constituted.[31]

As with other Petrarchan poets, Wroth's recurring subject is the self, with
the (in this case, male) beloved providing the means by which she can be
"doubly resounded" and, as it were, hear or see herself. Mary B. Moore puts
forward the interesting argument that Wroth "takes as her medium of reflection the echo, an aural, not visual, mode of reflection" – and further, that a
specifically "female Echo," enables her (or at least the heroine of her romance
and poems, Pamphilia) to find a "woman's community" to "provide the self-
reflection that their frequent roles as mirrors may prevent them from finding in
relationships with men."[32] Her argument certainly points to an emergent
strand in Wroth, even though the overwhelming emphasis of her poems is
on Pamphilia's desire for Amphilanthus who, like the traditional object of
Petrarchan yearning, remains frustratingly unattainable, and usually absent.

If we follow the logic of Moore's argument, Wroth's seeking for an
"aural" self may, though certainly somewhat at a distance, reflect a characteristic Protestant emphasis on the Word rather than the image. But
although permeated with the vocabulary of theologically tinged Neoplatonism, Wroth's poems are curiously indifferent to direct theological
references. There are a few obligatory references to saints of love and
occasional anti-Catholic references (there is a sideswipe at "popish law" in
one sonnet), but by the time she is writing, such remarks are part of

---

[31] For Wroth, see Waller, *Sidney Family Romance*, chapters 4, 6, and 8. The most recent biography is
   Hannay, *Wroth*.
[32] Moore, *Desiring Voices*, 138.

Protestant England's commonplaces. Toward the end of *Pamphilia to Amphilanthus,* however, she wrote a "crowne of Sonetts dedicated to Love." The "crown" is an echo of the "Little Crown of the Blessed Virgin," a devotional "chaplet" or string of beads, such as the Rosary, and the reference is based on the woman clothed with the sun, with the moon under her feet, and a crown of twelve stars on her head (Revelation/Apocalypse 12:1) which Catholics read as symbolizing the Virgin's motherhood and queenship. John Donne's *La Corona* (1607) consists of seven sonnets, meditations on the mysteries of Christ's life, the last line of each constituting the first line of the next, and possibly based on Southwell's sonnets on the Virgin; Wroth's "crowne" consists of fourteen sonnets, with only the most distant echo of Marian devotion.[33] But as with her father's adaptation of the Walsingham Ballad, that absent original continues, though more distantly, to haunt her poems. Another group of poems playfully brings Love, or Cupid, together with his mother Venus, Wroth imagines a world where the two reign harmoniously together and where the goddess graciously, and with motherly fondness, intercedes with the God of Love for suffering lovers. As Mary Paulissen notes, it is a world "where Love rules with his Mother, something like the Christ Child and the Virgin." In one poem, in what for Wroth is an oddly domestic scene, the speaker finds Cupid, a child abandoned in the forest, "cold, wett, and crying." She becomes the rescuing mother, drying him, nurturing him – until, typically in Wroth, he feels strong enough to betray her into the anxieties of desire.[34]

My argument in this chapter is not that Petrarchism and Marian devotion are identical, nor that one is simply the source of the other. But there are certain uncanny interminglings and echoes which unquestionably grow from a dominant pattern by which desire was structured and experienced in the period – and, arguably, well beyond. What happened in England to the wondrous and miraculous power of the Virgin when its source faded? When she was no longer accessible not just for prayers but for the unexpected transformative intervention in and out of time, where did that desire go? What stories emerged to (literally) embody it? There remained, after all, as the Petrarchan tradition shows, echoes of a deeply religious liminality within the yearnings of erotic love. But its objects are, finally, human, not divine. Such devotion is therefore all the more fragile, all the more obviously an idolization. As Frances Dolan comments, "for Protestants, it is particularly inappropriate to revere Mary, as opposed to Queen Elizabeth or

[33] Brownlow, "Holy Sonnets," 89–92.
[34] Paulissen, *The Love Sonnets of Lady Mary Wroth,* 38; Wroth, *Poems,* 139.

one's mistress, precisely because to do so confers on her a kind of divinity to which she is not entitled."[35] Catholic commentators pointed out that the "idolatry" which Protestants vilified when Catholics addressed the Virgin Mary, was being transferred to mortal "goddesses," most notably, they pointed out, in the cult of Elizabeth, for instance in Spenser, and also in the "profane" love poets. But in a universe that is bereft of divinity except for the stern Protestant God, perhaps sexual love provides the most powerful illusion we have? Otherwise, as Greville's poems repeatedly say, despair awaits us.

The longevity of both these interconnecting discourses is based on the remarkable extent to which they incorporate many of the major fantasies of patriarchal sexual and gender assignments arising from our culture. Perhaps, however fascinating it may be, the Petrarchan diagramming of how we interact when we encounter desire should finally be seen as a constricting, destructive distortion of the possibilities of human desire, a "perversion" in the sense I have tried to exclude from my analysis. Such a schematization of desire and the relationships it throws us into reinforces gender hierarchies and dichotomies; it registers pain rather than fulfillment as central to our being; it allows for autonomy to be ascribed predominantly to a beloved who is superior at the same time that it enacts the opposite; it valorizes unfulfillment and avoids the possibility of mutuality as the basis for fulfilling relationships. It enacts some of the most destructive, "perverse," scenarios of interrelationships in our history. And the reformers, it now needs to be admitted, would have said, and did say, comparable things about the idolization of the Virgin.

There is, however, a positive side to that moral, perhaps even moralistic, analysis – and the implied comparison with Marian devotion. What they have in common is a feature that may be seen as countermanding their destructiveness as human discourses, and that is their desire to recognize and evoke a sense of "wonder." Greville, it will be recalled, used the term ironically, as an indication of the self-deception involved in valorizing any female figure, human or divine. A much debated concept in sixteenth-century academic circles, "wonder" was discussed in Plato, Aristotle, Longinus and in some of the Schoolmen as both an aesthetic and a religious experience. Aristotle makes wonder "at once a goal of poetry and prelude to philosophy,"[36] an experiential opening of meaning rather than the analysis of meaning, based on the acceptance that rationality is only a means, not the goal. In Chapter 7, I will explore the staging of wonder,

---

[35] Dolan, *Whores of Babylon*, 118.   [36] Bishop, *Shakespeare and the Theatre of Wonder*, 4–5.

which became central to Shakespeare's late dramaturgy, and in which the returning traces of the Virgin become increasingly powerful. But "wonder" has a longer tradition behind it than its revival as an aesthetic term in both poetry and dramatic theory, and is most dramatically illustrated in the unification of theology and poetry we have seen in Petrarch – and before him, in Dante. It is what Dante famously described when he first saw Beatrice as a young girl, in the Chiesa di Santa Margherita, and then when she was older, in stray meetings, and if we are to believe the passionate imaginings of the Kabbala scholar Charles Mirsky, secretly and passionately and physically before she died.[37] "At that moment," when he sees Beatrice, Dante says, "I say truly that the spirit of life, which dwells in the most secret chamber of the heart," is truly felt. Thus, "*Incipit Vita Nuova*. The new life begins." He is not just momentarily struck but stricken with amazement, and knows not only has his bliss appeared, but also, like Petrarch, "Woe is me, wretched! because often from this time forth," he will be disturbed. He meets her in his poems as he struggles throughout the *Vita Nuova* to explain what has happened to him, how he loses his wits when he tries to explain to her, and is so afraid that he invents "screens," others whom he asserts he loves in order to escape the impact of the wonder that grows within him whenever he thinks of her or sees her.[38] She dies. He describes how he struggles through Hell to reach her and meets her in the extraordinary scene in *Purgatorio* 31, when she turns to him and says "*Ben Sem. Ben Sem*": "Look on us well: we are indeed, we are / Beatrice" and then conducts him throughout the *Paradiso*, teaching him and cajoling him and teasing and illuminating him – probably, despite Mirsky's speculations, in ways that she did not in "real" life have the opportunity to do.[39] Finally, she departs, fondly but firmly warning him that he gazes on her with such adoring looks that he may forget the God from whom she has come on her mission.

This is wonder, say Dante and Petrarch: not just the momentary flash, the shock of recognition, but the recognition that continues to shock. It is as if we are reading the world aright for the first time – a formulation I borrow from Carol Neely (in turn quoting from T. S. Eliot) in her advocacy of feminist readings of early modern texts. Or, in the words of the Dante critic, Charles Williams, both intensely personal and commonplace: Williams calls it the "way of affirmation," the recognizing of, and even a sense of being summoned by, the divine in the person of a fellow human being,

---

[37] Mirsky, *Dante, Eros, and Kabbalah*, e.g. 27, 60.   [38] Dante, *New Life*, 1–2, 8.
[39] Dante, *Purgatory*, canto 30, *Comedy*, II: 309.

not – as in traditional mysticism – through the way of negation.[40] Dante characterizes Beatrice's effect on him as being smitten, invaded, transfixed; his feelings are sexual, aesthetic, moral, devotional; he acknowledges changes that are occurring in him over which he has no control and which he did not seek. In Heidegger's famous phrase, he has been "thrown" into being. That she is a woman and not just an idea, and indeed very specifically a woman, is part of the order of things as he presents it. For Dante, being reborn in the new life is something that is caused by the "wonder" of her female, nurturing, erotic, and mothering body.

Beneath the rhetoric, speaking through the clumsy or sometimes laughable fetishization of the Petrarchan tradition, and before it, in the blend of Christian devotion and *amour courtois* in Dante, through the self-destructive masochism, the obsessive and invasive gaze, and even the masculinist competition over the displaying and dismantling of the beloved's body, then, within the wonderment claimed by both Marian devotion and poetry from Dante and Petrarch and into the English Petrarchans, there is arguably a story deeply rooted in human needs and desires, the desire for transformation and wonder within human experience. Medieval popular religion's emphasis on miracles and the sudden inbreaking of the divine into the otherwise seeming inexorability of time expresses its religious dimension, but "wonder" is also the goal of Dante and Petrarch and the serious Petrarchans after him – those such as Sidney, even though he is scorned by Greville (and occasionally by Sidney himself), by the Wyatt of some of the Anne Boleyn lyrics, by Spenser's Ann Boyle sonnets, and above all by Shakespeare as he explores the effect of being overwhelmed by emotions that at times call forth sentiments that defy mortality and time "even to the edge of doom" (Sonnet 116). Such poems try to capture the astonishment of encounters, memories, rare or recurring moments of ecstasy that Marian devotion had projected upon the figure of the Virgin. Grant Williams sees the Petrarchan blazon in such terms, quoting Irigaray to good effect that the lover encounters "sexual difference unintelligible to prior knowledge" or past experience. Wonder is "the face of the unknowable" momentarily known.[41] It is an inevitable temptation, as Greville would point out, to take such a moment and turn it to possession, and claim it has some kind of truth value or "knowledge" for it. But for the serious Petrarchan, as for the devoted worshiper of the Virgin, such moments are complete within themselves, opening up stories rooted deep within our beings without

[40] Neely, "Loss and Recovery," 180 and "Constructing the Subject," 15; Williams, *Figure of Beatrice*, 100.
[41] Williams, "Early Modern Blazons and the Rhetoric of Wonder," 126–7.

which we fall short of our human possibility. They defy explanation – "since why to love I can allege no cause," as Shakespeare affirms in Sonnet 49.

These are traces, then, in the Petrarchan tradition, with its multiple origins and many variations, of a re-experiencing, "negotiations," to repeat Christine Peters's term, over the seemingly fading place of Mary in early modern English culture. The Virgin's traces – what she had represented, what she had gradually ceased to represent – lie tantalizingly behind and provide much of the energy of late English Petrarchism. But an ideological shift of major proportions is occurring. Perhaps the late medieval world that had nourished devotion to the Virgin had been largely delusionary; but it had at least provided stories in which men and women had roles of comfort and delight to play. Southwell and Constable continue to affirm that world in the face of a changing cosmology and the emergence of a new, more isolated sense of selfhood. The worlds evoked by Fulke Greville and Walter Ralegh are more immediately fragmented, grim, anxiogenic; Donne's a world of divinized passion that is momentary, even though bound to time, as Dante's and Petrarch's was; Robert Sidney's momentary connection with an older world transforms it virtually unknowingly, in ways that his daughter wrestled painfully to re-discover. I now turn to the writer who in an age of skeptical post-modernism continues to fascinate (and annoy) many of us by seemingly being so powerfully insightful about such matters. That is Shakespeare.

CHAPTER 7

Traces: Shakespeare and the Virgin – All's Well That Ends Well, Pericles, and The Winter's Tale

Medieval drama was, as I suggested in Chapter 3, the major popular cultural form in which the contradictions of the late medieval religious world concerning the Virgin were played out, despite the best intentions of a tightly controlled civic and ecclesiastical theatrical environment. As the Reformation in England ebbed and flowed, the Protestant authorities seized upon the inherited cultural forms for their own propagandist purposes, but whereas a Protestant poetic was able to be created, using the more obviously poetical books of the Bible, especially the Psalms, as the model, in the drama no easy compromise proved possible. As Collinson notes, "the religious drama and pageantry treated divine things with a homely familiarity that was shocking and obnoxious to Protestants who had recovered their sense of God's awe-inspiring otherness."[1] From the late 1540s, as the Protestant revolution went forward in England, the drama went through a major transition. Protestant theologians attacked what they saw as the excesses of both biblical and non-biblical subjects on the stage, including the non-scriptural stories of the Virgin's life and powers. The official view of the older religious drama is epitomized by Dean Matthew Hutton of York's 1567 decree that a proposed "creed play" went against the "the sinceritie of the gospel," acknowledging that "it was plausible" some years ago, and "would now also all of the ignorant sort be well liked, yet now in the happie time of the gospel," neither the "learned" nor the "state" would likely tolerate it.[2]

Attempts to create a Protestant polemical drama, adapting medieval morality to Protestant nationalism, made some temporary headway – the devil is identified as the the pope, God with the monarch. Yet significant remnants of the cycle plays continued to be acted, especially in the

---

[1] Collinson, *Birthpangs of Protestant England*, 99, 101. [2] Tydeman, *Theatre in the Middle Ages*, 241.

provinces. The guilds were abolished in 1547, Corpus Christi was taken off the religious calendar in 1548, and so when economic hardships hit, the infrastructure that had for two hundred years supported religious plays crumbled. Theologically, plays dealing with the Virgin were among the most vulnerable. They faded from the York cycle early, and removing her presence from plays was an obvious concession to the new orthodoxy. But some local parishes, towns, and private houses reluctant to give up on traditional beliefs and practices did continue some of the less controversial plays. In Shrewsbury, the Passion was played before large audiences into the 1560s; a selection of the cycle plays is recorded in Coventry in the 1570s, a record much beloved of Shakespeareans, who imagine (plausibly) that the young William might well have been taken to see the last remnants of the old drama and thereby (so the sentimental version of the story goes) acquired his taste for the theater; and there are isolated instances of religious plays being staged as late as the first decade of the new century.

The rise of the commercial theater, at least in London, gave the reformers and political authorities their greatest opportunities to influence the content of a new drama in the way the medieval Church had attempted to use the old plays to coerce popular feelings. Over the course of the next fifty to seventy years, as medieval religious theater faded, one of the most popular ingredients of the new drama became a raw anti-Catholicism, frequently expressed in racy rhetoric familiar in religious polemic. By the 1590s, although a series of acts and decrees had forbidden the staging of religious matters, and censors watched the theaters moderately carefully, anti-Catholic sentiment was permitted, and patriotic history plays and Italianate revenge plays could readily exploit anti-Catholic prejudice. Foxe's reading of English Church history provided material for a host of plays, including the anonymous *Thomas Lord Cromwell* (1602), Rowley's *When You See Me, You Know Me* (1603), Heywood's *If You Know Not Me, You Know Nobody* (two parts, 1605) and Dekker's *The Whore of Babylon* (1607), all of which repeat the commonplace sexual slurs against Rome.[3] By the reign of James, notes Carol Wiener, "no good Englishman could have defined his national identity without some mention of his distaste for Rome, and this remained the case for the greater part of the seventeenth century." In a similar vein, the Shrine of Walsingham becomes identified with sexual scandal and scurrility in a number of early seventeenth-century plays – in contradiction to its association with Catholic England in the continuations of the musical version of the ballad.[4]

[3] Robinson, *Writing the Reformation.*
[4] Wiener, "Beleaguered Isle," 27; Chapman, "Met I with an old bare Mare," 222–9.

Paradoxically, dramatists who embraced (or exploited) the mood of anti-Catholic prejudice did so against a background of Protestant attacks on the theater itself as yet another instance of idolatry. What plays present, complained George Whetstone, "is too holye," since it puts on the "common Stage" matters "which Preachers should pronounce in Pulpits." A play, says Stephen Gosson, "is a pollution of idols."[5] Relentless Puritan iconophobes attacked the depravity of the stage and welcomed accidental (or deliberate) burnings in theaters as the punishments of a just and vengeful God against a godless activity.

Nonetheless, the Old Religion started to creep back into the drama, not least in the work of one of Dean Hutton's "ignorant sort," the son of a lapsed Catholic or "church papist,"[6] from Warwickshire, one William Shakespeare, who may have heard Herod bluster his way through his lines in a biblical play in Coventry, and remembered to make reference to the player, in an Erasmian manner, satirical yet fond, in *Hamlet*. Shakespeare came to the London theater scene in the late 1580s or early 1590s. He is therefore writing sixty to eighty years after the Dissolution, but the figure of the Virgin haunts many of his plays. In some plays, the Virgin's "pryvytes" have been transformed into the bodily allure and fragile mortality of a woman. "That's a fair thought," as Hamlet puts it, "to lie between maids' legs" (III. ii. 127), but the ladies in question are ones from whom Robert Sidney's pilgrim knight or Shakespeare's Danish prince are cut off – in one case far away, in the other mad and drowned, in both cases, mortal, mutable, subject to time. The universe of *Hamlet* is a lonely one: the world of magic, miracle, pilgrimages, and devotion to the female as a source of good and reconciliation is "out of joint" (I. v. 188–9).

The recognition of the Walsingham Ballad as the source of Ophelia's opening "mad" lines adds one more piece to our puzzlement over Shakespeare's relationship with Catholicism, which has become a fashionable topic since the 1980s. For hundreds of years, Shakespeare was integrated into a dominant patriotic and firmly Protestant reading of British cultural history. In recent years, encouraged by the re-positioning of Catholicism within English history, in the eyes of many revisionist biographers, Shakespeare has become seen a crypto-Catholic, even (in some more extreme versions) presented as an agent for the Counter-Reformation. The so-called missing years between approximately 1584 and 1590, a period from which we have little documentation of his whereabouts, is now quarreled over by advocates of Shakespeare's having Protestant Sidney–Leicester

---

[5] Izard, *George Whetstone*, 71; O'Connell, *Idolatrous Eye*, 14.   [6] Walsham, *Church Papists*.

Circle sympathies and employment, and those who see him in Catholic Lancaster, in touch with recusants and Jesuits.[7] The early plays, from *Henry VI* through *Romeo and Juliet*, or *King John*, and often as far into his career as *Measure for Measure* or *Macbeth,* have been mined to support both extremes and positions between, on the assumption that he came to London after being imbued in the beliefs of one or other religious faction.

Regardless of his whereabouts in those years, there seems to be an emerging consensus that, quite apart from the question of any personal commitment, Shakespeare's plays show that he was unusually sensitive to the continuing traces of Catholicism in late Elizabethan and Jacobean England. Recent scholars choose a variety of metaphors to describe this awareness. Beatrice Groves speaks of Shakespeare's "transferring to the theatre what remained of Catholicism's charisma." Richard Wilson asserts that Shakespeare slipped "from Rome to Romeo" and exchanged "Mary for Apollo."[8] More subtly, Stephen Greenblatt argues that the plays remain "haunted" by the Catholic past, by "rituals and beliefs that have been *emptied out.*" For Elizabeth Mazzola, late Elizabethan England was a "Protestant world" still "coated with symbolic residue." Regina Buccola and Lisa Hopkins choose metaphors that suggest leaking: they speak of the "vestiges of Catholic tradition and culture that leak out ... via stage imagery, plot devices, and characterization," instancing such "leakages" as Shakespeare's generally benign attitude to nuns and friars (as in *Measure for Measure*) and the radiant parody of religious devotion by an erotic pilgrim in *Romeo and Juliet.*[9]

In fairness, we are all – with the exception of some crass proselytizers – grasping uneasily for the most helpful metaphors to describe the unquestionable traces of Catholicism in Shakespeare's works. What can be usefully said is that Shakespeare was interested in religious history, theology, and devotional practices for their theatrical possibilities; and like any good dramatic productions (this is true, as we have seen, even with the seemingly didactic religious plays of the late Middle Ages or those by his contemporaries that exploit anti-Catholic sentiments), his plays revel in staging multiple and contradictory points of view. As Michael Questier quips, theatre is a "sort of playpen in which participants could adopt and lay aside, ventriloquise and caricature, try on for size, test and discard a

---

[7] See, e.g., for the "Protestant" claims, McCarthy, *Pseudonymous Shakespeare.*

[8] Groves, *Texts and Traditions*, 57; Wilson, *Secret Shakespeare*, 156.

[9] Greenblatt, *Shakespearean Negotiations*, 104, 112; Mazzola, *Pathology of the English Renaissance*, 7; Buccola and Hopkins, *Marian Moments*, 1. See also Duffy, "Bare Ruined Choirs," and Marotti, "Shakespeare and Catholicism."

whole variety of subject positions."[10] Nowhere is this more obvious than in *Hamlet* itself. When Ophelia enters singing her snatches of the Walsingham Ballad, a powerful moment of anguish and nostalgia takes on a deeper cultural resonance, as if in a few lines Shakespeare is recording and compressing a major, though unfathomable, cultural loss and the bewilderment that went with it. But there is no didacticism, no "staging faith," lost or found. We might even characterize the presence of Hamlet's father's ghost – often triumphantly paraded as proof of Shakespeare's Catholicism – as an example of his deliberate ambiguity. Is the Ghost a dweller in a Catholic Purgatory in a stark and grim Protestant universe? A devil come to tempt him, as Protestant theologians would have insisted? Or simply a melodramatic theatrical ghost speaking from under the stage? Or is Shakespeare using the theatrical power of these great opposing cosmologies of his time, and is not concerned with theological consistency? As Groves comments, he is not returning to Catholic residues either "as deconsecrated tropes nor to generate the outrageous and exciting frisson of the forbidden." It is as if what Catholic practices once represented have become "almost ordinary and accepted" in the material reality of the day to day, fully immanent.[11]

Hamlet, then, in its cryptic references to Catholicism, as in everything else, is an unambiguous affirmation of total ambiguity. In three of Shakespeare's other plays, however, we find the "staging" of particular Mariological moments that very definitely link with both the medieval affirmation of the Virgin and her supposed loss to Protestant England. In one of them, *All's Well That Ends Well,* a character announces that "miracles are passed" (II. iii. 1): it is as if Shakespeare accepts that aphorism as a given, and yet he looks within human experience for some continuities – not merely as echoes, but as emphatic points of human growth.

All's Well That Ends Well (probably 1604–5) was based partly on Boccaccio's *Decameron* (Day 3, story 9): it tells of how Helena, a poor physician's daughter, wins the hand of the young Count Bertram of Rousillion, and then, when he repudiates her, wins him for a second time by tricking him into getting her pregnant. In the climactic scene of the play, the Florentine girl Diana – who has helped Helena in her plot by means of a "bed-trick" when Helena takes her arranged place in Bertram's bed – turns to the scene's onlookers, both on stage and off, and announces a "riddle" that involves an apparent impossibility:

---

[10] Lake and Questier, *Antichrist's Lewd Hat,* xxxi. [11] Groves, *Texts and Traditions,* 31.

He knows himself my bed he hath defiled,
And at that time he got his wife with child.
Dead though she be, she feels her young one kick,
So there's my riddle: one that's dead is quick.

Diana then announces the entrance of the person who will provide the riddle's answer: "And now," she proclaims, "behold the meaning" (v. iii. 295–304). Helena enters.

To most of the stage witnesses, who have just been mourning her death, Helena is remembered as a young virgin who had been a compelling though somewhat disturbing interloper into the court of France, who had (at least to some) miraculously cured the king of a fistula, had subsequently (apparently) died, and whose marriage to Bertram was unconsummated. Her widower husband is about to be remarried at the instigation of the king and his mother, the elderly Countess of Roussillion. But now, this carefully manipulated conclusion is disturbed by a group of Florentine women claiming that Bertram has seduced Diana, and promised marriage to her. Then, even more disruptively, Helena herself enters, alive, claiming her husband and clearly pregnant. The king voices the sense of wonder the shocked spectators feel: "Is there no exorcist / Beguiles the truer office of mine eyes? / Is't real that I see?" (v. iii. 304–6). Empirical perception seems countermanded by magic or sorcery: for the second time in the play a "miracle" associated with Helena has occurred.

In my description of the scene, I have used language that deliberately stresses the play's links with the mixture of folktale and miracle play on which Shakespeare frequently drew for theatrical and emotional effects, if not for any specific theological content. Helena presents herself as the resurrected heroine, the miraculously restored wife, the virtuous healer. Her reappearance is an instant of wonderment set (and it is part of the fascination of this play) within realistic social tensions to create the effect summarized by the old lord Lafew: "Mine eyes smell onions, I shall weep anon" (v. iii. 320). The occasion of Lafew's "onions" – the resurrection of a person presumed to be dead – is a common motif to which Shakespeare was frequently drawn, most spectacularly at the end of *The Winter's Tale*, and which, we may recall, is one of the miracles attributed to the Virgin at her shrines, which, by the early seventeenth century, are to be witnessed only in Catholic countries, in places such as Loreto, and no longer at Ipswich or Walsingham or any of the other lost Marian pilgrimage sites.

However, the momentary tableau of Helena's reappearance links the play with a specific Mariological tradition. Helena is the Pregnant Virgin, exemplified most famously by Piero della Francesca's fresco, the "Madonna del Parto" (*c.* 1465).[12] I make no claim that Shakespeare knew Piero's work. But he would have certainly been aware of the artistic tradition of the representations of the pregnancy of the Virgin Mary and, as Gail Gibson shows in her discussion of East Anglian drama, the pregnant Madonna was a favorite motif in churches and drama in medieval England, intended to affirm the incarnational principle of God becoming man.[13]

Like Shakespeare's Helena, Piero's Virgin's body also thrusts itself dramatically at the spectator with a powerful combination of naturalism and ritual symbolism. Two identical angels gaze at us as they hold back the curtains, gesturing (like Diana in *All's Well* announcing Helena's entry) that we should "behold the meaning." Like Shakespeare, Piero shows a maternal body anticipating birthing, caught in exaltation, but tinged with anxiety, precisely the combination no doubt felt by many of the women who came to pay their devotions to the image at Marian shrines and to which Shakespeare alludes briefly in a series of short scenes before the play's culmination, where we see Helena pregnant, urging on her supporters, determined to bring her pilgrimage to a successful conclusion, defining in effect her own alternate "pathway" built on her sexuality and assertiveness.

Mary the Virgin Mother focused the paradox of the Incarnation, a miraculous anomaly, detached by dogma from sexual desires, menstruation, and the physicality of human life.[14] Historically, therefore, in her momentary role of pregnant Virgin, Helena embodies some aspects of the medieval affirmation of dedicated virginity. However, she is also a "Reformed" Virgin, representing both the emergent woman of humanistic learning and the Protestant affirmation of marriage and procreation as a woman's primary role. At the start of the play, Helena and Bertram's companion Parolles have a battle of wits over the uses of virginity. Although the debate is won by Helena, both discussants share commonplace Protestant attitudes that virginity is but a stage of a woman's life that should lead dutifully to marriage.

But Helena is not the virgin who announced, as Mary did, "be it according to thy word," either dutifully because it was predestined with no recourse except to respond dutifully, or by her own free will so that if "she chose the quiet life, she would be left at peace." According this second, Catholic, reading, "the decision was hers and hers alone . . . The history of the world hung in the balance as a young girl considered the options before

---

[12] Cole, *Piero della Francesca*, 76–7.
[13] Gibson, *Theatre of Devotion*, 174–6. For a more extensive analysis of the "Reformed Virgin" motif, see Waller, "Shakespeare's Reformed Virgin."
[14] Neyrey, "Mary: Mediterranean Maid and Mother," 70.

her."[15] Helena, in short, is different from both the Protestant and the Catholic Mary. She is also an assertive young woman who announces her own determination to preserve her virginity in order to lose it, as she asserts to Parolles, only "to her own liking" (I. i. 153). Now, through her own ingenuity and determination, she has done so. There is a subversive level to Shakespeare's pregnant virgin that challenges the dominant ideologies of both old and new religions, and which links her with other emergent aspects of the evolving "strong" Shakespearean heroine. Under the surface of a story that can be read as the affirmation of procreative heterosexual marriage, then, is another story, that of a woman's right to make sexual choices. Helena is carving out for herself one of Simon Coleman's alternate or even "subversive" pathways. Her entry is an affirmation of the pregnant subject who is not merely a container for a child; rather, she embodies Christine Battersby's concept of the "birthing self."[16] Where both medieval and post-Reformation theology, in different contexts, worked to assimilate women's sexuality to reproduction, what Helena affirms is the primary importance of choice. What is new, even radical, about *All's Well* is Helena's questioning of who may ultimately make the choice of person, time, and place in the "loss of virginity" (I. ii. 139).

The right to control her own body was rarely seen as a legitimate goal for a woman in early seventeenth-century England, and Helena's provocative response to Parolles at the end of their debate in the opening scene strikes at the heart of hundreds, perhaps thousands, of years of patriarchal presumptions about the control of women's bodies by men. In *All's Well*, the claim for sexual choice and control is made and the initiation undertaken by the woman herself, fulfilling or at least advancing the fantasies of autonomy that late medieval female pilgrims to a Marian shrine may well have entertained as they contemplated their own identification on pilgrimage. Kristeva speaks eloquently of women's "inner solitude" as a woman's first move toward such autonomy; such a concept has been widely recognized in a variety of places in the late medieval and early modern period, from what Theodora Jankowski terms "resistant virgins" to what Alison Jaggar terms "womanspace," arguing that "the significance of the spatial metaphor for a woman is likely to be a ... discovery of her own, inner desire, without fear of impingements, intrusions, or violation."[17] Here, almost a century

---

[15] For Protestant and Catholic positions respectively, see Svendson, "Is Mary Co-Redemptress?" and Beattie, *Rediscovering Mary*, 23.

[16] Battersby, *The Phenomenal Woman*, 16.

[17] See e.g. Jankowski, "Pure Resistance," 218–55; Jaggar, *Feminist Politics*, 271; Bassin, "Woman's Images of Inner Space," 191–203.

after the heyday of women pilgrims to shrines such as Walsingham or Woolpit, is a concrete instance of what kinds of desires women pilgrims might have been reaching for. An alternative pathway is emerging, or at least momentarily becoming clearer.

But there is even a further dimension to *All's Well* in which we can sense the presence (and cultural transformation) of the Virgin as well as the opening of new cultural possibilities for women. Another of the stories designed to "awake" our emotional "faith" at the play's end (to anticipate a celebrated phrase from the final scene of *The Winter's Tale*) and perhaps the play's most crucial story, is the return of the apparently dead Helena to life. Near the start of the revival of *All's Well*'s reputation in the mid twentieth century, G. Wilson Knight argued for its being saturated in religious language and allegory, and described Helena as "a semi-divine person, or some new type of saint." R. G. Hunter even more pointedly argued that Helena is a "literary descendant of the Virgin" typically found in medieval narratives and dramatic "miracles of Our Lady"; she is what Pierre Maquerlot terms "the Providential Agent" figure whose return "is shrouded in an atmosphere of miracle."[18] *All's Well* is certainly not alone among Shakespeare's plays in using one of the great stories of Western culture, the desire to overcome death, nor in associating that fantasy with a redemptive woman figure. The motif occurs repeatedly in the comedies, and even though we in the audience know that Hero, Marina, Thaisa, Imogen, Claudio, and others are not "really" dead, the plays' actions are structured to create identification, relief, and triumph when they reappear. Many accounts of Mary's miracles, it will be recalled, attributed the raising of the dead to her. In Shakespeare's plays of redemption through female figures, it is as if a medieval Madonna has been transformed and reintegrated into popular culture, no longer explicitly associated with the Virgin or one of her "madonnine" images, but humanized, embodying a more fragile but concrete humanity. The process of numinous secularization which I observed with the "Lady" of Robert Sidney's poem is similarly a trace of the apparently lost presence of the Virgin from England.

My other two examples of the traces of the Virgin in Shakespeare are from the late romances. Angela Carter speaks of the "consolatory non-sense"[19] of their underlying pattern, mocking their affirmation of the salvific power of martyr-like suffering, youthful female virginity, and providential

---

[18] Knight, *The Sovereign Flower*, 146; Hunter, *Shakespeare and the Comedy of Forgiveness*, 129–30; Maquerlot, *Shakespeare and the Mannerist Tradition*, 151.
[19] Carter, *The Sadeian Woman*, 5–6.

redemption. In both substance and tone, her scorn echoes the impatient iconoclasm of the Protestant reformers attempting to remove traditional religion from the minds of believers. Some defenders of the plays acknowledge such patterns but see them as signs of Shakespeare's reconciliation with Catholicism. Richard Wilson points out that three of the plays end with key scenes in "some curtained recess of the stage," an "isolated female place," where the faithful come to do homage to a powerful female figure. According to such an argument, all the plays incorporate a pattern of a journey, in pain and penitence, to this "discovery space" which is presented, like a traditional pilgrimage site, as a place of sacred revelation.[20] Shakespeare does seem to return over and over to such motifs – and yet there is a difference between any affirmation of traditional piety and the open-ended but numinous humanism of his late plays. They enact less a traditional religion, let alone a defiant return to it, and more a transformation of some aspects of it which Shakespeare finds tantalizing as explorations of the human condition and its utopian possibilities, especially as embodied in women and women's experience, but all too rarely able to be realized. The evocation of such recurring fantasies and yearnings about the place of the female – as virgin, mother, wise woman, and redemptrix – underlies the recurring significance of the Virgin in Shakespeare's late plays.

A major part of three of the four late romances (it is present but far less central in *The Tempest*) is the recurring male fantasy of salvation through the redemptive return of a woman to rescue and intercede for his erring behavior. Such a pattern is clearly derived from late medieval devotion to the Virgin, with its patterns of masochism and intense fetishization I examined in Chapter 3, but goes far beneath conventional surface pieties. It is rather as if Shakespeare wants to reclaim the human dimension of the fading magical world without its doctrinal underpinnings. *Cymbeline* provides a case in point. Like the other late plays, it is full of Catholic references, but as Groves points out, when Imogen speaks of her orisons, "she is not thinking about the Virgin, but about Posthumous . . . she hopes to encounter not Mary or God," but her husband,[21] just as Robert Sidney wished to return to his wife, and even, perhaps, despite their obvious incorporation within medieval Catholic beliefs, Dante and Petrarch wish to be united with Beatrice and Laura.

To examine this recurring pattern in the late plays, I turn first to *Pericles* (*c.*1608–9). Notwithstanding its highly problematic authorial status, its overall structure is clear. It involves a series of journeys by its hero, who

[20] Wilson, *Secret Shakespeare*, 248.   [21] Groves, *Texts and Traditions*, 29.

in effect acts out a spectrum of views of pilgrimage emerging in early modern England. Each journey has at its end a female figure, placed there either as a known goal or by an ambiguous force which can be labeled providence, coincidence, fate or just chance. The first, Pericles's confident ceremonial pilgrimage to find a wife, reflects traditional medieval views of pilgrimage, long since gone from English life but returning here with an initial hope followed by appalled disillusion. His pilgrimage turns out to be a self-deceiving journey to what Protestant iconoclasts would have seen as a false, idolatrous, and blasphemous shrine, its central image of incestuous sexuality with a seductive female idol reminiscent of Protestant caricatures of Rome. That is followed by a seemingly more successful voyage that brings him to a woman who seems to fulfill all his desires but only after a series of lucky chances. Not Providence but Chance seems to rule this world. The apparent loss of Thaisa in childbirth in a storm, also by chance and contingency, is followed years later by further loss when Pericles learns that his daughter, the last reminder of his lost wife, is also apparently dead. What follows are years of regret and despair. Finally, in the middle of an increasingly despairing journey, without goals or direction, Pericles is reunited with both, once again by chance, enacting for the audience that fantasy that the seemingly impossible may be given to us through both daughter and wife, virgin and mother, in twin culminating discovery scenes that are saturated in suggestions of intercession, reconciliation, and restoration.

Only the first of these pilgrimages, Pericles's voyage to find a wife in Antioch, is a traditional journey to reach a specific place or person. By the reign of James I, pilgrimage to a shrine or site of miracles was, for most English men and women, a distant memory, either an archaic and quaint habit of another time or a nostalgic reminder of a pattern of devotion that had virtually disappeared in England, even though it continued in Catholic Europe. But, as Tiffany has shown, for Protestants, the concept of pilgrimage had not disappeared but had become internalized. We see echoes of that process in the play. *Pericles* alludes to both the traditional and the emergent senses of pilgrimage, the one a journey to a specific, apparently holy, place, the other an internal journey not tied to place but open to possibility and chance.[22] Neither Protestant nor Catholic, the later scenes of *Pericles* incorporate elements of both, as if Shakespeare is feeling for ways to articulate a human experience that he believes conveys a sense of the numinous with being tied to a specific doctrine, and culminating with a

---

[22] Tiffany, *Love's Pilgrimage*, e.g. 179.

remarkable emphasis that neither Catholic nor Protestant could have easily accepted – the primacy of chance in human affairs. Shakespeare's universe is not that of either Aquinas or Calvin; if anything, it is closest to that of Giordano Bruno, an infinitely open universe where the goddess Fortuna is the presiding deity – but where the transformative role of a divine woman as virgin, mother, seer, bearer of wisdom and reconciliation remains central. The Virgin may have "disappeared" or been "lost," but it is as if she has re-emerged in the very changes and chances of being human.[23]

One of the traditional titles of the Virgin that is central to this play is Our Lady Star of the Sea – a title that was traditionally associated with the Virgin in her care for mariners. After his initial disillusioning pilgrimage, Pericles casts himself out onto the sea. The sea is closely associated with the women characters: Thaisa is lost at sea, and her body thrown overboard; Marina is named for her birth at sea, and it is the sea which eventually brings Pericles back to his daughter and his wife. Theweleit comments that "in all of European literature (and literature influenced by it), desire, if it flows at all, flows in a certain sense *through women*. In some way or other, it always flows in relation to the image of women." "Over and over," he asserts, Western culture has associated women with water – "the women-in-the-water, woman as water, as a stormy, cavorting, cooling ocean ... as a limitless body of water ... where we are a part of every ocean." It is as if what men ask women to be is somehow involved at a very primitive level with the sea.[24]

Pericles, then, sails the seemingly endless and unpredictable sea. After Marina's apparent death, with his wife and then his daughter taken from him, he drifts aimlessly. He has sworn "never to wash his face, nor cut his hair / He [puts] on sackcloth, and to sea. He bears / a tempest, which his mortal vessel tears, / And yet he rides it out" (IV. iv. 28–31). It is only by luck, by the power of chance, that he comes to Mytilene, where he is rescued by his fortuitous meeting with Marina in a scene that, like the climactic appearance of Helena in *All's Well*, or like the undeserved intervention of the Virgin in a medieval miracle tale, culminates in an unexpected reve-lation. Marina is frequently interpreted as a valorization of transcendent virginity whose radiant virtue in the brothel – in the tradition of medieval virgin martyr stories – triumphs over every kind of vice with which she may be assaulted. The mechanisms of the scene may be derived from medieval virgin martyr stories, with their crude and prurient humor, but (and here we can perhaps see Shakespeare gradually shaping the

[23] Bruno, *Expulsion of the Triumphant Beast*, 169.   [24] Theweleit, *Male Fantasies*, I, xxvi, 272, 28.

unpromisingly unsubtle material he inherited from his collaborator) his heroine also emerges as a young woman of energy and autonomy. Deanne Williams goes further and sees Marina as one of Shakespeare's many articulate heroines, even reflecting the emerging, new, educated ideal of early modern women. By the play's end, the play's father figure has been restored to his wife, has established a healthy relationship with his daughter, who has herself entered a new relationship with a lover/husband, and has had her mother and father restored to her. The play's initial claustrophobic scene of incest and idolatry is transformed into an image of father–daughter relations by which "father daughter incest, the subject of tragedy," is transformed into a "reaffirmation of 'family values,' the matter of comedy."[25]

Such a reading smoothes out what are unquestionable textual and conceptual difficulties with the play, but the structural thrust of the ending is clear enough. All three journeys that Pericles has undertaken – traditional pilgrimage, internalized pilgrimage, and unfocused, fortuitous voyaging – culminate in two scenes that evoke many of the traditional roles of the Madonna: daughter, mother, intercessor, and miraculous renewer of life. It is as if at the center of whatever view of the universe we may have, the Virgin (or what, in wish-fulfillment, the Virgin represents) awaits us. She evokes where we came from, and where we yearn to return. The restoration of his daughter is hailed by Pericles in terms that echo the Dantean (and common medieval paradox) that the Virgin "begetst" Christ, Dante's "*Virgine madre, figlia in tua figlio*":

> O, come hither,
> Thou that beget'st him that did thee beget;
> Thou that was born at sea, buried at Tarsus,
> And found at sea again . . . This is Marina.   (v. i. 188–93)

At the culmination of the *Paradiso*, Beatrice appears to Dante who, like Pericles, has proceeded on a long journey of self-discovery and instructs him not so much to look at her, but through her to the Virgin and ultimately to God. She has been lost and now, after trials, challenges, and losses, is restored to him. For Pericles, Marina is at once his daughter and his own "begetter" or restorer.

Some critics read the progress of the play after Pericles's initial disillusionment as a specifically Christian vision, a representation of trust in Providence through the gracious gift of faith as he learns painful lessons

---

[25] Williams, "Papa Don't Preach," 202.

about perception and presumption. Is Pericles's outburst on losing Thaisa – "O you gods! / Why do you make us love your godly gifts / And snatch them straight away?" (III. i. 22–4) – answered by a providential force eventually giving the "gifts" back? Is that a reward for his patience? A gift from the gods (or God)? Or just chance? For Christian-oriented critics, it is as if Pericles, like Dante in the *Commedia*, has gone through hell, Purgatory, and is now being shown a heavenly vision. In Tillyard's words, it is "almost as if [Shakespeare] aimed at rendering the complete theme of *The Divine Comedy* in miniature."[26] *Pericles* can just as plausibly be read as a fantasy, a fable, written specifically by a man (and in a sense offered as a confirming story to other men) of men's supposed "need" for women. The reification of gender roles that have dominated Western patriarchal thought and which were so heavily reinforced by the cult of the Virgin is a major focus of the play. Pericles gets not a vision of the divine – in Dante's poem Beatrice points beyond herself to the Virgin, and to God – but of a reunited human family. The play's conclusion sends the protagonist back into the world, to work out the future, much as at the end of *The Tempest,* Prospero breaks his magic staff, drowns his book, and returns to the risky but real world of time, history, and unpredictability. Pericles likewise must now work on making his restored relationships function within human rather than mythical time. At the play's end the hero is not shown heaven, but a very temporal space and set of relationships in which he must work his human fulfillment.

A qualification about the optimism of the play's final act, voiced by feminist critics, is needed here. The fantasy of loss, rescue, and reconciliation – whether by means of the youthful hope represented by the daughter, or the mature power of the mother – on which the play is built is intensely male-centered. I see no way of avoiding this observation, to which Theweleit's analysis of "male fantasies" is again relevant. Shakespeare explores the male fixation with Woman as rescuers or bearers of salvation in all the late plays, especially *Cymbeline* and *The Winter's Tale*; in *Cymbeline*, at least, he subjects it to intense critique and through the character of Posthumus shows its destructiveness. But here, in *Pericles*, he is interested in the pattern without serious critique; it is sketched out, as if, working with an existing, only partly finished script, he were gradually testing its theatrical possibilities. The return of Thaisa, beloved wife as well as mother, is presented as a religious ritual: heralded by Diana, accompanied by serenading virgins and marveling attendants, it is as if this male fantasy were a universal truth. A man has suffered unjustly, undergone terrible torments and

---

[26] Tillyard, *Shakespeare's Last Plays*, 59.

losses, and now, the central fantasy figures of his inner world, the virgin daughter/whore/mother/wise woman, appear to reassure him. This is a fantasy of over-valuation, involving the projection of deep and largely gender-based insecurities upon women as a need somehow justified by the universe itself. Cryptically, in these final scenes but with extraordinary effect, *Pericles* stages some of the great male fantasies of our history, which for nearly a millennium and a half had been projected upon the Virgin Mary.

The power of *The Winter's Tale* (1610–11), a play which in the past fifty years has frequently been seen as one of the most important works of Shakespeare's career, rests on its intellectually demanding and emotionally disturbing treatment of some of our most basic human realities – especially the dangerous combination of male insecurities and sexuality, memories of childhood and early family relationships, and how they impact on our adult lives. Like *Pericles,* it culminates in a spectacle that bears witness to the continuing presence of the Virgin in England. In no other Shakespearean play is the renewed and transformed Virgin expressed so explicitly as in the revival of Hermione. Here, in 1610–11, three generations after the 1538 destruction of the "sisters," accompanied by the triumphant gloating prurience of Latimer at their destruction and at their powerlessness, the Virgin's transformed presence – not her return, but something, as Ariel sings in *The Tempest,* even more "rich and strange" (*The Tempest,* I. ii. 565) – is set forth in one of Shakespeare's most powerful works. Transformed into a momentary vision of a statue of an apparently dead queen coming to life, the Virgin returns within an image of human intercession, restoration, and resurrection, as metaphors for human change and responsibility in a needy human world from which the supernatural power of the female had been, supposedly, banished.

I make no apology for the slightly ecstatic tone of the preceding paragraph. In our time, productions of *The Winter's Tale,* more than most of Shakespeare's plays, have reverberated with an aura of transformative religious feeling. But that is not to say the play explicitly advocates or represents any particular dogma: that impression applies to "humanist" and "religious" readings, and even those who see the reconciliation of Leontes and Hermione at the end as tentative, partial, or even impossible. Many recent critics (and not a few productions) have pointed to the uncanny psychological accuracy of Shakespeare's portrayal of Leontes, most notably in Antony Sher's performance in the 1999 Royal Shakespeare Company production directed by Greg Doran, where the actor consciously strove to enact someone beset with morbid jealousy, or the extraordinary pairing of Simon Russell Beale and Rebecca Hall in Sam Mendes's 2009 Bridge production.

Long before Freud or modern developmental psychology, Shakespeare provides remarkable insight into the anxieties of being gendered male in a patriarchal society and the places women have been asked to occupy in the ideologies that swirl around in male fantasy structures.

Shakespeare's interest in these primitive contradictions within masculine identity focuses on a male figure, Leontes, whose separation has been incomplete or problematic and for whom anxiety arises when he is called upon as an adult to be a friend, a husband, or father. Throughout the play, we are reminded of how the idealization of childhood, the time when we rely most on mothering, functions as an avoidance of the complexities of adulthood. As a husband, Leontes finds himself once again dependent upon a woman to confirm his identity, and he may easily re-enact, either positively or negatively, in displaced or disguised forms, his early crises of masculine identity. Leontes's and Polixenes's nostalgic idealizations of boyhood are the subject of fond teasing by Hermione. She listens to the two "twinn'd lambs" identify their "temptations" as the onset of sexuality and meeting their wives, jesting that their perceived loss of security makes Polixenes's queen and her into "devils" (1 .ii. 80). She has, as Sanders puts it, "an elasticity and largeness," a "free 'play' of spirit" that shows no such dark insecurities, and when she persuades Polixenes to stay longer in Sicilia, she does so with generosity and without suspicion of any unconscious complexities in her husband. Leontes's reactions, on the other hand, come from a very "primitive and very powerful" place in the psyche which includes a pathetic, though terrifying, reversion to childhood as a time in which such complexities did not threaten him.[27] Such fantasies that are unrealizable are projected upon women: their origins may not be immediate or concrete but may involve a fantasy of maternal omnipotence, combined with the inability to recognize a woman as relating to a man in a relationship built on mutuality, not hierarchy. Undifferentiated bliss was in childhood, in the fantasy a timeless world before the complications of parental relations interfered. It is painful for him, beyond his understanding, to leave this world and acknowledge that the "she" on whom he now blames his insecurities is the "she" who sustains him. He attacks precisely what we are attracted by, her mature sexuality and easy friendship, her apparent oneness with her family and the unborn child. Leontes repudiates her because he is threatened by this ease, and he adds the irrationality of the child to the arbitrariness of the political tyrant and the destructiveness of the authoritarian male. His abjection when he believes her to be dead evokes

---

[27] Sanders, *Winter's Tale*, 17, 25.

the rage of the child against the person whom he most loves and yet from whom he must assert his independence. It is the anguished regret and belated repentance of the iconoclast who realizes too late what he has destroyed. Broader cultural parallels are not difficult to project upon the play: Leontes voices the Protestant iconoclasts' desire to break from the motherhood of the Virgin, but in doing so, cutting off the deeper reaches of that relationship. He is destructive of the relationship in the way the Protestant iconoclasts were destructive of the Virgin's shrines and relics. As Huston Diehl similarly notes, "inasmuch as the male lovers rage against what they desire and kill what they love, they resemble the Protestant iconoclasts who 'bewhore' and 'kill' sacred images they had once adored."[28]

Hermione is one of Shakespeare's most complex women characters, not merely in the play's dramatic development, but in what she stands for in its moral scheme and broader historical significance. Once again, Freud's insight into what the over-valuation of women, of which the adulation of the Virgin has historically been a prime manifestation, gives us an important clue to understanding her. In Western culture – certain psychoanalysts would say universally – men tend to idealize women for needs such as those Leontes so tragically displays. In doing so they "over-value" women, whether as mothers, lovers, wives, daughters or as embodying some transcendent cosmic force. As we saw in *Pericles*, but with far more suggestiveness in this play, woman, or a succession of women, are asked or "needed" to complete or compensate for men's insecurities, to a degree that is inevitably unattainable, or impossible. When, at Hermione's trial, Leontes speaks of her as "too much beloved" (III. ii. 5), he uses a phrase that points to his impossible level of "need" for Hermione to fulfill insatiable demands, "Too much beloved" turns all too rapidly into too much hated. Sanders comments ironically that "from that fine and ancient made mess created by first deifying women as 'precious'/'gracious'/'sacred' and then treating them as property, the males flee in confusion . . . They leave Hermione, as it were, holding the baby. Or (if we count Leontes) – the babies."[29]

Familiarity in a relationship may overcome a man's primitive mystification of woman, but the implication is that fantasy of awe and even dread of woman's power always remains alive ready to be activated. To abandon the fantasy of Woman as omnipotent (whether that is experienced as negative or positive) and to recognize women as independent subjects is often difficult for men, who tend to remain in an infantile state rather than accept

---

[28] Diehl, *Staging Reform*, 172; see also Dunn-Hensley, "Return of the Sacred Virgin," 194.
[29] Sanders, *Winter's Tale*, 33.

the more disturbing but revolutionary appreciation of the other's independent subjectivity. Modern feminist scholarship has generally followed the Protestant reformers in seeing the Virgin as, at the very least, reinforcing such destructive stereotypes. But do they lie deeper in the male psyche than that? The origins of the fantasies imposed upon Mary may well be rooted far deeper than we like to admit and we might see the Virgin as constructed by such primitive fantasies rather than as their origin or cause. Those considerations are, at least, brought into the discussion through Shakespeare's play.

The Winter's Tale is conventionally characterized as "comedy" (as in the Folio) or "romance" (as in the taxonomies of many modern accounts of the late plays). But arguably "tragedy" is just as relevant a category, at least in its first half. Traditionally, tragedy is centered on a heroic male character, and the first half of *The Winter's Tale* may be thought of as the tragedy of Leontes. But Hermione's plight is more singularly tragic: unjustly accused, trapped in circumstances that destroy her integrity, relationships, and family, she is a victim not only of her husband's tyranny, but also of a whole masculinist world that all the men (and perforce, the women) in the play take for granted. Shakespeare gives Hermione some of the most dignified, emotionally controlled lines in all his plays, showing enormous courage before the catastrophic events which victimize her. She proves to Leontes what all the others see and are helpless to change, that he is dangerously childish and destructively tyrannical. The play is written so that we are asked to believe that the tragedy is complete by the end of Act III, that Hermione is "really" dead. Like Leontes, we hear Paulina's report. We also hear him demand to see his wife's and son's bodies and hear his determination to have them buried together (III. ii. 232–4). The Folger (Washington, DC) production of 2009 stressed the finality of Hermione's death by having her body on stage, with Leontes cradling her head and starting his long anguished repentance over her dead body. To this point in the play, we have witnessed a tragic end to the action. Death is where the destructiveness of both idealization and denigration have led. Leontes condemns himself to serving painful years of regret and repentance. It would have not taken much difficulty to read the death of Hermione as the death of the True Queen and the true Church in England. No doubt many Catholics and church-papists in the first decade of the seventeenth century wished and prayed for such a pattern of recognition and repentance to occur in England.

Emerging strongly in the later scenes of the play's first half is its second significant woman character, Paulina, who represents another aspect of woman as maturing agent, but not in any sense as transcendent goddess so much as woman as mature companion. She is initially Hermione's supporter and defender, taking Leontes's abuse for her frank opposition to him and then, as his repentance deepens, stepping forward to act as his counselor. Of course, she, too, is fulfilling a male need – that of the wise woman who will step forward to repair the damage of male destructiveness, even if she herself has been the victim of his primitive insecurities and rages. The wise woman embodies a maturity that the men of the play find extraordinarily difficult to match, even if they can finally be led to acknowledge its importance and attempt to emulate it.

The second half of the play highlights the third of the play's women figures. She too is created in part from recognizable images of the Virgin. Complementing the roles of mother, wife, wise friend, and intercessor is the figure of the young and idealistic daughter – in *The Winter's Tale* a much more developed figure than in *Pericles*. Perdita has grown up as if embodying the ideals of innocence to which Leontes and Polixenes looked back. In Time's words, she has "grown in grace" (IV. i. 24) and we are shown, in the longest scene of all Shakespeare's plays, how that grace is constituted within traditional male fantasies of women. But Perdita is not a straightforward embodiment of nostalgic purity, pastoral joy, and seasonal celebration: she has a fastidious, even puritanical, side to her, as if Shakespeare wants to complicate our responses and recognize that purity, integrity, and even a mild iconoclasm, are not unimportant. Where Hermione has been "overvalued" by Leontes – simultaneously idealized and denigrated – Perdita insists on her lover being as honest and straightforward as she can. When Perdita meets Leontes, we get similarly an intriguing reminder of both the play's opening scenes and Shakespeare's peculiar fascination with fathers and daughters. On seeing Perdita, Leontes immediately thinks of Hermione. Shakespeare's source, *Pandosto,* makes much of the incestuous tinge to the relationship: sensing a memory of his dead wife, Pandosto propositions his daughter without knowing her identity and then kills himself when he discovers his error. But like Hermione's warm but totally appropriate affection toward Polixenes at the play's start, Leontes's attraction to his daughter now comes from a mature, mothering, place in the psyche. He has a new sense of what his dead wife represented and perhaps what a new kind of relationship with real women, not just idealized fantasy forms, might have been. However briefly, it is a deconstruction of the masculine myth of Woman. Neely argues that in the final scene "all of the characters need to recover Hermione."[30] Leontes's maturation shows how that might be possible.

[30] Neely, *Broken Nuptials*, 206.

At the play's end, the central importance of Time and the crucial cosmic force of Chance that seems to rule the world of *Pericles* is once again stressed. We are living no longer in magical time, but in human time. It takes the lost sixteen years not just for Perdita to grow up and for Leontes to repent, but also for Hermione to age and show that she is not a timeless symbol, somehow reflecting a lost, "fixed" ideal, to be worshiped and denigrated but, as Jessica Benjamin explains, a person within "independent subjectivity" within a "shared reality" rather than part of an "omnipotent fantasy." From being what Kristeva terms the fantasy of a "lost territory" for the only partially separated male ego, she can now through the process of time become a genuine relational object. In developmental terms (and *The Winter's Tale* is about development), the passing of time shows how a relationship of mutuality might be able to develop.[31] This breakthrough is represented in the statue scene, choreographed by Paulina in her role as the healer–priestess of this particular place of pilgrimage. Renaissance theorists of "wonder," mentioned in Chapter 6, were especially focused on drama. Aristotle's *admiratio* – what Philip Sidney termed "a well-raised admiration" – saw stage performance and spectacle as key elements in creating wonder, which many saw as leading from amazement to knowledge. Bishop points out that the early seventeenth century, absorbing the discoveries and speculations not just of Erasmus's "new learning," but Donne's "new philosophy," the discoveries and speculations of Copernicus, Galileo, and Bruno, "was especially primed to welcome an aesthetics of *admiratio*."[32]

G. K. Hunter notes that given the religious paranoia of Protestant Jacobean England, "a straightforward reference to the Virgin as intercessor" would have been "too Popish to be acceptable" on the Jacobean stage, which may account for why many scholars suggest that the first acted version of the play in November 1611, recorded by Simon Forman in his diary with no mention of the statue scene, might not have included it. It was, however, included in the 1623 Folio, so that in other court performances recorded in 1613, 1618, 1623 and 1634, in the increasingly liberal religious atmosphere of James's court, with his Catholic queen, and especially in that of Charles I, it was increasingly likely to have been performed. The scene has, as Overton puts it, an "unnerving aptness": as I noted earlier, a recurring structure of the romances is a movement toward "isolated female places," discovery spaces, that are all centered upon a woman to whom

---

[31] Benjamin, *Like Subjects, Love Objects*, 31, 43, 93; Kristeva, *Tales of Love*, 234.
[32] Sidney, *Defence*, 118, 120; Donne, *Complete English Poems*, 276; Bishop, *Shakespeare and the Theatre of Wonder*, 37.

characters make a pilgrimage.[33] Paulina's gallery is "lonely, apart" (v. iii. 18), but it is the means of integrating what the pilgrims learn there back into the world. Like the now long-lost pilgrimage sites, this sacred space takes us away from the world but eventually directs us back into it.

The language surrounding the return of Hermione is full of unmistakable Mariological connections. Hermione, Ruth Vanita suggests, has been hidden and preserved the way Catholics secreted statues, rosaries, and other reminders of Catholic devotion from the iconoclasts: historians have often noted how quickly some of the trappings of Catholicism reappeared under Mary Tudor, and how in Elizabeth's reign discoveries of hoarded remnants of the Old Religion were continually discovered, with some hidden so well that they were not discovered until the eighteenth or nineteenth centuries.[34] Hermione's memory has been revered in the same way as that of a saint: Leontes enters formally, led in procession, while her memorial is presented and extolled, "As she lived peerless, / So her dead likeness, I do well believe, / Excels whatever yet you look'd upon / Or hand of man hath done." The first impression is that much as the "image" of Our Lady of Walsingham and her "sisters" destroyed in 1538 had affected pilgrims, at least as described in the Pynson Ballad, all must acknowledge that there is "magic in thy majesty, which has / My evils conjured to remembrance and / From thy admiring daughter took the spirits, / Standing like stone with thee" (v. iii. 14–17, 39–42).

Huston Diehl fairly protests that the "catholicizers" of Shakespeare (and I acknowledge this chapter in some part to be one such) all too readily "assume that there is no place for wonder in the Protestant imaginary," and that Perdita's place in the play is to represent restraint and to protest that what we witness is not "superstition" or idolatry (v. iii. 43–4).[35] But, having set Perdita up to represent a cautious, even puritanical, inclination to iconoclasm, Shakespeare has her overcome by wonder at the statue, the "image" of her mother and to be converted to the wonder of the image:

> And give me leave,
> And do not say 'tis superstition, that
> I kneel and then implore her blessing. Lady,
> Dear queen, that ended when I but began,
> Give me that hand of yours to kiss.   (v. iii. 42–6)

---

[33] Shakespeare, *All's Well That Ends Well*, ed. Hunter, 145; Overton, *Winter's Tale*, 83; Wilson, *Secret Shakespeare*, 248. For Forman's account, see Chambers, *William Shakespeare*, 337–41.

[34] Vanita, "Mariological Memory," 311–37.   [35] Diehl, "'Strike All that Look Upon with Marvel'," 19.

As Susan Dunn-Hensley notes, Perdita's kneeling before the statue and kissing it certainly suggests pre-Reformation devotional practice.[36] Rejecting the concept of "superstition" here – and in effect showing Perdita's conversion to the validity of images and the positive power of art – is a direct challenge to Protestant iconoclasm toward the Virgin. The act of magical transformation, Paulina affirms emphatically, is not superstitious or unlawful, though, as Leontes affirms, "If this be magic, let it be an art / Lawful as eating." Like a guardian of a shrine, or a priestess, Paulina calls on the onlookers to "awake" their "faith" just as the writer of the Pynson Ballad exhorted pilgrims to Our Lady of Walsingham to marvel at the miracles of the Virgin. Only then, in the atmosphere of reverence, and with an affirmation of "faith," can Hermione "descend" and "be stone no more." Looking at the statue, Leontes acknowledges that the stone rebukes him "for being more stone than it." Now, the healing and completely human "miracle" can occur: "O, she's warm," exclaims Leontes (v. iii. 110–11, 99, 37–8, 109). Sanders argues that "this is the single most important discovery" of *The Winter's Tale* – the "discovery of warmth."[37] The resurrection scene is remarkable, not just as a piece of theater, but because it blurs the distinction between the statue and the reality of flesh. It is a resurrection, the bringing to life in the body of what has been dead and what has been turned into a statue, a mere image. Occasionally, productions will have Leontes and Perdita go against Paulina's warning not to touch the statue in order to show, at that point, she is still a statue (there is, after all, nothing "in" the text to forbid such a reading). Only when she descends does she become flesh: we can then witness directly "look, she's warm" as the incarnate miracle of *The Winter's Tale*.

The return, revival, or resurrection of Hermione (the terms directors or critics use may be a clue to their own stance before issues far broader than the play's theatrical effects) reaches back to the complex and overlapping traditions of the Virgin as the source of miracles. In medieval miracle stories, women's miracles are often associated, as Anne-Marie Korte explains, with "a change in her body or brought about by her body" (or, one needs to add, with masculinist fantasies of them). The association of women's bodies and miracles underlies much of the reformers' hostility to veneration of the Virgin and the attempt in England and other Protestant countries to domesticate and demythologize the image of the Virgin in theology, liturgy, and popular devotion.[38] *The Winter's Tale* clearly returns, if not to the theology, at the very least to its richly numinous associations.

[36] Dunn-Hensley, "Return of the Sacred Virgin," 196.
[37] Sanders, *Winter's Tale*, 118.   [38] Korte, *Women and Miracle Stories*, 352–3.

The modern revival of the reputation of *The Winter's Tale* and the other late plays (and the point applies to other so-called "problem plays" that have climactic scenes of resurrection and renewal such as *All's Well*) is a striking phase in the history of Shakespearean reception. The play can produce in readers and spectators an uncanny mixture of what Time calls "joy" and "terror" (IV. i. 1). It seems to provide a safe haven for the acknowledgment and then the therapeutic release of pent-up primitive anxieties concerning gender, family, and the possibility of spirituality within the material world. At the end of the play that safe haven is, as in the other late romances, identified with human relationships and the family. Such an ending does not always fit well with modern assumptions – as can be seen in a number of recent productions that settle for less than full reconciliation between Leontes and Hermione, or even for none, thus deliberately refusing the logic of the play. Such endings, of course, are a reader's or director's choice, even if they do not appear to be the play's.

The assumption the play seems to make is that when we respond to and in a sense re-produce these plays within our own histories, we are led to draw on some of our most primitive and our most deeply encultured memories, a core part of which is the "place" where the Virgin had been available for pre-Reformation men and women. The continued fascination of the late plays is, I suspect, based on the ways they draw out those experiences, whether we describe those as built into our basic biogrammar or (as some psychoanalysts argue) our fundamental psychological patterns, or as culturally determined, or as a mixture of all these. Indeed, if a combination of biopsychological and cultural layering makes up what Freud called the unconscious, then the late romances are among those works that draw most deeply on what that often contentious term stands for. That is, of course, why we call them "great"– not because they are somehow "universal," above the material or psychological details of our histories – but because they are deeply embedded in those histories and have consequently been read in intriguingly different ways.

In her discussion of the loss of Catholicism in post-Reformation England, Frances Dolan sees Hermione as representing the "vanishing Catholic" and "mourns" that loss in the context of what she also sees as the "vanishing feminist" today. Perhaps naively, I see her views as too pessimistic. When Dolan advocates "seek[ing] out ... feminism's new manifestations," my view is that the ending of the play points precisely in such directions.[39] The conclusion of *The Winter's Tale* directs us back to the

---

[39] Dolan, "Hermione's Ghost," 229, 231.

ending of *All's Well*. In both, the Virgin plays a major transformative role. The final "story," which establishes the "wonder" of the ending is, as in so many Shakespeare plays, that of the theater itself. The culmination is a deliberately staged, self-consciously theatrical moment. Shakespeare draws attention not just to the magic of Helena's or Hermione's resurrection but that of his own art. What the statue scene enacts is the craft of the dramatist in articulating those stories and drawing them out in our experience of the play. "Is there no exorcist / Beguiles the truer office of mine eyes? / Is't real I see?" (v. iii. 298–300), says the King of France of Helena. Or as Leontes affirms here, if this is magic, it should become as "lawfull as eating" (v. iii. 111). That magic is, increasingly, why modern critics have seen *The Winter's Tale* as one of Shakespeare's great plays – and as evidence for not the disappearance but the traces and transformation of the Virgin into early modern culture.

CHAPTER 8

Multiple Madonnas: traces and transformations in the seventeenth century

In this chapter, at least at first, I turn back to "history," to Sidney's "truth of a foolish world," and give what I would hope is a fairly consensual account of the place of the Virgin in the first half of the seventeenth century. Then, as I start to interrogate the period's major poetical figures – Donne, Milton, Herbert, Crashaw – I will become more speculative, preparing for a return at the end of the chapter to a more theoretical re-engagement with questions posed by Kristeva, Beattie, Carroll, and others whom I introduced in my opening chapter, and up to whom I have, on and off, "sidled" throughout the intervening chapters.

In the early 1530s, for most English men and women – the exceptions were largely the small though growing minority of reformers and the strong supporters of the royal supremacy, including Cromwell's growing team of humanist bureaucrats – the central beliefs and devotional practices of the late medieval Church must have been a seemingly permanent reality, with the place of the Virgin inextricably engrained in the ideological assumptions and practices of their lives. But we have now moved on three or more generations, through what I have termed the "century of iconoclasm." Insofar as there is a consensus among modern historians, it is that following the upheavals of the 1530s and Henry's decision to pursue independence from Rome, the Reformation in England was not one momentous change but a series of mainly small, often unremarkable, events that cumulatively constituted a major cultural revolution. Beattie's claim of the Virgin's eradication "from Protestant consciousness" is slightly extreme, but there is unquestionably what MacCulloch terms a "general Protestant silence falling over Mary."[1] Except where the level of polemic becomes shrill, among Protestants she is revered because she is the savior's mother – not for any inherent qualities and certainly not for the highly visceral, sexualized projection of her body as the center of theology and devotion that the

---

[1] Beattie, *Eve's Pilgrimage*, 138; MacCulloch, "Mary and Sixteenth-Century Protestants," 213.

181

reformers perceived in medieval Mariological devotion or when they looked across at what they saw as the excesses of Catholic Europe. In a parallel development in Lutheran Germany, Bridget Heal sees her gradual transformation from "divine intercessor" to exemplary "humble *Hausmutter*."[2] The dominant Protestant image of Mary is the dutiful wife and self-effacing mother, unambiguously subordinate to her son; she is pared down to the largely silent figure the reformers perceived in the Scriptures and which, as they saw it, had blasphemously and superstitiously been distorted in medieval theology and popular devotion. Her presence is spiritual rather than physical, her body less central to thought and devotion than her spiritual significance.

In England, in what only gradually became a predominantly Protestant society, what had been the universally available, local, material manifestations of the Virgin's presence and power – shrines, chapels, statues, "images" of many kinds – were, except among a dwindling though tenacious minority, treated with hostility, derision or, after the initial phase of destruction, simply neglect or embarrassment. Shrines such as Walsingham and Woolpit, Willesden, Penrhys or Ipswich faded into ruins or else were appropriated and used to reward supporters of the Reformation. The rich tradition of legend, tales, and stories of the Virgin's miracles and interventions into human affairs was ridiculed and such stories were gradually reduced, as Alexandra Walsham puts it, to "merely ... foolish 'dotages,'" especially of women, eventually to attract some interest, in a "mixture of anti-Catholic prejudice, nostalgia, and condescension" from the antiquarians and folklorists of the eighteenth and nineteenth centuries.[3]

Holy wells, which we have seen were frequently associated with Marian shrines such as those at Woolpit or Walsingham, provide a case in point. Most gradually evolved into "wishing wells," and were adapted to local folktales and leisure activities such as "taking the waters." As Walsham notes, "holy wells and healing springs may have as much [as ruins] to tell us about how England became a Protestant nation": in her study of early modern fountains, Hester Lees-Jeffries notes that although wells and springs become "reinvented by medicine and science," they do retain a vague, sometimes nostalgic, sense of religious significance, often politicized as "vital signs of God's grace and favour towards the English people." She shows how as early as Spenser's *Faerie Queene* in the 1590s, wells and fountains were already being adapted to a nationalistic providentialism – though something of the older associations between fountains and

[2] Heal, *Cult of the Virgin Mary*, 109.
[3] Walsham, "The Reformation and 'The Disenchantment of the World'," 520.

eroticized women figures is retained, although largely negatively, in the Bower of Bliss, which is described by Spenser with a strong dose of Protestant disapproval of the Catholic idolization of the female. The displays of the fountain nymphs as Guyon approaches the center of the Bower are part of the idolatrous provocation offered to Spenser's Knight of Temperance, who then, very intemperately, proceeds to destroy the whole Bower in the way that many fountains were destroyed, blocked, or simply adapted to local folklore. Stories of miraculous cures at holy wells may have continued in Catholic Europe, but in England such beliefs were mocked as superstitious, as by Barnabe Rich in 1610, who sarcastically observed that the stories of miraculous cures would more than rival the tall tales of Mandeville's medieval accounts of strange and amazing monsters encountered in foreign travels.[4]

The two main Walsingham wells, for example, were not ruined or filled in – another, just outside the walls of the priory, was filled with rubbish and not unblocked until the revival of the shrine in the twentieth century[5] – but remained as part of the estate, and gradually became simply decorative attractions rather than miraculous manifestations of the Virgin's power. By the nineteenth century, it could be proclaimed that the wells had been known as "Wishing Wells" from "time immemorial." Some degree of ritual did remain. Petitioners would kneel on a stone between the two wells and "plunge one hand in each well," so that the water reached their wrists, and all the while, they might "wish for anything" they desired. After making the wish, petitioners must "drink as much of the water of the wells as may be held in the hollow" of their hands. Secrecy was of the utmost importance: "if he never tells his wish to any other – never utters it aloud, even to himself" – within a year the wish would come true.[6]

It is easy to look ahead from the religious turbulence of the Reformation era to later centuries toward such accounts and understand how Regina Mara Schwartz can speak of the "loss of mystery" and "the dawn of secularism,"[7] a process incorporating the transference of the medieval religious rituals to "superstitious" or quaintly primitive folk practices. In protestantized England, visiting wishing wells had certainly, by the eighteenth-century's rediscovery of the medieval, taken on the cast of an exercise in nostalgia, an excursion for the well-to-do country families of Jane

---

[4] Walsham, "Reforming the Waters," 229; Lees-Jeffries, *England's Helicon*, 146–7, 148, 152–3.
[5] Lee-Warner, "The Walsingham 'Wishing Wells'," 51–5.
[6] Glyde, *The Norfolk Garland*, 74–5; Walsham, "Reforming the Waters," 255.
[7] Schwartz, *Sacramental Poetics*, 29.

Austen's novels, with ruins and abbeys to provide a mannered backdrop for them to act out their anxieties over property acquisition and vacant country livings. There would be no need to make reference to the Virgin, except in a patronizing tone dismissing the primitive though charming superstitions of the past, as is the case in Agnes Strickland's romantic novel, *The Pilgrims of Walsingham* (1834), in which a court party of Henry VIII, Queen Catherine, Wolsey, Ann Boleyn, Thomas Wyatt, and others make their way through four hundred lugubrious pages to the Virgin's shrine, where they partake of the excitement of the wishing wells. In the later revival of the wells, there are still sexualized echoes in the obvious eroticization of the instructions at Walsingham: kneeling before them, plunging into them, expressing one's desire, drinking from them, and then maintaining secrecy. Wells remain rooted in the strong associations of women and water, a commonplace in classical as well as Christian mythologies, and in the long-standing patriarchal observation of women as unstable, fluid, and (as Theweleit's analysis of male fantasies makes clear) associated, at least in the male imaginary, with some absolute origin, some vast and primeval maternal interior.[8] But there are no extravagant public vows to the Virgin, no ex-votos or offerings, even though the year's wait for a wish to be fulfilled is perhaps not unrelated to the purgatorial waiting time before achieving "heaven." Walsham suggests that such sites "were slowly desacralized and reconsecrated to leisure,"[9] but the religio-magical aura continues quietly though it is more associated with individual experience rather than a sacred community. If we can still see the echoes of a magical universe, it is no longer presided over by the Virgin, let alone triumphantly embodied in her.

But the onset of the "dawn of secularism" in the mid seventeenth century should not be over-simplified. Set in a European-wide context, the Virgin certainly does not, of course, disappear, either in the seventeenth century or later. Indeed, the surging Counter-Reformation, in Europe and increasingly in the Hispanic Americas and parts of Asia, intensified her role in Catholic theology and devotion. The cult of the Virgin became "the chief symbol and agency of Counter-Reformation renewal," MacCulloch notes. Despite some careful attention at the Council of Trent to what were described as misunderstandings of core Catholic beliefs and practices, the Catholic Church allowed and at times encouraged a militant Marianism that included many of the aspects of popular religion that Protestants found so objectionable. A typical Catholic formulation was that "we have resolved to

---

[8] Theweleit, *Male Fantasies*, 1. 185, 241. For an analysis of Strickland, see Waller, *Walsingham*, ch. 6.
[9] Walsham, "Reforming the Waters," 245.

particularly honor the Virgin, seeing that the heretics defame her and destroy her images."[10] St. John Eudes, founder of the Society of the Heart of the Mother Most Admirable and influential in the establishment of the feast of the Holy Heart of Mary in 1648, envisaged the Virgin looking down, as Queen of Heaven, at the "numberless multitude and frightful enormity" of heretics and blasphemers who had rejected her: "She sees this earth of ours which should be a paradise . . . yet it is filled with innumerable atheists and blasphemers making every effort to exterminate the Holy Church," who "blaspheme . . . without ceasing, even more than the devils and the damned in hell. For the devils, being deprived of liberty, cannot add to their sins, whereas living sinners heap crime on crime, impiety on impiety, murder upon murder, abomination upon abomination." The Virgin, "our heavenly Mother," is "Queen of Heaven and earth, and God has given her sovereign power over all created things; therefore she would not lack the power, if such were her will, to avenge most justly the many atrocious insults offered by men to their God and Savior."[11]

The late sixteenth and seventeenth centuries in Catholic Europe see an extraordinary flowering of Baroque art, poetry, devotional tracts, and music. In part this was at least an inadvertent outcome of the Council of Trent. In authorizing an aggressive defence of the Virgin that differentiated the Catholic Church from Protestantism and the emerging world of rationalism and enlightenment, Trent's first session, in 1546, affirmed the importance of the unwritten traditions of the Church as authoritative in establishing doctrine and practice. As Haskins points out, this decree gives, "though not explicitly, canonical authority to traditional beliefs such as the tales and miracles that had informed the figure of Mary." Protestant theologians had a far more cautious understanding of Christian "tradition," typically limiting its authority to the decrees of the first few Councils of the Church, or even to their own readings of Scripture, and rejected any more widely ranging sense of the *consensus fidei*, especially any acceptance of popular beliefs, tales, legends, and folk traditions. The basis of popular Marian religion in desire, wish-fulfillment, and fictions was implicitly validated by Trent's valorization of tradition, and the rich tradition of Marian "story" continued to be a core part of what Andrew Greeley terms the Catholic as opposed to the Protestant imagination.[12]

[10] MacCulloch, "Mary and Sixteenth-Century Protestants," 214–15.
[11] Eudes, *Admirable Heart of Mary*, 140–1.
[12] Haskins, *Who is Mary?* 35; Carroll, *American Catholics in the Protestant Imagination*, 163–8; Greeley, *Catholic Imagination*. For an extended discussion of this later period in relation to Walsingham, see Janes and Waller, *Walsingham* chs. 5, 6, 9, 10, 15.

As part of its intensification of Marianism, the Counter-Reformation sees the emergence of what is in effect a new theological genre, the Mariological treatise, its development also in part motivated by Protestant attacks on the Virgin. Early examples include Peter Canisius's *De Maria Virgine Incomparabili* (1577), and Counter-Reformation Mariological theology culminates, Boss argues, in the work of the Spanish Jesuit Frederico Suárez (1548–1617), who sees the Virgin as the embodiment of the unique relationship between God and the creation. Mary "stands for creation in what is supposed to be its right relationship with the Creator"; she is "humanity's final destination," showing how a human may be "joined to God in the most complete manner possible." The Incarnation holds out the hope that it "is always within the grasp of a man or a woman to increase in merit and come nearer to perfection," and that the whole material universe is a creative, mothering embodiment of God's divine creativity. On a more popular level, despite Trent's cautions, Mary continues to be portrayed according to local preferences of female form and fashion, as she had been in pre-Tridentine art. In 1652, José de Jesús Maria provided a description of the Virgin's features that reflects a sentimentalized amalgam of the dominant features of Renaissance portraiture, not unrelated to many of the clichés of Petrarchism: she is of average height, is "perfectly proportioned," has blonde hair, green eyes, with curved eyebrows, a long nose, soft red lips, white and even teeth, a long, pale pink face, neither too round or sharp.[13]

A number of Catholic women wrote lives of the Virgin as part of this Counter-Reformation response to Protestant attacks on Mary, including the distinguished Petrarchan poet Vittoria Colonna and two later women writers influenced by the Counter-Reformation, Chiara Mattraini and Lucrezia Marinella. Their varied emphasis shows the confidence and the variety of Madonnas that were encouraged by Trent and as part of the counter-propaganda directed against the reduced Mariology of the Reformation: Colonna's earthy early sixteenth-century life is a product of the Catholic "new learning," sparse, mainly scriptural, Christocentric; the others, written well into the period of the post-Tridentine offensive, more imaginatively, even flamboyantly, incorporate legend and speculative tales, and also direct their focus to issues reinforcing women's interests and powers, presenting a view of Mary as a powerful romance heroine, working miracles and marvels.[14]

As part of this "message of resistance against Protestant iconoclasm," accounts of the Virgin's spectacular apparitions and miracles multiplied, as

---

[13] Boss, "Francisco Suárez and Modern Mariology," 260–1; Johnson, "Mary in Early Modern Europe," 370.
[14] Haskins, *Who is Mary?* 2–4.

did replicas of the Holy House. Walsingham's sister (or rival) shrine in the fifteenth century, that of Our Lady of Loreto's miraculously transported *casa sacra*, became the object of enthusiastic papal approval and attracted increasing numbers of pilgrims. Orazio Torsellino's *History of our Lady of Loreto* (translated into English in 1608) assured the faithful that contrary to the assertions of iconoclastic heretics, the "great miracles" and "rare wonders," the curing of diseases and even the revival of the dead – miracles which less than a century before had been attributed to Walsingham and celebrated in the Pynson Ballad – were triumphantly continuing.[15] In 1657, the German Jesuit Wilhelm Gumppenberg published the *Atlas Marianus*, a collection, with copious illustrations, of over 1,200 Marian pilgrimage sites, with detailed descriptions of over one hundred, headed by Loreto. Frequently revised, it included stories of apparitions and miracles by the Virgin, and its multiple editions were adapted to highlight shrines in different countries.[16] It lists examples of a newly militaristic militant Virgin, intervening (as at the Battle of Lepanto in 1571) to defeat the infidels from the East. A few examples in England are listed, including the statue of Our Lady of Tewkesbury which "survived all the fury of the heretics" during the upsurge of Protestantism, and in 1625 chose the moment to retaliate against further attempted desecration by causing an impious Protestant who tried to destroy it to throw himself, "in a state of frenzy," into a well to his death.[17]

For Catholics living in England, however, the "disappearance" of the Virgin was more, indeed, immediately apparent and painful. Catholic worship and devotion were largely driven underground. Catholic propagandists attacked the reformed services in part because of their excision of the Virgin: the Jesuit William Bishop clashed with the Calvinist William Perkins over Mary's role in salvation, and scorned "the poore short prayers" of the Church of England as "a certayne mingle-mangle, translated out of the old portaise and Masse book, patched up with some fewe of their own inventions," and "backward in his blessed Mother the holy Virgins praises."[18] Those who wished to remain faithful to the Catholic Church were largely left to pursue their piety privately, with their rosaries, hopes, and memories. There were a few permitted Catholic sanctuaries at court that provided occasional and (for most Protestants) highly suspicious

[15] Ellington, *From Sacred Body to Angelic Soul*; Torsellino, *Lady of Loreto*. For Loreto, see also Phillips, *Loreto and the Holy House*.
[16] Gumppenberg, *Atlas Marianus centuriis explicantur*.
[17] Waterton, *Pietas Mariana Britannica*, II, 147.
[18] Patterson, "William Perkins versus William Bishop," 256.

opportunities for Catholic worship, such as the chapel of Charles I's queen, Henrietta Maria, or the residences of Catholic ambassadors.

As Barry Spurr's survey of Marian poetry shows, immediately following the spectacular burst of Southwell's poems in the 1590s, the Virgin continues to appear in a number of poems by Catholics, but in England, even in Catholic texts, she tends to be portrayed as a model of virtuous behavior, deserving reverence for her spiritual qualities. Ben Jonson's moving tribute to his daughter, who died as an infant, stands out for its quiet, moving evocation of the Virgin's traditional roles:

> Here lyes to each her parents' ruth,
> Mary, the daughter of their youth:
> Yet, all heauen's gifts, being heauen's due,
> It makes the father, lesse, to rue.
> At sixe moneths end, shee parted hence
> With safetie of her innocence;
> Whose soule heauens Queene, (whose name shee beares)
> In comfort of her mothers teares,
> Hath plac'd amongst her virgin-traine:
> Where, while that seuer'd doth remaine,
> This graue partakes the fleshly birth,
> Which couer lightly, gentle earth.[19]

English Protestants may have been instructed by their Calvinist theologians not to consider their departed love ones as being in Heaven (or Hell) but waiting for the final resurrection; the older, Catholic view of being able to communicate with or at least join (with or without a notion of Purgatory, which like the Virgin's intercessory capacities only slowly faded in English popular religion) was a more consoling view and in this poem by an occasional in-and-out Catholic, it narrates a story of grief, caring, and hope that the infant Mary is welcomed by her heavenly namesake.[20]

However, the second decade of the new century, now a hundred years after the Dissolution, sees a gradual revival of Marian presence in the English Church in the increasingly influential Laudian or "High Church" movement. In 1639, English Catholics were still hopeful of a reunion between the Church of England and Rome, despite the widespread anti-papal feelings and growing hostility to the monarchy. Mary Ward, the founder of an order of sisters and schools for Catholics on the continent, returned to England, looking to continue her work in London – but

---

[19] Jonson, *Works*, VIII, 33–4. For a brief discussion of other Marian references in Jonson's poems see Spurr, *See the Virgin Blest*, 97–9.
[20] For post-Reformation beliefs about death and dying, see Marshall, *Beliefs and the Dead*.

eventually retreated to Yorkshire where, after the victories of the parliamentarians, she died in 1645.[21] A high point of this optimistic period is the Anglican Anthony Stafford's ebullient book *The Femall Glory* (1638). "I professe that I am her admirer, not her Idolator," he writes, and "I believe the under-valuing of one of so Great, and Deare in Christ's Esteeme, cannot but to be displeasing to Him." He attacks the French Jesuit Justus Lipsius for asserting that as much grace proceeds from Mary's milk as from Christ's blood – as, it will be recalled, though far more virulently, had William Crashaw and other reformers – but once a few theological niceties designed to distance his views from papistry are established, Stafford's praises are indistinguishable from Counter-Reformation praise. He sees Mary as the peak of creation, a "Transcendent Creature," with a place above "any of her sexe," and not a "Meere Woman." They include an intense focus on the visual, the sensual, and the combination of intense physicality and highest spirituality:

Her Breasts white as their owne Milke, pressed by her delicate fingers, as white as either, he softly pats, and playes with. Sometimes He repaires to them for sport, sometimes for necessity; and He who feeds all things else, draws thence His nourishment.[22]

Other treatises such as Austin's *Haec Homo* (1637) show, Graham Parry argues, that in some Anglican circles, "there was an emergent enlargement of the doctrinal and emotional range of devotion" that would open the way for the Virgin Mary as a figure to be more honored and admired than in earlier stages of the Reformation.[23] In the early 1640s, however, the Laudian reforms were swept away in the resurgence of republican Protestantism, the establishment of anti-episcopal legislation in 1643 and 1644, and culminating in the execution of the king in 1649. The century of iconoclasm had been but slumbering. Toleration of a wide variety of Christian dominations was proclaimed – but predictably excluded were Catholics and Anglicans, along with more extreme Protestant sectaries such as Quakers. By 1646, Presbyterianism was the official religion of England, and the Virgin was firmly and officially marginalized.

I turn now to English poetry of the period, where we see the Virgin's transformations and contradictory roles, and where her emergence and transformations are multiple, varied, and show how many of the poets at least were exploring the stories beneath the theological confrontations.

[21] Littlehales, *Mary Ward*, chapters 27, 28.   [22] Stafford *Femall Glory* (1869), cxxvi, 168, lxxxvi, xv, 114.
[23] Parry, *Glory, Laud, and Honour*, 129; Stafford, *Femall Glory*.

As I noted in discussing Steinberg's analysis of late medieval and Renaissance artists in relation to orthodox medieval theology, it was the theologians who tried to enforce a rigid indoctrination upon the rapidly changing culture; it was the poets who pulled them back, providing points of growth and alternate modes of thought and feeling.[24]

In modern overviews of English poetry of the seventeenth century, the tolling of the bell for Petrarchism in England is conventionally attributed to John Donne. Donne is also widely seen as a major contributor, at least in English poetry, to what Anthony Low terms "the 'reinvention of love,' from something essentially social and feudal to something essentially private and modern."[25] Yet however much admirers (or idolizers) of Donne would wish to agree, it is difficult to generalize about any consistent philosophy of love from Donne's career or writings. In his long period of apparent repentance for the extremes of his early life, Donne repeatedly calls his period of erotic love poems his "idolatry," a term he also used to refer to his earlier veneration of his wife, and in one of his marriage sermons he warns that "there is not a more uncomely" or "poorer thing, then to love a Wife like a Mistresse."[26]

More theologically aware than Sidney or Ralegh, for Donne the fusion of religion and sexuality was a never-ending preoccupation. Donne's direct references to the Virgin in the poems are generally cautious, except for the striking reference in "Good Friday, 1613: Riding Westwards," where she is accorded, at least on a plausible reading, the role of co-redemptrix that was characteristic of Catholic devotion, if not yet doctrine: she, the "miserable mother," is described as "God's partner here, and furnished thus / Half of that sacrifice, which ransomed us." As Spurr points out, however, the lines can be read simply as indicating that Mary was a cooperative participant in the Incarnation, but Donne's characteristic enthusiasm for the female certainly moves the reference toward the Catholic devotions from which he was attempting to separate himself.[27] Growing up as a Catholic, Donne may well have muted his devotion to the Virgin as he struggled to find a place at court, and projected those residual feelings upon not simply his lovers, real or fictional, but a series of aristocratic women patrons, including Lucy Countess of Bedford and Magdalene Herbert, as gracious and influential Protestant worldly equivalents to the Virgin.[28]

[24] Steinberg, *Sexuality of Christ*, 110.   [25] Low, *Reinvention of Love*, 33.
[26] Donne, *Complete English Poems*, 306, 314; *Sermons*, II, 345.
[27] Donne, *Complete English Poems*, 330; Spurr, *See the Virgin Blest*, 92–3.
[28] See the forthcoming study by Chapman, *Early Modern Patrons*.

In his two "Anniversary" poems, written to commemorate the death of the young child Elizabeth Drury, Donne projects something of being caught between these two worlds, clearly using the commission to honor an otherwise insignificant child in ways similar, although on a far less ambitious level, to Dante's Beatrice and Petrarch's Laura. He consoles the bereft parents that marriage and motherhood may not always be God's will for the virtuous Protestant daughter, and assures them that virginity had once had a valorized role in salvation. Maureen Sabine argues that behind the poems Donne is wrestling with his childhood reverence for the Virgin, that he writes not merely for income but is using the poems for working through to a more immanentalist view of what Mary had once represented for him and his family. A seemingly public tribute, the poems contain "retrospective veneration" for the Virgin. But if the poems were what Sabine calls "work of reluctant iconoclasm,"[29] what is destroyed is not so much of his former faith as the insights of his own greatest poems.

But there is more to be said about Donne and the Virgin than such explicit and disappointingly reactionary references. The Dissolution and the burning of Our Lady of Walsingham and her sisters in 1538 itself was by now two generations past, and is not mentioned by Donne: any nostalgia for a lost universe was no doubt soberly tempered by the persecution of his Catholic family, and outweighed by his desire for employment, which meant, whether willingly or not, expressing loyalty to the Jacobean Protestant authorities. Walton's life of Donne, written half a century after his death, claims that he had a painting of the Virgin in his study; he certainly possessed or had read a number of Counter-Reformation Mariologists, and even though he denounced the Catholic belief in Mary's intercessory role in some of his sermons, there is a recurring and often wistful Mariological strain that surfaces in his writings. In the absence of the Virgin, what George Klawitter calls Donne's perpetual "wrestling with the idea of 'woman' in general as mediatrix, and with women as individual embodiments of salvation" becomes a recurring theme of his love poems.[30]

In some of Donne's poems, however, it must be admitted that such an obsession turns into mere compliment or misogynic denigration, as if in embarrassed bravado for having momentarily taken the "centrique part" of a woman (what, it will be recalled, Erasmus referred to coyly as the Virgin's "pryvytes") too seriously. In some of his more masculinistic squibs, and

---

[29] Sabine, *Feminine Engendered Faith*, 19, 37–8, 85, 104.
[30] Klawitter, "John Donne's Attitude toward the Virgin Mary," 131.

often explicitly later in his life in his sermons, Donne falls back on the long misogynic tradition of viewing women's bodies as dangerous to the fragile male ego and therefore requiring ordering. Elizabeth Hodgson has pointed to the recurring pattern of Woman as mother, daughter, and bride as animating Donne's work, all aspects of the orthodox image of the Virgin, and a structure by which he could keep the threatening aspects of women at bay and by which he could (ironically, like a good Petrarchan) try to construct a stable masculine self.[31] Apart from the "idolatry" of some of his early love poems, to adapt Beattie's critique of the dominant masculinist theological tradition, Donne "never accommodated the fertile, sexual, bleeding female body into [his] symbolic life."[32] There is a more disturbing misogynic strand in his later writings that even his greatest admirers should not overlook. He can wittily attack religious communities and dedication to celibacy: "When God had made *Adam* and *Eve* in Paradise," he "did not place *Adam* in a Monastery on one side, and *Eve* in a Nunnery on the other."[33] Yet his consistent emphasis as a preacher was on the threatening and finally corrupting power of women's sexuality, which needed constant disciplining: "shee sinned, we bear" is the stark observation in the "Metempsychosis" section of "The Progress of the Soul." H. L. Meakin comments that Donne is not only diminishing the role of the Virgin, but is retaining the "especially negative view of Eve, proportional to the Catholic faith's positive view of Mary, yet out of all proportion when she is left standing alone in the Protestant landscape."[34]

Yet in what, perhaps sentimentally, we still might see as his core love poems, he postulates a transcendent and equal love – what Schwartz describes as spaces of "most exquisite intimacy"[35] – that loses sight of gender differences as it triumphantly separates itself from lesser loves, moving away from the "dull sublunary love, whose soul is sense" ("A Valediction, forbidding Mourning") to a love in which the two are merged, "One neutral thing both sexes fit" ("The Canonization").[36] A handful of poems, so this argument goes – "The Anniversary," "Air and Angels," "Love's Growth," "The Canonization," "The Relique," for instance – celebrates what in one of his holy sonnets he calls the "holy thirsty dropsy"[37] of relational love where he wants passionately for that which has been accorded in the past to the Virgin now to become embodied in the wonderment of the flesh. The

---

[31] Hodgson, *Gender and the Sacred Self*, 164.   [32] Beattie, *Woman*, 118–19.
[33] Donne, *Sermons*, III, 242.
[34] Donne, *Complete English Poems*, 180; Meakin, *Articulations of the Feminine*, 178.
[35] Schwartz, *Sacramental Poetics*, 79.   [36] Donne, *Complete English Poems*, 47–8, 84–5.   [37] *Ibid.*, 316.

unacknowledged (and perhaps unacknowledgable) adoration of the Virgin becomes transformed, immanentalized, as a striking part of Donne's passion. Wonder strikes the lover and, instead of (or often as well as) being derided, is shared. Much as Erasmus did with the veneration of the Virgin's milk at Walsingham, even in late Elizabethan England, with its long suspicion of idolatry, Donne can play breezily with the mutual sainthood of lovers, half mocking the concept but also taking it very seriously as a discourse to try to capture some of the wonderment of love and articulate the uniqueness as "saints" of love in a world where sainthood has lost its intercessory powers:

> . . . by these hymns, all shall approve
> Us canonized for love ;
>
> And thus invoke us, "You, whom reverend love
> Made one another's hermitage ;
> You, to whom love was peace, that now is rage ;
> Who did the whole world's soul contract, and drove
>   Into the glasses of your eyes;
>   (So made such mirrors, and such spies,
> That they did all to you epitomize)
>   Countries, towns, courts: beg from above
>   A pattern of your love![38]

Through the fond, almost Erasmian satire, comes a wistful need to replace the lost saints, and in particular to replace the faded glory of a revered woman. In this poem, whether it is bravado or theology or (in Donne's case, most likely a combination of both), it is not the absence of sexuality but the power of its expression that becomes the chief criterion for sainthood. As Grace Jantzen quips, in these poems, "it is not for abstinence" that sainthood will "be accorded, but for sexual pleasure and prowess."[39] While it is by no means a consistent note, if we look at the whole of his career and writings, in these poems Donne is unquestionably looking to sexuality not as associated with the untrustworthiness, monstrosity, and death-drive of traditional misogyny (as occurs in so many of his later sermons on sexuality and the body), but with wonder.

The "sentimental" reading of Donne associates these poems celebrating the "way of affirmation," to use Charles Williams's phrase, with Donne's marriage.[40] Thomas Hester suggests that Anne More functioned not only as a "sacralizing power" to transform mundane existence by connecting him to sacred space and time, but their life together was itself "the sacralizing force"

[38] *Ibid.*, 48.   [39] Jantzen, "Canonized for Love," 185.   [40] Williams, *Figure of Beatrice*, 11.

that transformed his cosmos. For the later Donne, especially after the death of his wife, such radical immanentalism becomes seen as idolatry. But in his early life, and certainly in these poems, it was an error to which he had been wholeheartedly committed. Especially important is the intensity with which he sees sexual love as the source of infinity in the present moment – his "desire of" (in a wonderful pun on his wife's family name) "more," and not just as sacramental but as redemptive and transformative – but rather as the source of "wonder." As Sabine notes, if for Protestants marriage was no longer an official sacrament, "the corpus *mysticum* survived, concealed in lovers' bedrooms, sexed bodies, and amorous sonnets." From this perspective, as Sabine contends – and as Donne's later contradictions all too readily illustrate – if "death brings our personal loving to an end, it may mean the death of God as well."[41]

Donne's contradictions are therefore not merely idiosyncratic, or part of a process of one man growing old, but point to broader contradictions in English society about the place of the Virgin and female experience generally, and to the multiplicity or "splitting" of the Virgin in an increasingly diverse culture. As Spurr points out, ironically it was the eventually unrepentant Puritan John Milton who perhaps best summed up the feeling of the Church of England in the late 1620s in his ode "On the Morning of Christ's Nativity." Unambiguously Christocentric, Milton has the Virgin respectfully in the background. Mary is acknowledged at the opening: the babe is "Of wedded Maid, and Virgin Mother born," but then she fades until the final stanza when she resumes her function of dutiful caregiver: "But see! The Virgin blest / Hath laid her babe to rest." Although Nature is evoked throughout the poem, there is no sense whatsoever that the Virgin is identified with, let alone the high point of, Creation. Alison Chapman argues that among Milton's many early flirtations with the surface of Catholicism, specifically here the idea of canonization, is his *Arcades* (1632?), in effect a draft of what becomes *Comus* (1634), and performed at Harefield, north-west of London, in honor of the Countess of Derby, who forty years earlier had been addressed by another Protestant poet, Edmund Spenser, as Amaryllis in *Colin Clouts Come Home Again*. Chapman argues that Milton's hagiographic and Petrarchan language (the countess is described as a "deity," a "goddess bright," who lives in a "shrine") is intended, as with Donne and his patronesses, to make "the Lady of this place" the Protestant alternative to the Virgin commemorated in the title of

[41] Hester, *Donne's "Desire of More"*; Sabine, "No Marriage in Heaven," 236; Malpezzi, "Love's Liquidity in 'Since She Whome I Lovd'," 249.

the Mary the Virgin Church in Harefield where the countess's impressive tomb can be found. Miltonic reticence toward the Virgin, however, hardens into hostility in *Paradise Lost*, where in his seduction of Eve Satan uses phrases that Milton parodies from Marian hymns, thereby implying an attack on Catholic idolatry.[42]

Also contemplating the Virgin in similar terms to Milton in the seemingly calm 1630s was George Herbert, who plays with Mary's name in an anagram, which is little more than a trivial verbal doodle – "How well her name an ARMY doth present / In whom the Lord of Hosts did pitch his tent" – but who wrestled with some of the wider cultural contradictions that were emerging in English life in the 1630s in a rich poetical meditation in which he surveys the court of Heaven, and wishes he was permitted to "addresse / My vows to thee most gladly, Blessed Maid, / And Mother of my God." Herbert tentatively, at a courtly and almost envious distance, praises the Virgin in traditional devotional terms, as if acknowledging their sensual power over him but knowing that they are, sadly, forbidden. Mary is "the holy mine, whence came the gold, / The great restorative … the cabinet where the jewell lay." But he cannot "unfold" himself to her

> But now, alas, I dare not; for our King,
> Whom we do all joyntly adore and praise,
> Bids no such thing.[43]

Yet he acknowledges that others – obviously enough, Catholics – do so; those who, like Herbert himself, "do not so" may perhaps nonetheless take vicarious advantage of that forbidden but tempting devotion. How could that be, however? Does he imply that he envisages Mary's intercessory prayers for him being effective? The poem is generally read as a rejection of Mariolatry, but the wistful concession at the end with its rich interplay of courtesy, negotiation, and ambiguity opens up a place for the increasing nostalgia for the magical world that Herbert's Church has partly abandoned. As Bishop George Bull put it a little later in the century, good Protestants should affirm that the Virgin "was more blessed by conceiving Christ in her heart by faith, than conceiving him in her womb," a view shared with the Protestant poet, Aemilia Lanyer.[44] Rowan Williams observes, with perhaps a little contemporary wish-fulfillment (not least perhaps because he is Archbishop of Canterbury in an Anglican Church never free from controversy and contradiction) that Herbert's poem is not

---

[42] Gardiner, "Miltan's Parodies of Catholic Hymns"; Milton, *Poems*, 156–61. I owe the general reminder not to neglect Milton in this context to Alison Chapman. See, "Milton's Genii Loci," "Milton's Nuns."
[43] Herbert, *Works of George Herbert*, 77.   [44] Bull, *Works*, 1, 110–12; Lanyer, "Salve Deus," pt. 4.

"the sad or wistful expression of a rather shrunken Protestant spirituality," but rather is playfully transgressive: "he is deliberately courting the forbidden, celebrating it by saying he cannot, and then rather impudently suggesting at the end that he might yet 'disburse' – as of course he has just done in the poem."[45]

No such coyness distracts Richard Crashaw, the son of one of the period's most forthright anti-papist propagandists. Although Crashaw left England and the Anglican Church for Rome and died as a canon of Loreto, most of his Marian poetry was written while he was still in England. His poetry marks a high point in English post-Reformation poetry on the Virgin, both returning to the extravagances of pre-Reformation devotion and at the same time pointing to the cultural fragility of the world he is attempting to evoke. The Virgin and other female figures, including Mary Magdalen and St. Teresa, are as powerful presences in Crashaw's verse as they had been in devotional verse before the Reformation.

Susannah Mintz justly warns that just because "Crashaw made women the primary subjects of his religious verse," "it is not enough to claim repetition as valorization." Crashaw's repeated celebrations of the Virgin have traditionally been termed excessive, extravagant, vulgar, shocking, eccentric, undecorous, and unEnglish.[46] As Fellow of Peterhouse and curate at Little St. Mary's in Cambridge, where one of his admirers termed him "chaplaine of the virgine myld," who "lived to dye / In th'virgines lappe," he was accused by Puritan investigators of superstition and idolatry, and on the feast of the Annunciation "credibly reported to have turned himselfe to a picture of the Virgine Mary and to have used these words *Hanc adoramus, colamus hanc.*"[47] His devotional extravagance and the intensely sexualized metaphors go back unabashedly to medieval gynotheology, but they also betray Crashaw's increasing sense of aloneness in the English Church and the resurgence of the iconoclasts as the Civil War approached. His anxiety – again, not simply a personal idiosyncrasy – spills over in the repetitive urgency of his poems, as if affirmations of loyalty and admiration of the Virgin need to be repeated as vehemently as possible as the iconoclasts close in. Crashaw's most celebrated poem, the hymn to St. Teresa, also establishes the characteristics of his Marian verse: a dynamic level of intensity toppling into anxiety and evocations of

---

[45] Williams, "George Herbert and Henry Vaughan."

[46] Mintz, "Crashavian Mother," 112. For objections to Crashaw, see the summary in Rambuss, "Sacred Subjects and the Aversive Metaphysical Conceit," 497–500, 503, and Spurr, *See the Virgin Blest*, 99–100, 101, 104, 105.

[47] Thomas Car, "Crashawe, the Anagramme," in Crashawe, *Complete Poetry,* 653; Pritchard, "Puritan Charges against Crashaw and Beaumont," 578.

ecstasy, a strong, fetishistic, emphasis on visualizing physical detail, repeated and accelerating excitement, usually involving masochistic exchanges, the interweaving of extremes, including sexuality and death, as well as the familiar Petrarchan paradoxes of fire and water, pleasure and pain, and an attempt to achieve a climax of wonder through the evocation of spectacle. Rambuss terms Crashaw an "incarnationalist," one "prone to converting operations of the soul into spectacles of the body."[48] But the "conversion" is by no means precise: the distinction between physical sensation and spiritualization is blurred, in part deliberately, and in part because Crashaw does not believe or see, finally, that there is a distinction. Is the spiritual immanent in the material? Or does the material become spiritualized by desire or fantasy? Crashaw is characteristically drawn to what Kristeva terms "abjection," experiences that fuse attraction and repulsion for "the desirable and terrifying," especially physical encounters that bring the subject to the blurring of ecstasy and repulsion, and so to the "edge of non-existence and hallucination."[49]

Crashaw especially searches for these extreme experiences through what Netzley terms his "obsessive attention to orifices,"[50] in relation to both a feminized Christ and the female body, whether of St. Teresa, Mary Magdalen or the Virgin herself. As Sabine comments, "the body of Christ and those of his female suppliants are shown to possess mouths, eyes, breasts, wombs, and wounds, and to emit milk, blood, tears, saliva, and feces." Often these liquefactions blend, just as a variety of sexual acts to which the poems refer combine and blur. Bowels discharge, tears rise upward, blend with milk, blood and milk flow together, as in the epigram "Upon the Infant Martyrs":

> To see both blended in one flood
> The Mothers Milke, the Childrens blood,
> Make me doubt if Heaven will gather,
> Roses hence, or *Lillies* rather.[51]

Crashaw's poems specifically on the Virgin include "Hymn in the Assumption" of Mary, which characteristically is an urgent, dramatic blurring of the earthly and heavenly, the natural and supernatural, and is expressed in one paradox after another, reminiscent of both Marian and Petrarchan rhetoric. She, "a peice of heav'nly earth ... must goe home." As she rises through the stars, she "makes a farre more milkey way." Earth

---

[48] Rambuss, "Sacred Subjects," 501.
[49] Kristeva, *Abjection*, 1, 2, 54. Although our emphases differ, I draw in part here from Maureen Sabine's provocative article, "Crashaw and Abjection," 423–43.
[50] Netzley, "Oral Devotion," 248.   [51] Crashaw, *Complete Poetry*, 10.

loses her yet still retains her; heaven is complete and yet lacks her, "so sweet
a Burthen," until she arrives. The whole of nature weeps to lose her but
rejoices in that she takes us with her:

> We in thy prayse will have our parts.
>
> Thy pretious name shall be
> Thy self to us; and we
> With holy care will keep it by us.

We will give her our "sweetness" and she will reciprocate; she is Queen of
Heaven, yet she also remains "mistresse of our song."[52] None of the compar-
isons or conceits are without precedent and the parallels with Petrarchan lyrics
are unmistakable: it is the level of intensity, what Kristeva calls the gathering
together of perversion and beauty, that is so distinctive of Crashaw's response
and contribution to the titillating interplay of sexuality and spirituality that he
takes from the gynotheological edge of medieval and baroque Mariology.[53]

The "Hymn in the Holy Nativity . . . sung as by the Shepheards," makes a
fascinating contrast with Milton's Nativity Ode. The voice of Milton's poem
is restrained, distanced from the physical intimacy of the scene, as if deliberately keeping the reader away from its potential physicality. The Virgin is kept
soberly in the background as nursemaid and caregiver. Crashaw brings us
directly to the intimacy of physical touch and introduces a playfulness, and a
level of public exhibitionism as mother and child display for the shepherds:

> See, see how soon his new-bloom'd CHEEK
>   Twixt's mother's brests is gone to bed.
> Sweet choise, said we! no way but so
>   Not to ly cold, yet sleep in snow.

In Milton, Nature is a demure and decidedly unmagical background; in
Crashaw, it is part of the sensual fulfillment identifying the Mother with
Creation. Both are part of "LOVE's architecture": "The BABE, whose birth
embraves this morn, / Made His own bed e're He was born." With his
fixation on female liquidity and flow, for Crashaw Mary's breasts are "Two
sister-seas of Virgin-Milk," and the child "Warmes in the one, cooles in the
other." Every action is sexualized:

> Shee sings thy Teares asleepe, and dips
>   Her Kisses in thy weeping Eye:
> Shee spreads the red leaves of thy Lips,
>   That in their Buds yet blushing lye.[54]

---

[52] Crashaw, *Complete Poetry*, 115, 117, 119.   [53] Kristeva, *Powers of Horror*, 155.
[54] Crashaw, *Complete Poetry*, 77.

A similar intensification of both the sensual and the specifically sexual occurs in "Sancta Maria Dolorum," Crashaw's expansion of the traditional Stabat Mater hymn. Following medieval precedents, he imagines the Mother experiencing the pains of childbearing (which of course by legend, as in the *Protevangelium*, Mary was spared) during the Crucifixion: "in his woes / And Paines, her Pangs and throes. / Each wound of His, from every Part, / All, more at home in her owne heart." The blend of emotions incorporates pain and pleasure, sexuality and death: "O costly intercourse / Of deaths, and worse," a typical Crashavian note implying a level of unstatable perversity beyond death, which includes a shared pain as the two, Mother and Son:

> Discourse alternate wounds to one another,
> > Quick Deaths that grow
> > And gather, as they come and goe.
> His Nailes write swords in her, which soon her heart
> > Payes back, with more than their own smart ;
> Her Swords, still growing with his pain,
> Turn Speares, and straight come home again.

With such a build-up, the poem's final petition for mutual wounding does not come as a surprise: "O teach those wounds to bleed / In me."[55]

Crashaw's most distinctive Marian poem is the celebrated epigram, written first in Latin and published in 1634, and then made considerably more dramatic in its English version, and published in 1646 as "Blessed be the paps which Thou hast sucked":

> Suppose he had been Tabled at thy Teates,
> > Thy hunger feels not what he eates;
> Hee'l have his Teat e're long (a bloody one)
> The Mother then must suck the Son.[56]

The poem has sometimes been explained away biographically: Sabine sees a progression from a motherless childhood and a grimly authoritarian father – William Crashaw, she comments, would have rolled over in his grave at his son's sentiments – to fusion with a polymorphously sexual Mother Church, represented by the melodramatic picture of Christ as Mother, suckling the Virgin with what is both a "teat" and the side-wound. Biographical reductionism aside, Sabine is right to stress how the poem deliberately provokes a strong response of abjection, as extreme, sexual, and other "perverse" acts are compressed into the image we are asked to "suppose." Crashaw shifts the

---

[55] *Ibid.*, 165, 167.   [56] *Ibid.*, 14.

viewpoint from the relatively ordinary pleasure of a mother or nurse to the Christ Child, to that of becoming a participant in the extremity of poly-morphously perverse devotion that expresses the relationship with the Virgin and her Son. Kimberly Johnson points out that in the later English version of the poem, Crashaw chooses language, notably "suck" for the Latin "*bibet*," that takes it "outside the sacramental system" of the original Latin epigram, and forces upon the reader images that are so "resolutely physical that it is perhaps only possible to imagine the scene visually."[57] The poem is reaching to encompass as much sexual and bodily extremity as possible and to fuse that not just into the spiritual but *as* the spiritual. Each detail is chosen precisely for its evocation of extremity. But the effect – even if the criticisms of tastelessness or repulsiveness are set aside as instances of Leo Steinberg's "modern oblivion"– is a disturbing combi-nation of the idealization and denigration of the female that comes from medieval Marian devotion. As William Empson, somewhat gleefully, spelled it out, we are inveigled into "a wide variety of sexual perversions . . . the sacrificial idea is aligned with incest, the infantile pleasures, and canni-balism."[58] Sabine adds a rather tentative question: "did the poet intend his conflation of this mystical vision . . . to give rise to depictions of incest, fellatio, and sodomy?"[59] The answer, of course, is yes, and more. The child has eaten the mother; the mother now eats the son in an extreme extension of the Eucharist. We should add the allusions to the pre-genital pleasures of oral gratification, where "sexual activity has not yet been separated from the ingestión of food," genitality, digestion, and (as Susan Morrison would insist) therefore of waste and excretion. To repeat Kristeva's description of abjection, it involves sidling up to the most intense and extreme experi-ence – the blurring of the supposedly revolting and loathsome with the highest ecstasy, revulsion with transformation.[60] Crashaw's poetry heightens the physicality of the virgin's body as the center of religious experience.

Crashaw's poems were published, after his death in Italy, in 1648. They bring to a climax, in many senses, my look at the ways in which the Virgin is fragmented in the waning years of what we loosely call early modern England. They circle back to medieval gynotheology, and take my argu-ment back to the questions I posed in my preface and opening chapter as I

[57] Johnson, "Richard Crashaw's Indigestible Poetics," 36.
[58] Steinberg, *Sexuality of Christ*; Empson, *Seven Types of Ambiguity*, 221.
[59] Sabine, *Feminine Engendered Faith* and "Richard Crashaw."
[60] Phillips, "Opening the Purple Wardrobe," 143–8: Kristeva, *Powers of Horror*, 153.

"sidled" up to issues posed by some cultural psychoanalysis and feminist theology. I resume that discussion here.

Tina Beattie asserts that "by the seventeenth century, Mary had all but been eradicated from Protestant consciousness."[61] It is clear that such apocalyptic pronouncements over-simplify the transitions and transformations that are occurring in early modern England. However much we can observe her fading and pick up just traces of her, it would be fairer to say that in addition to the continuities of traditional devotions among the Catholic remnant, the Virgin representations and embodiments continue to surface, even in some surprising places. Beattie's remark, however, is part of a more cosmic argument which deserves further consideration. The history of ideologies inevitably consists of histories of struggles and contradictions, claims of truth and assertions of power, and what "comes through," to use one of Raymond Williams's favorite phrases, is that human social experience is always "in solution," not yet or never quite precipitated out in the form of the "known relationships, institutions, formations, positions" or other residual formulations of human experience. History is always *presentness*, which includes both the pasts and what stories we have imagined of those pasts, and incorporates our changing readings of the lived experiences and the "structures of feeling" by which our contradictions are lived.[62] We need, therefore, however briefly, to look back to early modern England from our own present.

What has "come through" from what Peter Matheson calls the "great shattering" of the Reformation in England is what we loosely call a "secular" and, more latterly, a "post-human" world. To speak of the secularization or (in its earlier phase) the "protestantization" of English culture in the seventeenth and eighteenth centuries, let alone the "eradication" of the Virgin as a key aspect of that transition, we are entering into a hugely controversial, apocalyptic-sounding area much argued in historical and theological studies. What is the force of Keith Thomas's classic distinction between the worlds of "magic" and "religion"? Was the disappearance or at least the diminution or splitting of the magical universe of the Catholic Middle Ages a historical phenomenon? Is there some inherent distinction between "Catholic" and "Protestant" views of the material universe, as Andrew Greeley and Michael Carroll, among others, maintain? Can we rather observe surges of re-sacralization or different modes of the sacred in different histories and cultures? As Schwartz puts it, do gods (and I would add, goddesses) disappear and reappear?[63]

---

[61] Beattie, *Eve's Pilgrimage*, 138; see also Boss, *Empress and Handmaid*, 95–6.
[62] Williams, *Keywords*, 288; Goodman, *Georgic Modernity*, 1, 96.
[63] Walsham, "The Reformation and 'The Disenchantment of the World'," 498.

The supposed desacralization of English society, indeed (in the views of some theologians) of the whole cosmos, supposedly brought about by the Protestant revolution, is a change famously enshrined in Weber's phrase, "the disenchantment of the world," with the Reformation a "milestone on the road towards modernity."[64] According to this reading of early modern history, the Protestant regimes of Europe encouraged, actively or by default, a desacralization of a magical universe that was associated closely with medieval Catholicism. Some modern Catholic apologists have even seen "secularization" as a punishment inflicted on England for its unfaithfulness to the Mother of God. Charlotte Spretnak claims that the loss of the Virgin from Protestantism was a profound "symbolic link between humans and the larger reality," and that Western man has subsequently "framed the human story" as a "tragic alienation from the unfolding story of the cosmos." Sara Jane Boss and other contemporary Catholic theologians point to what they see as the tragically empty universe created by Protestantism, which they link explicitly to the Reformation rejection of the Virgin. Mary, says Boss, "who stands for creation in relation to God, and so corresponds to nature in relation to humanity," has lost the "terrible sacred power she once held in the Christian imagination."[65] For modern Catholics, both Roman and Anglican, therefore, the burning of the statues of the Virgin in 1538, and the longer process of the destruction of the shrines and religious establishments was a tragedy of enormous proportions that could not even start to be healed until Our Lady returned to England in the past hundred years, as the shrines and statues, pilgrimages and devotions, many of which have been at the center of this study, have been revived in the late nineteenth and twentieth centuries in a series of invented traditions much like those that established the credentials of Walsingham in the fifteenth century.

Stories of the Virgin have been inextricably linked to the history of sexuality and gender roles. The last five hundred years, so the argument goes, have seen remarkable progress in the material well-being of Western men and (far less fully and more slowly) women, though (it needs to be added) at enormous cost to other whole cultures and their members and accompanied by, and even dependent on, the ruthless exploitation of the

---

[64] Weber's phrase, quoted from *The Protestant Ethic and the Spirit of Capitalism,* is central to Alexandra Walsham's finely wrought arguments concerning the fading (rather than the disappearance) of the magical or "enchanted" world: see especially "Recording Superstition," "The Disenchantment of the World," and "Reforming the Waters." Yet Weber's concept is less about the loss of magic than the rise of bureaucracy, though the phrase has often become a shibboleth of secularization: see Aldridge, *Religion in the Contemporary World,* 70–3, and Carroll, *American Catholics in the Protestant Imagination,* 171–2.

[65] Spretnak, *Missing Mary,* 52; Boss, *Empress and Handmaid,* 112.

eco-structure and therefore the world's future viability. This mastery, the argument continues, has also been achieved as part of an increasingly masculinist and mechanical view of the universe which, argues Boss, has made Western men "peculiarly susceptible . . . to a tendency towards the domination of others, and of women in particular." Pre-Reformation society moved from "having a strong and maternal focus – one in which men and women experienced themselves as continuous with" the natural world, and one which was instead oriented "towards the fathers."[66] Reacting to a generation of feminist critiques and a generation of theologians who continue to work today on the boundaries of religion, culture, and psychoanalysis, Beattie argues that "all present constructs of sexual difference" within traditional Christian theology have been "products of masculinity," and therefore "what poses as the feminine in western culture is in fact the masculine imaginary." Mary has been, she continues, "an object that can be filled with all kinds of fantasies, which then become the normative way of seeing her." She looks at the process by which male Church authorities "created" the Virgin in ways that involve the "erasure of the body and especially of the sexed female body" and the continued and intensified authority of masculinist control of the environment. This process, she asserts, was intensified by Protestantism, which purged Christianity of its "material and maternal dimension." How then, she continues, can women have more adequate "access to the symbolics of their own subjectivity"? And can we find indications of those alternative symbolics in the past?[67]

So, the argument goes, in the Reformation, we watch Mary the mother–queen–goddess being replaced by the meek and obedient vehicle of the father's will – and we observe the violence with which the mother figure herself is reviled. Protestantism's displacement of female experience involved a fear of male ego dissolution in a universe empty of comfort, without maternal reassurance, and providing no possibility of creative acknowledgment of the originating feminine – except through violence and explosion. As I argued in Chapter 2, one reaction to the fear of being overwhelmed – especially when one is concerned, theologically, that abandonment to the power of the woman is an endangerment to eternal salvation – is to destroy it, to revenge oneself on its power. The iconoclast attempts to master threats to his integrity by destroying them, a process that is a distortion of the healthy tension and release of sexuality and a replacement by what Theweleit terms the iconoclastic "tension followed by explosion." The absolute transcendence of the God of Protestant theology gave

---

[66] Boss, *Empress and Handmaid*, 176.   [67] Beattie, *God's Mother*, 32; *Eve's Pilgrimage*, 108.

Protestants the pretext for repudiating the Mother. They did so by relying on an "external agency" to give them an individuation of a particularly lonely kind, ceasing to be part of the maternal body by a savage wrenching away from its power – and by turning violently upon it. Secularization and the Enlightenment paradoxically served to disenchant us not just from the universe but also from ourselves.[68]

The eco-feminist argument, as it is sometimes called, since it identifies the Virgin with or even as the high point of the Creation, is just one of an increasing number of reactions to post-modernism that radically call into question the optimistic myth of material progress on which the affluent Western world has probably irretrievably placed its bets in the post-modern (or supposedly post-human) "incredulity towards metanarratives."[69] It is also an argument that may all too easily lend itself to nostalgia and sentimental apathy, thereby furthering the repression against which it protests. Weber's (or for that matter, Greeley's) understanding of the dynamics of the Protestant as opposed to a Catholic universe (or imagination) is an abstraction, or at best a schematic of differing world views that have never been fully absorbed by its adherents. One can certainly abstract from Reformation theology and polemic the vision of a desacralized material world, divinely created and guided but closed to human and material intervention. Intercessory prayer, holy relics, and the worship of images have no effective place in that world, though they may come to be mentioned by some (such as Herbert) with nostalgic fondness, not merely as vehicles of damnation. Perhaps, as we have seen the reformers and iconoclasts claim, the Reformation was part of an intervention by God into human affairs but (even granting that for the sake of argument, or politeness) the consequent disenchantment of the world has happened only piecemeal, and has never been completed. The great error of the Reformation was perhaps not that it pointed out how intellectually wrong or silly many of the aspects of medieval Catholicism may have been, but that in its attempt to replace the idolatry of the visual and sensual by the idolatry of the word, the reformers distorted and destroyed some of humanity's most creative and nurturing religious feelings – and worse, not just within their own threatened, anxious reformist selves but for the generations that followed as well. Perhaps, as Kristeva quips, the English were always an emotionally repressed people, but the Reformation has much blame for reinforcing that tendency.[70]

---

[68] Theweleit, *Male Fantasies*, II, 194.   [69] Lyotard, *Postmodern Condition*, 105.
[70] Kristeva and Clément, *Feminine and the Sacred*, 43.

What is the place of the Virgin in these speculations? Is Marina Warner correct when she concludes her classic study, *Alone of All Her Sex,* as follows:

[She] is not the innate archetype of female nature, the dream incarnate; she is the instrument of a dynamic argument from the Catholic Church about the structure of society, presented as a God-given code ... For as Barthes has written: "Some objects become the prey of mythical speech for a while, then they disappear, others take their place ..." the Virgin's legend will endure in its splendour and lyricism, but it will be emptied of moral significance, and thus lose its present real powers to heal and to harm.[71]

Do we have to accede to Warner's prediction of the Virgin's slow but inevitable irrelevance? It is hard to see that irrelevance when one looks at popular Catholic culture and the stories it promulgates and elaborates all around the world. The Virgin is reported to make daily appearances – in apparitions, sunlight, sandwiches, trees, freeway underpasses, and even more grossly material substances. It is easy to laugh at such stories, or even (as Erasmus did) smile politely but knowingly. Perhaps a better stance would be to try to create a more enlightened, fulfilling, and responsible set of stories from the needs and utopian yearnings of those all too often deeply negative, fearful, and misogynic narratives? As Beattie suggests, looking back at the theological battles of early Christianity, at times one feels that the wrong parties won out, and that Christian and Western history might have been very different had some of the early Church's theological battles ended differently: we might, she says, have a "different version of the same story, based on the recognition that the narrative of the Christian life might unfold differently from the perspective of women."[72] Beattie goes back to the patristic period when the Christian Church was taking shape and to the formation of what became the cult of the Virgin, and quotes Frost's famous metaphor (over-used but in this case apt) that there were paths "not taken." To indicate where the rejected paths might have led, she picks statements from some patristic theologians that stress Mary as beginning a new creation, the embodiment of the oneness of the creation and God.[73]

In Chapter 2, with help from some contemporary feminist theologians like her, I suggested that the Virgin's most powerful alternate or subversive "pathway," adapting Simon Coleman's phrase, centered on the possibilities of a repressed but not entirely invisible female sexuality. From the cultural margins – popular religion, song, drama, as well as the visual arts such as

---

[71] Warner, *Alone of All Her Sex*, 338–9.   [72] Beattie, *God's Mother*; *Eve's Advocate*, 50, 175.
[73] Althaus-Reid, *Indecent Theology*, 39, 45; Beattie, "A Man and Three Women," 97–105; "Mary in Patristic Theology," in Boss, *Mary*, 75–105.

painting and sculpture – there were traces in late medieval culture that show us what Raymond Williams called "pre-emergent" possibilities, alternatives in which the figure of the Virgin, despite hundreds of years of repression and exploitation, might have supported an affirmation of the body and a more positive endorsement of human sexuality that could have been associated with, not differentiated from, Mary. Althaus-Reid advocates that we look at our history to find "what has not been said or has been hidden" what she terms the theological "closets."[74] However fraudulent much of what the "magical universe" may have been, its abandonment signified a wider loss – perhaps the denigration of the nourishing role of the Virgin in English emotional life contributed to a wider denigration of what *Cymbeline* calls "the woman's part" (II. v. 20) in early modern life. To adapt Steinberg's observation on the visual artists' corrections of medieval theologians, the religious authorities drifted further toward a deep-rooted misogyny already all too pervasive in Western history, and it was the poets who (at least partly) pulled them back.

I started this book with a quotation from Kristeva on the power and persistence of the Virgin in Western history. In these final speculative paragraphs, I return to her observations. Kristeva asks a question which continues to fascinate me, just as I believe it does our time, and perhaps every time, in history: what are the stories which lie beneath the dogmas of Mariology, deeply buried in our being? Such an approach circumvents the question of metanarratives, even of "truth," and looks to the stories we tell of ourselves – as Aristotle suggested, we are story-telling animals. Rosemary Ruether assesses the efficacy of stories of Christianity, like any religion or meta-narrative, by stressing that "received symbols, formulas, and laws are either authenticated or not through their ability to illuminate and interpret experience ... If a symbol does not speak authentically to experience, it becomes dead or must be altered to provide a new meaning." When Warner argues that the Virgin's stories are now "emptied of moral significance," and have lost their "real powers to heal and to harm,"[75] intriguingly, Kristeva, the "Christian atheist," takes a more optimistic view about the potential for stories of liberation rather than oppression centered on the Virgin – and ones not just directed to women. In her passionate interchange of letters with her colleague, the "Jewish Atheist," Catherine Clément, Kristeva attempts to reevaluate the concept of the sacred in a post-Christian, secular world that has, at least in intellectual circles, often been dismissive of belief. It also raises the

---

[74] Williams, *Marxism and Literature*, 126; Althaus-Reid, *Indecent Theology*, 75, 88.
[75] Ruether, *Sexism and Godtalk*, 13–14; Warner, *Alone of All Her Sex*, 339.

traditional issue, so central to Mariology, of a special connection between the sacred and the female, asserting that not only has the contemporary world been diminished by that exclusion, but also so have the official theologies of religion. Kristeva observes that the exclusion or "breakdown" of the sacred is in part responsible for the alienation and depression of modern women, even while so many of their lives have been distorted and destroyed by the masculine-dominated authorities of official religion.[76]

She proceeds, both in her letters to Clément, and her closely connected Versailles lectures on religion, to examine the powerful stories that underlie the manifestations of the Virgin in our history. We do not have to accept these as the only stories that the Virgin embodies, but they are worth listening to. One, says Kristeva, is the fantasy that we can overcome "the unthinkable of death by postulating maternal love in its place." In the traditional image of Mary as perpetual virgin, Kristeva sees a very different story from the ones that dominated late medieval Christianity, though, as I have suggested, there are recurring hints of alternate stories. She sees in the Virgin Birth, for instance, an underlying desire for "our mothers to be virgins, so that we can love them better or allow ourselves to be loved by them without fear" of any rival. We want not to be "excluded from the act of pleasure that is the origin" of our own existence. Such a fantasy, she argues, opens possibilities for both men and women. Getting behind the dogma of the Virgin Birth, asking not whether it is "true," but what stories lie beneath it, may help us get to the "primal bedrock" of "the mother–child dyad" and move beyond the rule of the father. Before the father–child struggle and the painful process of renunciation of the "maternal paradise" is the desire to become, at least in fantasy, central to our own creation – in Theweleit's terms, to achieve a positive transition to becoming more fully born.[77]

Second, there is the issue of women's sexuality. Kristeva views the "censorship of Mary's sexuality" as the most devastating erasure of human pleasure and fulfillment in our history. Yet she looks to the Middle Ages and sees signs that the increasingly powerful presence of the "(w)hole," as potentially both humanizing and feminizing, can be envisaged. Behind the seeming alienation of the Virgin Mother is a further fantasy about "having a child without the aid of a father." The Virgin provides women with the additional fantasy of the "only human being who does not have to die (even her son must endure the cross)," and so Mary becomes a "representation, a fantasy, of an immortal biology."[78] So the underlying story here

[76] Kristeva and Clément, *Feminine and the Sacred*, 175.   [77] *Ibid.*, 178.
[78] Kristeva, *Tales of Love*, 251–2; Kristeva and Clément, *Feminine and the Sacred*, 176.

is for a desire for autonomy, for "owned" language and for a woman's access to and control of her own body and its pleasures. A re-envisioning of the Virgin might, as the Liberation theologians put it, help bridge the gap between Mary and ordinary women and, more importantly, directly help "ordinary women."

The transition from "late medieval" to "early modern" is therefore a blurred but (despite so many attempts to close down options for humanity) open-ended one. About the same time as the elder William Crashaw is delivering himself of his dyspeptic sermon on the corrupt femaleness of the Virgin and the Catholic Church, Donne is begging that the true Church show herself like a woman, open to all men, begging his profane mistress to show herself to him as to a midwife, and secretly keeping a painting of the Virgin in his study, and Shakespeare is staging an ecstatic image, humanized and immanentalist, of the Virgin in *The Winter's Tale*. Jane Caputi calls for a theology of gynocentrism and for "taking back" the "holy sites" of the body, particularly of women from a destructively phallocentric culture.[79] Where does (the younger) Crashaw advise the Virgin to look for heaven? To her lap: "on her lap she casts her humble eye," where she and we can see "Heaven." Donne, Sabine points out, had also called Mary's womb a "strange heav'n," and Crashaw in one of his Latin epigrams called it a "small heaven." In an obvious sense the "heaven" in her lap is the Christ Child – but, as usual, Crashaw blurs the two, and what we also look at is Mary's own lap. We "looke downe" in order to look up.[80]

By the middle of the seventeenth century, then, the Virgin has assumed many different shapes and been integrated into multiple stories. Among Tridentine Catholics, she has become spiritualized, a glorious soul rather than a glorified body. Among more extravagant versions of popular (and some scholarly) Catholicism – rare in England, perhaps, but triumphantly set forth in Crashaw's poetry – she is the embodiment of the glorious physicality of Creation. For most English Protestants, Mary has become a solemn bystander, a solemn repressed figure, almost without soul or body. But there are alternate Marys coming through, and in strange, unexpected places that may wait two or three hundred years to emerge as dreams or utopian possibilities. As Matheson comments, "when a 'great shattering'" such as the Reformation "takes place and an enchanted world is lost, it can free us up to step out in new directions but can also toss us into the abyss.

[79] Caputi, "Naked Goddess," 186–7.
[80] Crashaw, *Complete Poetry*, 9; Sabine, *Feminine Engendered Faith*, 150.

Dreams and nightmares frequently interweave."[81] For, regardless of the continuities and adaptations today's historians may ingeniously find between the late Middle Ages and the post-Reformation, something had happened to English religion and English society. What came through was a new society and new ways of constructing the self. In the long Reformation, 1538 may have been just part of a larger and slow-moving pattern of contradiction, change, surge and re-surgence, but in 1538 (at some time) there was (probably) a fire (or more than one). Sometimes (to parody Freud) a fire is just a fire. Not so, perhaps, in 1538.

[81] Matheson, *Imaginative World of the Reformation*, 4.

Works cited

Aldridge, Alan. *Religion in the Contemporary World: A Sociological Introduction*. New York: Polity Press, 2007.

Althaus-Reid, Marcella. *Indecent Theology: Theological Perversions in Sex, Gender and Politics*. London: Routledge, 2000.

"Queer I Stand: Lifting the Skirts of God." In *The Sexual Theologian: Essays on Sex, God and Politics*. Ed. Lisa Isherwood and Marcella Althaus-Reid. London: Continuum, 2005, 99–109.

Althusser, Louis. *Lenin and Philosophy and Other Essays*. Trans. Ben Brewster. New York: Monthly Review Press, 1971.

Amirav, Hagit, and Hans-Martin Kirn. "Notes on the Reformation, Humanism, and the Study of Hebrew in the Sixteenth Century: The Case of Theodore Bibliander (1505–64)." *Church History and Religious Culture* 87.2 (2007), 161–71.

Anger, Jane. "Protection for Women." In *First Feminists: British Women Writers, 1578–1799*. Ed. Moira Ferguson. Bloomington: Indiana University Press, 1985, 58–73

Aston, Margaret. *Lollards and Reformers: Images and Literacy in Late Medieval Religion*. London: Continuum, 1984.

England's Iconoclasts. Volume 1: Laws Against Images. Oxford: Clarendon Press, 1988.

Faith and Fire: Popular and Unpopular Religion, 1350–1600. London: Continuum, 1993.

"English Ruins and English History: The Dissolution and the Sense of the Past." *Journal of the Warburg and Courtauld Institutes* 36 (1973): 231–55.

"Public Worship and Iconoclasm." In *The Archaeology of Reformation 1480–1580*. Ed. David. R. M. Gaimster and Roberta Gilchrist. Leeds: Maney, 2003, 9–28.

Bassin, Donna. "Women's Images of Inner Space: Data toward Expanding Interpretative Categories." *International Review of Psycho-Analysis*, 9 (1982): 191–203.

Battersby, Rosemary. *The Phenomenal Woman: Feminist Metaphysics and the Patterns of Identity*. Cambridge University Press, 1998.

Baumeister, Roy. *Social Psychology and Human Sexuality*. Philadelphia: Psychology Press, 2001.

Beattie, Tina. *Rediscovering Mary: Insights from the Gospels*. Liguori: Triumph Books, 1995.

Eve's Pilgrimage: A Woman's Quest for the City of God. London: Burns & Oates, 2002.

God's Mother, Eve's Advocate: A Marian Narrative of Women's Salvation. London: Continuum, 2002.

Woman. London: Continuum, 2003.

New Catholic Feminism: Theology and Theory. New York: Routledge, 2006.

"A Man and Three Women – Hans, Adrienne, Mary and Luce." *New Blackfriars* 79 (1998): 97–105.

"Redeeming Mary: The Potential of Marian Symbolism for Feminist Philosophy of Religion." In *Feminist Philosophy of Religion: Critical Readings.* Ed. Pamela Sue Anderson and Beverley Clack. London: Routledge, 2003, 107–22.

"Queen of Heaven." In *Queer Theology: Rethinking the Western Body.* Ed. Gerard Loughlin. Oxford: Blackwell, 2007, 293–307.

"Mary in Patristic Theology." In *Mary,* ed. Boss, 75–105.

Benjamin, Jessica. *The Bonds of Love: Pychoanalysis, Feminism, and the Problem of Domination.* New York: Pantheon Books, 1988.

Like Subjects, Love Objects: Essays on Recognition and Sexual Difference. New Haven: Yale University Press, 1998.

Bennett, Tony. "Texts, Readers and Reading Formations." *Bulletin of the Mid-Western Modern Languages Association* 16.1 (Spring 1983): 3–17.

Bernard, G. W. *The King's Reformation: Henry VIII and the Remaking of the English Church.* New Haven: Yale University Press, 2006.

"Vitality and Vulnerability in the Late Medieval Church: Pilgrimage on the Eve of the Break with Rome." In *The End of the Middle Ages? England in the Fifteenth and Sixteenth Centuries.* Ed. John Lovett Watts. Stroud: Sutton, 1998, 199–233.

Bicks, Caroline. *Midwiving Subjects in Shakespeare's England.* Aldershot: Ashgate, 2003.

[Binham Priory] www.binhampriory.org/ruinstour/ladychpl.html. Accessed February 15, 2010.

Bishop, T. C. *Shakespeare and the Theatre of Wonder.* Cambridge University Press, 1996.

Blackledge, Elizabeth. *The Story of V: Opening Pandora's Box.* London: Weidenfeld and Nicholson, 2003.

Boss, Sarah Jane. *Empress and Handmaid: On Nature and Gender in the Cult of the Virgin Mary.* London: Cassell, 2000.

Ed. *Mary: The Complete Resource.* Oxford University Press, 2007.

"Francisco Suárez and Modern Mariology." In *Mary,* ed. Boss, 256–78.

Bowie, Fiona. *The Anthropology of Religion: An Introduction.* Oxford: Blackwell, 2006.

Brant, Sebastian. *The Ship of Fools,* vol. 1. Trans. A. Barclay. Edinburgh: William Paterson, 1874.

Brett, Philip. "Edward Paston (1550–1630): A Norfolk Gentleman and His Musical Collection." *Transactions of the Cambridge Bibliographical Society* 4 (1964–8): 51–69.

Brookshire, Bradley. "Bare ruin'd quiers, where late the sweet 'Byrds' sang: Covert Speech in William Byrd's 'Walsingham' Variations." In *Walsingham,* ed. Janes and Waller, 199–216.

Brownlow, F. W. "Holy Sonnets." In *Donne and the Resources of Kind.* Ed. A. D. Cousins. Madison: Fairleigh Dickinson University Press, 2002, 87–105.

Bruno, Giordano. *The Expulsion of the Triumphant Beast.* Trans. Arthur D. Imerti. Lincoln: University of Nebraska Press, 2004.

Buccola, Regina and Lisa Hopkins, eds. *Marian Moments in Early Modern British Drama.* Aldershot: Ashgate, 2007.

Bugslag, James. "Local Pilgrimages and Their Shrines in Pre-Modern Europe." *Peregrinations* 2.1 (2007): http://peregrinations.kenyon.edu/vol2-1/ SpecialSection/ Local_Pilgrimage. Accessed February 1, 2010.

Bull, George. "Sermon IV: On the Mean and Low Condition of the Blessed Virgin Mary." In *The Works of George Bull,* 1. Oxford University Press, 1846, 120–2.

Bynum, Carolyn Walker. *Jesus as Mother: Studies in the Spirituality of the High Middle Ages.* Berkeley: University of California Press, 1982.

Holy Feast and Holy Fast: The Religious Significance of Food to Medieval Women. Berkeley: University of California Press, 1987.

"The Body of Christ in the Later Middle Ages: A Reply to Leo Steinberg." In *Fragmentation and Redemption: Essays on Gender and the Human Body in Medieval Religion.* New York: Zone Books, 1991, 79–117.

Calvin, John. *A Treatise on Relics.* Trans. Valerian Krasinski. Edinburgh: Johnston and Hunter, 1854.

Caputi, Jane. "On the Lap of Necessity: A Mythic Reading of Teresa Brennan's Energetics Philosophy." *Hypatia* 16.2 (2001): 125–50.

"The Naked Goddess: Pornography and the Sacred." *Theology & Sexuality* 9.2 (2003): 180–200.

[Cardigan, Our Lady of]. www.ourladyofthetaper.org.uk. Accessed February 1, 2010.

Carroll, Michael P. *The Cult of the Virgin Mary: Psychological Origins.* Princeton University Press, 1986.

Catholic Cults and Devotions: A Psychological Inquiry. Kingston: McGill-Queens University Press, 1989.

Madonnas that Maim: Popular Catholicism in Italy Since the Fifteenth Century. Baltimore: Johns Hopkins University Press, 1992.

Veiled Threats: The Logic of Popular Catholicism in Italy. Baltimore: Johns Hopkins University Press, 1996.

Irish Pilgrimage: Holy Wells and Popular Catholic Devotion. Baltimore: Johns Hopkins University Press, 1999.

American Catholics in the Protestant Imagination: Rethinking the Academic Study of Religion. Baltimore: Johns Hopkins University Press, 2007.

"Interview: Praying the Rosary." *Journal for the Scientific Study of Religion* 27 (1988), 429–41.

"Pilgrimage at Walsingham on the Eve of the Reformation: Speculations on a 'splendid diversity' Only Dimly Perceived." In *Walsingham,* ed. Janes and Waller, 35–48.

"Robin Hood." Unpublished paper. Privately communicated, 2010.

Carter, Angela. *The Sadeian Woman.* London: Virago, 1979.

Cartwright, Kent, ed. *A Companion to Tudor Literature.* Malden, MA: Wiley-Blackwell, 2010.

Caviness, Madeline. *Visualizing Women in the Middle Ages: Sight, Spectacle, and Scopic Economy*. Philadelphia: University of Pennsylvania Press, 2001.

Certain Sermons Or Homilies Appointed to be Read in Churches in the Time of Queen Elizabeth. Philadelphia: H. Hooker, 1855.

Chambers, E. K. *William Shakespeare: A Study of Facts and Problems*. Oxford: Clarendon Press, 1930.

Chandlery, P. J. *Mary's Praise on Every Tongue: A Record of Homage Paid to Our Blessed Lady in all Ages and throughout the World*. London: Manresa Press, 1924.

Chapman, Alison. "Early Modern Patrons and Medieval Saints." In *English Literature 1550–1660*. Forthcoming

"Milton's Genii Loci and the Specter of the Medieval Saints." *Milton Studies*, forthcoming.

"Ophelia's 'Old Lauds': Madness and Hagiography in *Hamlet*." *Medieval and Renaissance Drama in England* 20 (2007): 111–35.

"Met I with an old bald Mare": Lust, Misogyny, and the Early Modern Walsingham Ballads." In *Walsingham*, ed. Janes and Waller, 217–32.

"Milton's Nuns." Unpublished paper, Sixteenth Century Studies Conference, Montreal, October, 2010.

Chaucer, Geoffrey. *The Riverside Chaucer*. Ed. Larry D. Benson. Boston: Houghton Mifflin, 1987.

Chidley, Rev. *Our Lady of Penrhys*. London: Catholic Truth Society, 1962.

Cole, Bruce. *Piero della Francesca: Tradition and Innovation in Renaissance Art*. New York: Icon Editions, 1991.

"Pilgrimage to 'England's Nazareth': Landscapes of Myth and Memory at Walsingham." In *Intersecting Journeys: The Anthropology of Pilgrimage and Tourism*. Ed. E. Badone and S. Roseman. Urbana: University of Illinois Press, 2004, 52–67.

Coleman, Simon. "Do You Believe in Pilgrimage?" *Anthropological Theory* 2 (2002), 355–68.

"Tradition as Play: "Pilgrimage to 'England's Nazareth.'" *History and Anthropology* 15 (2004): 273–88.

"Pilgrimage to Walsingham and the Re-Invention of the Middle Ages." In *Pilgrimage Explored*. Ed J. Stopford. Woodbridge: Boydell and Brewer, 1999, 189–214.

Coletti, Theresa. *Mary Magdalene and the Drama of Saints Theater, Gender, and Religion in Late Medieval England*. Philadelphia: University of Pennsylvania Press, 2004.

"Purity and Danger: The Paradox of Mary's Body and the Engendering of the Infancy Narrative in the English Mystery Cycles." In *Feminist Approaches to the Body in Medieval Literature*. Ed. Linda Lomperis and Sarah Stanbury. Philadelphia: University of Pennsylvania Press, 1993, 65–95.

Collinson, Patrick. *The Birthpangs of Protestant England*. New York: St. Martin's Press, 1988.

Constable, Henry. *Poems*. Ed. Joan Grundy. Liverpool University Press, 1960.

Cook, G. H., ed. *Letters to Cromwell and Others on the Suppression of the Monasteries*. London: John Baker, 1965.

Cooper, Helen. *The English Romance in Time: Transforming Motifs from Geoffrey of Monmouth to the Death of Shakespeare*. Oxford University Press, 2004.

Cooper, Trevor. *The Journal of William Dowsing: Iconoclasm in East Anglia during the English Civil War*. Woodbridge: Boydell 2001.

Corbet, Richard. *Poems*. Ed. J. A. W. Bennett and H. R. Trevor-Roper. Oxford: Clarendon Press, 1955.

Coulton, C. C. *Art and the Reformation*. New York: Harper, 1958.

Craig, Leigh Ann. *Wandering Women and Holy Matrons: Women as Pilgrims in the Late Middle Ages*. Leiden: Brill, 2009.

Cranmer, Thomas. *A Short Instruction into Christian Religion*. Oxford University Press, 1829.

Crashaw, Richard. *The Complete Poetry of Richard Crashaw*. Ed. George Walton Williams. New York University Press, 1972.

Crashaw, William. *The Jesuites Gospell*. London, 1610.

The Sermon Preached at the Cross, Feb 14, 1607. New York: Johnson Reprint Company, 1972.

Cruickshank, Dan. *The Story of Britain's Best Buildings*. Buffalo: Firefly Books, 2003.

Cuffel, Alexandra. *Gendering Disgust in Medieval Religious Polemic*. South Bend: University of Notre Dame Press, 2007.

Dalton, Anne Marie. "The Challenge of Violence: Toward a Theology of Women's Bodies." Catholic Network For Women's Equality Newsletter, 2008. www.cnwe.org/articleWin3.htm. Accessed February 1, 2010.

Dante Alighieri. *The New Life of Dante Alighieri*. Trans Charles Eliot Norton. Boston: Houghton Mifflin, 1920.

The Comedy of Dante Alighieri, the Florentine. Trans. Dorothy L. Sayers, and Barbara Reynolds. 3 vols. Harmondsworth: Penguin, 1950–63.

Davis, J. F. "The Trials of Thomas Bilney and the English Reformation." *Historical Journal* 24 (1981): 775–90.

Dickinson, J. C. *The Shrine of Our Lady of Walsingham*. Cambridge University Press, 1956.

"'Strike All that Look Upon with Marvel.'" In *Rematerializing Shakespeare*. Ed. Bryan Reynolds and William N. West. New York: Palgrave, 2005, 19–34.

Diehl, Huston. *Staging Reform, Reforming the Stage: Protestantism and Popular Theater in Early Modern England*. Ithaca: Cornell University Press, 1997.

Dolan, Frances. *Whores of Babylon: Catholicism, Gender, and Seventeenth-Century Print Culture*. Ithaca: Cornell University Press, 1999.

"Hermione's Ghost." In *The Impact of Feminism in English Renaissance Studies*. Ed. Dympna Callaghan. New York: MacMillan, 2007, 213–37.

Donne, John. *The Sermons of John Donne*. Ed. G. R. Potter and Evelyn M. Spearing. 10 vols. Berkeley: University of California Press, 1953–62.

The Complete English Poems. Ed. A. J. Smith. Harmondsworth: Penguin, 1971.

Dormer, Ernest W. *Gray of Reading: A Sixteenth-Century Controversialist and Ballad-Writer*. Reading: Bradley & Son, Ltd. 1923.

Dreyer, Elizabeth A. "Whose Story Is It? – The Appropriation of Medieval Mysticism." *Spiritus: A Journal of Christian Spirituality* 4.2 (2004): 151–72.

Driscoll, Catherine. *Girls: Feminine Adolescence in Popular Culture, and Cultural Theory*. New York: Columbia University Press, 2002.

Duffy, Eamon. *The Stripping of the Altars: Traditional Religion in England c. 1400–1580*. New Haven: Yale University Press, 1992. 2nd edn., 2005.

Faith of our Fathers: Reflections on Catholic Tradition. New York: Continuum, 2004.

Fires of Faith: England under Mary Tudor. New Haven: Yale University Press, 2009.

"Bare Ruined Choirs: Remembering Catholicism in Shakespeare's England." In *Theatre and Religion: Lancastrian Shakespeare*. Ed. Richard Dutton, Alison Findlay, and Richard Wilson. Manchester University Press, 2003, 40–57.

Duncan-Jones, Katherine. "Sir Philip Sidney's Debt to Edmund Campion." In *The Reckoned Expense: Edmund Campion and the Early English Jesuits: Essays in Celebration of the First Centenary of Campion Hall, Oxford (1896–1996)*. Ed. Thomas McCoog. Woodbridge: Boydell, 1996, 97–113.

Dunn-Hensley, Susan. "Return of the Sacred Virgin: Memory, Loss, and Restoration in Shakespeare's Later Plays." In *Walsingham*, ed. Janes and Waller, 185–98.

Eagleton, Terry. *Reason, Faith, and Revolution, Reflections on the God Debate*. New Haven: Yale University Press, 2009.

Easton, Pamela. "'Was It Good For You, Too?' Medieval Erotic Art and Its Audiences." *Different Visions: A Journal of New Perspectives on Medieval Art* 1 (September, 2008): 1–30.

Eire, Carlos. *War Against the Idols: The Reformation of Worship from Erasmus to Calvin*. Cambridge University Press, 1989.

Elizabethan Sonnet Sequences. Ed. Martha Foote Crow. New York: AMS Press, 1969.

Ellington, Donna Spivey. *From Sacred Body to Angelic Soul: Understanding Mary in Late Medieval and Early Modern Europe*. Washington: Catholic University of America Press, 2001.

Empson, William. *Seven Types of Ambiguity*. London: Chatto and Windus, 1949.

England, George, Alfred W. Pollard, and Eugen Kölbing, eds. *The Towneley Plays*. London: EETS, 1897.

Epiphanius, Bishop of Salamis. *The Panarion: Selected Passages*. Ed. Philip R. Amidon. New York: Oxford University Press, 1990.

Erasmus, Desiderius. *Pilgrimages to Saint Mary of Walsingham and Saint Thomas of Canterbury*. Trans. John Gough Nichols. Westminster: John Bowyer Nichols and Son, 1849.

The Pilgrimage of Pure Devotion. London, 1536. In *Tudor Translations of the Colloquies of Erasmus (1536–1584)*. Facsimile repr., introd. Dickie A. Spurgeon. Delmar: Scholars' Facsimiles and Reprints, 1972.

The Colloquies of Erasmus. Trans. and annotated Craig R. Thompson. *Collected Works of Erasmus*, vol. 40. University of Toronto Press, 1997.

"The Usefulness of the Colloquies (*De Utilitate Colloquiorum*)." In *The Colloquies of Erasmus*. Trans. Craig R. Thompson. Chicago: University of Chicago Press, 1965, 1095–119.

"Pean Virgini Matri (Paean in Honour of the Virgin Mother)." *Collected Works*. Ed. Elaine Fantham and Erika Rummel. University of Toronto Press, 1989, 33.

Eudes, Saint John. *The Admirable Heart of Mary*. Trans. Charles di Targiani and Ruth Hauser. New York: P. J. Kenedy, 1948.

Ferris, Lesley. *Crossing the Stage: Controversies on Cross-Dressing*. London: Routledge, 1993.

Finucane, Ronald C. *Miracles and Pilgrims: Popular Beliefs in Medieval England*. London: J. M. Dent and Sons Ltd, 1977.

Fissell, Mary E. *Vernacular Bodies: The Politics of Reproduction in Early Modern England*. Oxford University Press, 2004.

Ford, Judy Ann. *John Mirk's Festial: Orthodoxy, Lollardy, and the Common People in Fourteenth-Century England*. Cambridge: D.S. Brewer, 2006.

Forest, William. "An Edition of the Marian Poems of the Recusant Writer, William Forest, from MS. Harleian 1703." Ed. Joseph Patrick Keena. Unpub. Diss., University of Notre Dame, 1960.

Forster, L. W. *The Icy Fire: Five Studies in European Petrarchism*. Cambridge University Press, 1969.

Foskett, Mary F. *A Virgin Conceived: Mary and Classical Representations of Virginity*. Bloomington: Indiana University Press, 2002.

Foucault, Michel. *The History of Sexuality: An Introduction*. Vol 1. New York: Vintage, 1978.

Foxe, John. *The Actes and Monuments*. Ed. George Townshend. London, 1844.

Fraser, Russell A., ed. *The Court of Venus*. Cambridge University Press, 1955.

Freeman, Thomas S. "Offending God: John Foxe and English Protestant Reactions to the Cult of the Virgin Mary." In *The Church and Mary*. Ed. Robert N. Swanson. *Studies in Church History* 39 (2004): 228–38.

Freikel, Lisa. "Shakespearean Fetish." In *Spiritual Shakespeares*. Ed. Ewan Fernie. London: Routledge, 2005, 109–29.

Frere, Walter Howard, ed. *Visitation Articles and Injunctions of the Period of the Reformation*. 3 vols. London: Longmans, Green, 1910.

Fulke, William and Richard Gibbings. *Stapleton's Fortress Overthrown*. Cambridge University Press, 1848.

G., A. *The Widowes Mite*. London, 1619.

Gardiner, Anne Barbeau. "Milton's Parody of Catholic Hymns in Eve's Temptation and Fall: Original Sin as a Paradigm of 'Secret Idolatries'." *Studies in Philology* 91 (1994): 216–31.

Gatti, Hilary. "Petrarch, Sidney, Bruno." In *Petrarch in Britain: Interpreters, Imitators, and Translators over 700 Years*. Ed. Martin McLaughlin et al. Oxford University Press, 2007, 149–63.

Gaventa, Beverly Roberts. *Mary: Glimpses of the Mother of Jesus*. Colombia: University of South Carolina Press, 1999.

Genzoe, Lena. "The Feminization of Healing in Pilgrimage to Fatima." In *Pilgrimage and Healing*. Ed. Jill Dubisch and Michael Winkelman. Tucson: University of Arizona Press, 2005, 25–46.

Gibson, Gail McMurray. *The Theater of Devotion: East Anglian Drama and Society in the Late Middle Ages*. University of Chicago Press, 1989.

"Scene and Obscene: Seeing and Performing Late Medieval Childbirth." *Journal of Medieval and Early Modern Studies* 29 (1999): 7–24.

Gillett, H. M. *Walsingham and Its Shrine*. London: Burns, Oates & Washbourne, 1934.

Glancy, Jennifer A. *Corporal Knowledge: Early Christian Bodies*. Oxford: Oxford University Press, 2010.

Glyde, John. *The Norfolk Garland: A Collection of the Superstitious Beliefs and Practices Proverbs Curious Customs Ballads and Songs of the People of Norfolk*. London: Jarrold, 1872.

Goodman, Kevis. *Georgic Modernity and British Romanticism: Poetry and the Mediation of History*. Cambridge University Press, 2004.

Gössman, Elisabeth. "The Image of God and the Human Being in Women's Counter-Tradition." In *Is There a Future for Feminist Theology?* Ed. Deborah F. Sawyer and Diane M. Collier. Sheffield: Sheffield Academic Press, 1999, 26–56.

Graef, Hilda. *Mary: A History of Doctrine and Devotion*. London: Continuum, 1985.

Granger, Penny. *The N-Town Play: Drama and Liturgy in Medieval East Anglia*. Cambridge: D. S. Brewer, 2009.

Graziano, Frank. *Wounds of Love: The Mystical Marriage of Saint Rose of Lima*. Oxford University Press, 2004.

Greeley, Andrew M. *The Catholic Imagination*. Berkeley: University of California Press, 2001.

[Review of] Michael Carroll, *Madonnas that Maim*. *Contemporary Sociology* 22 (1994): 121–2.

[Review of] Michael Carroll, *American Catholics in the Protestant Imagination*. *American Catholic Studies* 119.2 (2008): 101–2.

Green, Charles and A. B. Whittingham. "Excavations at Walsingham Priory, Norfolk, 1961." *Journal of the Royal Archaeological Society* 125 (1968): 255–90.

Greenblatt, Stephen. *Shakespearean Negotiations: The Circulation of Social Energy in Renaissance England*. Berkeley: University of California Press, 1989.

Greville, Fulke, *Selected Poems*. Ed. Thom Gunn. University of Chicago Press, 1968.

The Prose Works of Fulke Greville, Lord Brooke, 1554–1628. Ed. John Gouws. Oxford: Clarendon Press, 1986.

Groves, Beatrice. *Texts and Traditions: Religion in Shakespeare, 1592–1604*. Oxford: Clarendon Press, 2007.

"Shakespeare's Sonnets and the Genevan Marginalia." *Essays in Criticism* 57 (2007): 114–28.

Gumppenberg, Wilhelm. *Atlas Marianus sive de imaginibus Deiparae per orbem Christianum miraculosis*. 4 vols. Ingolstadt, 1657–9.

Hackett, Helen. *Virgin Mother, Maiden Queen: Elizabeth I and the Cult of the Virgin*. New York: St. Martin's Press, 1995.

Hamrick, Stephen. "*Tottel's Miscellany* and the English Reformation." *Criticism* 44 (2002): 329–61.

Hannay, Margaret P. *Mary Sidney, Lady Wroth*. Farnham: Ashgate, 2009.

Harris, Silas M. *Our Lady of Cardigan*. Cardiff: Western Mail & Echo, 1954. www. ourladyofthetaper.org.uk. Accessed February 1, 2010.

Harrison, William. *The Description of England: The Classic Contemporary Account of Tudor Social Life*. Ed. Georges Edelen. Ithaca: Cornell University Press, 1975.

Haskins, Susan, ed. and trans. *Who Is Mary? Three Early Modern Women on the Idea of the Virgin Mary*. University of Chicago Press, 2008.

Heal, Bridget. *The Cult of the Virgin Mary in Early Modern Germany: Protestant and Catholic Piety, 1500–1648*. Cambridge University Press, 2007.

Herbert, George. *The Works of George Herbert*. Ed F. E. Hutchinson. Oxford: Clarendon Press, 1941.

Herolt, Johannes. *Miracles of the Blessed Virgin Mary*. London: Harcourt Brace, 1928.

Hester, M. Thomas, ed. *Donne's "Desire of More": The Subject of Anne More Donne in His Poetry*. Newark: University of Delaware Press, 1996.

Hildegard of Bingen. *Symphonia: A Critical Edition of the Symphonia armonie celestium revelatium*. Ed Barbara Newman. Ithaca: Cornell University Press, 1988.

Hill, Carole. "St Anne and her Walsingham Daughter." In *Walsingham*, ed. Janes and Waller, 99–112.

Hobsbawm, E. J. and T. O. Ranger, eds. *The Invention of Tradition*. Cambridge University Press, 1983.

Hodgson, Elizabeth M. A. *Gender and the Sacred Self in John Donne*. Newark: University of Delaware Press, 1999.

Holloway, Julia Bolton. *Saint Bride and Her Book*. Cambridge: D. S. Brewer, 2000.

Holmes, Megan. *Fra Lippo Lippi: The Carmelite Painter*. New Haven: Yale University Press, 1999.

Hughes, P. L. and J. F. Larkin, eds. *Tudor Royal Proclamations*. New Haven: Yale University Press, 1964.

Hunter, Robert G. *Shakespeare and the Comedy of Forgiveness*. New York: Columbia University Press, 1965.

Hussey, Maurice. *The Chester Mystery Plays; Sixteen Pageant Plays from the Chester Craft Cycle*. London: W. Heinemann, 1957.

Irigaray, Luce. *Speculum of the Other Woman*. Trans. Gillian C. Gill. Ithaca: Cornell University Press, 1985.

Isherwood, Lisa and Marcella Althaus-Reid. "Queering Theology." In *The Sexual Theologian: Essays on Sex, God and Politics*. Ed. Lisa Isherwood and Marcella Althaus-Reid. London: Continuum, 2005, 1–15.

Izard, Thomas C. *George Whetstone: Mid-Elizabethan Gentleman of Letters*. New York: Columbia University Press, 1942.

Jaggar, Alison M. *Feminist Politics and Human Nature*. New York: Rowman & Littlefield, 1983.

James, M. R. *The Sculptures in the Lady Chapel at Ely*. London: D. Nutt, 1895.

Janes, Dominic. *Victorian Reformation: The Fight over Idolatry in the Church of England, 1840–1860*. Oxford University Press, 2009.

and Gary Waller, eds. *Walsingham and English Culture: Landscape, Sexuality, and Cultural Memory*. Farnham: Ashgate, 2010.

Jankowski, Theodora A. *Pure Resistance: Queer Virginity in Early Modern Culture.* Philadelphia: University of Pennsylvania Press, 2000.

Jantzen, Grace M. "What's the Difference? Knowledge and Gender in (Post) Modern Philosophy of Religion." *Religious Studies* 32 (1996): 431–48.

"'Canonized for Love': Pleasure and Death in Modernity." In *The Good News of the Body: Sexual Theology and Feminism.* Ed. Lisa Isherwood. London: Continuum, 2000.

Johnson, Kimberly. "Richard Crashaw's Indigestible Poetics." *Modern Philology* 107 (2009): 32–51.

Johnson, Trevor. "Mary in Early Modern Europe." In *Mary: The Complete Resource*, ed. Boss, 363–84.

Jones, Malcolm. *The Secret Middle Ages.* Westport: Praeger, 2002.

Jones, Norman. *The English Reformation: Religion and Cultural Adaptation.* Malden, MA: Blackwell, 2002.

Jonson, Ben. *Works*, ed. C. H. Herford and Evelyn Simpson. Oxford: Clarendon Press, 1947.

Timber: Discoveries 1641: Conversations with William Drummond of Hawthornden 1619. Alcester: Read Country Books, 2008.

Julian of Norwich. *Showing of Love.* Trans. Julia Bolton Holloway. Collegeville: Liturgical Press, 2003.

Kamerick, Kathleen. *Popular Piety and Art in the Late Middle Ages: Image Worship and Idolatry in England 1350–1500.* New York: Palgrave Macmillan, 2002.

Kaplan, Louise. *Female Perversions: The Temptations of Emma Bovary.* New York: Doubleday, 1991.

Kaplan, Steven L. *Understanding Popular Culture: Europe from the Middle Ages to the Nineteenth Century.* New York: Mouton, 1984.

Klawitter, George. "John Donne's Attitude toward the Virgin Mary: The Public versus the Private Voice." In *John Donne's Religious Imagination: Essays in Honor of John T. Shawcross.* Ed. Raymond-Jean Frontain and Frances M. Malapezzi. Conway: UCA Press, 1995, 123–40.

Klein, Lisa M. *The Exemplary Sidney and the Elizabethan Sonneteer.* Newark: University of Delaware Press, 1998.

Klein, Melanie. *Envy and Gratitude and Other Works.* New York: Free Press, 1975.

Knight, George Wilson. *The Sovereign Flower: On Shakespeare as the Poet of Royalism.* London: Methuen, 1958.

Korte, Anne-Marie. *Women and Miracle Stories: A Multidisciplinary Exploration.* Leiden: Brill, 2001.

Kreitzer, Beth. *Reforming Mary: Changing Images of the Virgin Mary in Lutheran Sermons of the Sixteenth Century.* Oxford University Press, 2004.

Kristeva, Julia. *Desire in Language: A Semiotic Approach to Literature, and Art.* Trans. Thomas Gora, Alice Jardine, and Leon Roudiez. New York: Columbia University Press, 1980.

In the Beginning was Love. Trans. Arthur Goldhammer. New York: Columbia University Press, 1987.

Powers of Horror: An Essay on Abjection. Trans. Leon S. Roudiez. New York: Columbia University Press, 1987.

Tales of Love. Trans. Leon S. Roudiez. New York: Columbia University Press, 1987.

and Catherine Clément. *The Feminine and the Sacred.* New York: Columbia University Press, 2001.

Lake, Peter, with Michael Questier. *The Antichrist's Lewd Hat: Protestants, Papists and Players in Post- Reformation England.* New Haven: Yale University Press, 2002.

Lamb, Mary Ellen. *The Popular Culture of Shakespeare, Spenser and Jonson.* London: Routledge, 2008.

Lambarde, William. *A Perambulation of Kent.* Ed. Michael Zell. Bath: Adams & Dart, 1970.

Lanyer, Aemilia. *The Poems of Aemilia Lanyer: Salve Deus Judaeorum.* Ed. Susanne Woods. New York: Oxford University Press, 1993.

Latimer, Hugh. *Sermons.* Ed. George Elwes Corrie. Cambridge: Parker Society, 1855.

Lees-Jeffries, Hester. *England's Helicon: Fountains in Early Modern Literature and Culture.* Oxford University Press, 2007.

Lee-Warner, Henry James. "The Walsingham 'Wishing Wells'." *Norfolk Archaeology* 8 (1879): 51–5.

Leland, John. *The Itinerary in Wales of John Leland in or about the Years 1536–1543.* Ed. Lucy Toulmin Smith. London: G. Bell, 1910.

Lewis, Suzanne. "Images of Opening, Penetration and Closure and the *Roman de la Rose.*" *Word and Image* 8 (1992): 215–42.

Lipton, Emma. "Performing Reform': Lay Piety and the Marriage of Mary and Joseph in the N-Town Cycle." *Studies in the Age of Chaucer* 23 (2001): 407–35.

Littlehales, Margaret Mary. *Mary Ward: Pilgrim and Mystic.* Tunbridge Wells: Burns and Oates, 2001.

Lochrie, Karma. *Heterosyncrasies: Female Sexuality when Normal Wasn't.* Minneapolis: University of Minnesota Press, 2005.

"Mystical Acts, Queer Tendencies." In *Constructing Medieval Sexuality.* Ed. Karma Lochrie, Peggy McCracken, and James A. Schultz. Minneapolis: University of Minnesota Press, 1997, 180–200.

Lodge, Thomas. *Complete Works.* Ed. Edmund Gosse. 4 vols. Glasgow: Hunterian Club, 1883.

Lord, Peter. *The Visual Culture of Wales: Medieval Vision.* Cardiff: University of Wales Press, 2003.

Low, Anthony. *The Reinvention of Love: Poetry, Politics and Culture from Sidney to Milton.* Cambridge University Press, 1993.

Lumiansky R. M. and David Mills, eds. *The Chester Mystery Cycle.* 2 vols. London: EETS, 1974–86.

Luria, Maxwell S. and Richard L. Hoffman, eds. *Middle English Lyrics.* New York: W. W. Norton, 1974.

Luxford, Julian M. *The Art and Architecture of English Benedictine Monasteries, 1300–1540: A Patronage History.* Woodbridge: Boydell Press, 2005.

Lydgate, John. *A Critical Edition of John Lydgate's Life of Our Lady.* Ed. Joseph A. Lauritis, Ralph A. Klinefelter, and Vernon F. Gallagher. Louvain: E. Nauwelaerts, 1961.

Lyotard, Jean-François. *The Postmodern Condition.* Trans. Geoff Bennington and Brian Massumi. Minneapolis: University of Minnesota Press, 1983.

McAvoy, Liz Herbert, ed. *The Book of Margery Kempe.* Woodbridge, Suffolk: D. S. Brewer, 2003.

Authority and the Female Body in the Writings of Julian of Norwich and Margery Kempe. Woodbridge, Suffolk: D.S. Brewer, 2004.

McCarthy, Penny. *Pseudonymous Shakespeare.* Aldershot, Ashgate, 2006.

McCormick, Kathleen. "I Always Felt Like I Was On Pretty Good Terms With The Virgin Mary, Even Though I Never Got Pregnant In High School." *Phoebe: Gender and Cultural Critique* 20.1 (2008): 73–80.

MacCulloch, Diarmaid. *Reformation: Europe's House Divided 1490–1700.* London: Allen Lane, 2003.

"Mary and Sixteenth-Century Protestants." In *The Church and Mary.* Ed. R. N. Swanson. Rochester: Boydell Press, 2004, 190–217.

McEntire, Sandra J. "The Likeness of God and the Restoration of Humanity in Julian of Norwich's *Showings.*" In *Julian of Norwich: A Book of Essays.* Ed. Sandra J. McEntire. London: Routledge, 1998, 3–34.

Maitland, A. Fuller and W. Barclay Squire, eds. *The Fitzwilliam Virginal Book.* New York: Dover Publications, 1979.

Malpezzi, Francis M. "Love's Liquidity in 'Since she whome I lovd.'" In *Donne's "Desire of More."* Ed. T. Hester. New York, DE: University of Delaware Press, 1996, 196–203.

Mangrum, Bryan D. and Giuseppe Scavizzi, eds. *A Reformation Debate: Three Treaties in Translation.* Toronto: Centre for Reformation and Renaissance Studies, 1998.

Maniura, Robert. "Image and Relic in the Cult of Our Lady of Prato." In *Images, Relics, and Devotional Practices in Medieval and Renaissance Italy.* Ed. Sally J. Cornelison and Scott B. Montgomery. Tempe: Medieval & Renaissance Texts & Studies, 2005, 193–212.

Maquerlot, Jean-Pierre. *Shakespeare and the Mannerist Tradition: A Reading of Five Problem Plays.* Cambridge University Press, 1995.

Marks, Richard. *Image and Devotion in Late Medieval England.* Stroud: Sutton, 2004.

Marotti, Arthur. "Shakespeare and Catholicism." In *Theatre and Religion: Lancastrian Shakespeare.* Ed. Richard Dutton, Alison Findlay, and Richard Wilson. Manchester University Press, 2003, 218–41.

Marsh, Christopher W. *Popular Religion in Sixteenth-Century England: Holding their Peace.* New York: St. Martin's Press, 1998.

Marshall, Peter. *Religious Identities in Henry VIII's England.* Aldershot: Ashgate, 1988.

Beliefs and the Dead. Oxford University Press, 2002.

Matheson, Peter. *The Imaginative World of the Reformation.* Minneapolis: University of Minnesota Press, 2004.

Mathieu, Paul, *Sex Pots: Eroticism in Ceramics.* New Brunswick: Rutgers University Press, 2003.

May, Steven W. *The Elizabethan Courtier Poets: The Poems and Their Contexts.* Columbia: University of Missouri Press, 1991.

Mazzola, Elizabeth. *The Pathology of the English Renaissance: Sacred Remains and Holy Ghosts.* Leiden: Brill, 1998.

Meakin, H. L. *John Donne's Articulations of the Feminine.* Oxford: Clarendon Press, 1998.

Meredith, Peter. *The Mary Play from the N-Town Manuscript.* London: Longman, 1987.

Michalski, Sergiusz. *The Reformation and the Visual Arts: The Protestant Image.* London: Routledge, 1993.

Miles, Margaret R. *Image as Insight: Visual Understanding in Western Christianity and Secular Culture.* Boston: Beacon Press, 1985.

A Complex Delight: The Secularization of the Breast, 1350–1750. Berkeley: University of California Press, 2008.

Mills, David. *Recycling the Cycle: The City of Chester and its Whitsun Plays.* University of Toronto Press, 1998.

"'Some Precise Cittizins': Puritan Objections to Chester's Plays." *Leeds Studies in English* 28 (1998): 219–31.

Milton, John. *The Poems of John Milton.* Ed. John Carey and Alastair Fowler. London: Longmans, 1968.

Mintz, Susannah B. "The Crashavian Mother." *Studies in English Literature, 1500–1900* 39 (1999): 111–29.

Miravalle, Mark I. *Introduction to Mary: The Heart of Marian Doctrine and Devotion.* Santa Barbara: Queenship Publishing, 1993.

Mirsky, Mark. *Dante, Eros and Kabbalah.* Syracuse University Press, 2003.

Mitjans, Frank. "Thomas More's Veneration of Images, Praying to Saints, and Going on Pilgrimages." *Thomas More Studies* 3 (2008): 64–9.

Montfort, Louis-Marie Grignion de, Saint. *A Treatise on the True Devotion to the Blessed Virgin.* Trans. F. W. Faber. New York: P. J. Kennedy, 1909.

Moore, Mary B. *Desiring Voices: Women Sonneteers and Petrarchism.* Carbondale: Southern Illinois University Press, 2000.

Moore, Helen. "The Pilgrimage of Passion in Sidney's *Arcadia*." In *Pilgrim Voices: Narrative and Authorship in Christian Pilgrimage.* Ed. Simon Coleman and John Elsner. New York: Berghahn Books, 2003, 61–83.

More, Thomas. *The Complete Works of Sir Thomas More.* Ed. Gerald L. Carroll and Joseph B. Murray. New Haven: Yale University Press, 1963.

Morrill, John. "William Dowsing and the Administration of Iconoclasm." In *The Journal of William Dowsing: Iconoclasm in East Anglia during the English Civil War.* Ed. Trevor Cooper. Woodbridge: Boydell, 2001, 1–28.

Morrison, Molly. "Strange Miracles: A Study of the Peculiar Healings of St. Maria Maddelena de' Pazzi." *Logos: A Journal of Catholic Thought and Culture* 8 (2005): 129–44.

Morrison, Susan Signe. *Women Pilgrims in Late Medieval England.* London: Routledge, 2000.

Excrement in the Late Middle Ages: Sacred Filth and Chaucer's Fecopoetics. New York: Palgrave MacMillan, 2008.

"Waste Space: Pilgrimage Badges, Ophelia, and Walsingham Remembered." In *Walsingham*, ed. Janes and Waller, 49–66.

Morrongiello, Christopher. "Roads to Ralegh's *Walsingham* and the Figurative Passages of Edward John Collard and Francis Cutting." *Journal of the Lute Society* 37 (1997): 17–36.

Moser, Mary Beth. "Blood Relics: Menstrual Roots of Miraculous Black Madonnas in Italy." www.metaformia.org/files/Blood_Relics.pdf. Accessed February 1, 2010.

Mulvey, Laura. *Visual and Other Pleasures*. Bloomington: Indiana University Press, 1989.

Neely, Carol Thomas. *Broken Nuptials in Shakespeare's Plays*. New Haven: Yale University Press, 1985.

"Constructing the Subject: Feminist Practice and the New Renaissance Discourses." *English Literary Renaissance* 18 (1988): 5–18.

"Loss and Recovery: Homes Away from Home." In *Changing Subjects: The Making of Feminist Literary Criticism*. Ed. Gayle Greene and Coppélia Kahn. London: Routledge, 1993, 180–94.

Netzley, Ryan. "Oral Devotion: Eucharistic Theology and Richard Crashaw's Religious Lyrics." *Texas Studies in Literature and Language* 44 (2002): 247–72.

Newlyn, Evelyn S. "Between the Pit and the Pedestal: Images of Eve and Mary in Medieval Cornish Drama." In *New Images of Medieval Women*. Ed. Edelgard DuBruck. Lampeter: Mellen, 1989, 121–64.

Newman, Barbara. *God and the Goddesses: Vision, Poetry, and Belief in the Middle Ages*. Philadelphia: University of Pennsylvania Press, 2003.

Neyrey, Jerome H. "Mediterranean Maid and Mother in Art and Literature." *Biblical Theology Bulletin* 20 (1990): 65–75.

Noll, Mark A. *Confessions and Catechisms of the Reformation*. Vancouver: Regent College Publishing, 2004.

Norbrook, David and Henry R. Woudhuysen, eds. *The Penguin Book of Renaissance Verse 1509–1569*. Harmondsworth: Penguin. 1993.

Normington, Kate. *Gender and Medieval Drama*. Woodbridge, Suffolk: D. S. Brewer, 2004.

Obermeier, Anita. *The History and Anatomy of Auctorial Self-Criticism in the European Middle Ages*. Amsterdam: Rodopi, 1999.

O'Connell, Michael. *The Idolatrous Eye: Iconoclasm and Theater in Early-Modern England*. Oxford University Press, 2000.

O'Donnell, Anne M. "Mary and Other Women Saints in the Letters of Erasmus." *Erasmus of Rotterdam Society Yearbook* 11 (1961): 105–21.

Osherow, Michele. *Biblical Women's Voices in Early Modern England*. Farnham: Ashgate, 2009.

Overton, Bill. *The Winter's Tale*. Atlantic Highlands: Humanities Press International, 1989.

Paine, Clive. "The Chapel and Well of Our Lady of Woolpit." *Proceedings of the Suffolk Institute of Archaeology*, 38 (1996): 8–12.

Parish, Helen L. *Monks, Miracles, and Magic*. London: Routledge, 2005.

Parry, Graham. *Glory, Laud, and Honour: the Arts of the Anglican Counter-Reformation*. Woodbridge: Boydell and Brewer, 2008.

Pastoetter, Jakob M. "Tourism and Sex: Conceptualization of Foreign Countries as (S)exotic." *Sexuality and Culture* 5 (2001): 107–10.

Patterson, W. B. "William Perkins versus William Bishop." In *The Church and Mary*. Ed. R. N. Swanson. Rochester: Boydell Press, 2004, 252–69.

Paulissen, May Nelson. *The Love Sonnets of Lady Mary Wroth: A Critical Introduction*. Salzburg: Institut für Anglistik und Amerikanistik Universität Salzburg, 1982.

Peraino, Judith A. *Listening to the Sirens: Musical Technologies of Queer Identity from Homer to Hedwig*. Berkeley: University of California Press, 2005.

Perkins, William. *Works*. Ed. Ian Breward. Appleford: Sutton Courtenay Press, 1970.

Perry, Nicholas and Loreto Echeverría. *Under the Heel of Mary*. London: Routledge, 1988.

Peters, Christine. *Patterns of Piety: Women, Gender, and Religion in Late Medieval and Renaissance England*. Cambridge University Press, 2002.

Petrarch, Francesco. *Sonnets and Songs*. Trans. Anna Maria Armi. New York: Grosset and Dunlap, 1968.

Phillips, Bill. "Opening the Purple Wardrobe: A Psychoanalytic Approach to the Poetry of Richard Crashaw (1613–1649)." *Revista Alicantina de Estudios Ingleses* 12 (1999): 143–8.

Phillips, G. E. *Loreto and the Holy House*. Fitzwilliam, NH: Loreto Publications, 2005.

Pietz, William. "The Problem of the Fetish I." *RES: Anthropology and Aesthetics* 9 (1985): 5–17.

"The Problem of the Fetish II: The Origin of the Fetish." *RES: Anthropology and Aesthetics* 13 (1987): 23–45.

"The Problem of the Fetish IIIa: Bosman's Guinea and the Enlightenment Theory of Fetishism." *RES: Anthropology and Aesthetics* 16 (1988): 105–23.

Pilarz, Scott R. *Robert Southwell and the Mission of Literature, 1561–1595: Writing Reconciliation*. Aldershot: Ashgate, 2003.

Platt, Peter G. "Recent Studies in Tudor and Stuart Drama." *Studies in English Literature 1500–1900* 48 (2008): 443–517.

Price, Merrall Llewelyn. "Re-membering the Jews: Theatrical Violence in the N-Town Marian Plays." *Comparative Drama* 41 (2008): 439–63.

Pritchard, Alan. "Puritan Charges against Crashaw and Beaumont." *TLS* July 2, 1964, 578.

Pugh, Syrithe. "Sidney, Spenser, and Political Petrarch." In *Petrarch in Britain: Interpreters, Imitators, and Translators over 700 Years*. Ed. Martin McLaughlin et al. Oxford University Press, 2007, 243–58.

Purkiss, Diane. "Desire and Its Deformities: Fantasies of Witchcraft in the English Civil War." *The Journal of Medieval and Early Modern Studies* 21 (1997): 103–32.

[The Pynson Ballad.] Magdalene College, Cambridge, Pepys Library, 1254 (STC 25001).

Ralegh, Sir Walter. *The Works of Sir Walter Ralegh*. Ed. Thomas Birch. London, 1829.

The Poems of Sir Walter Raleigh. Ed. Agnes M. C. Latham. Cambridge, MA: Harvard University Press, 1962.

Poems of Sir Walter Ralegh: A Historical Edition. Ed. Michael Rudick. Ithaca: Cornell University Press, 2000.

Rambuss, Richard. "Sacred Subjects and the Aversive Metaphysical Conceit: Crashaw, Serrano, Ofili." *ELH* 72 (2004): 497–530.

Reay, Barry. *Popular Culture in Seventeenth-Century England*. London: Routledge, 1998.

Redworth, Glyn. *The She-Apostle: The Extraordinary Life and Death of Luisa de Carvajal*. Oxford University Press, 2008.

Ribas, Mario. "Liberating Mary, Liberating the Poor." In *Liberation Theology and Sexuality*. Ed. Marcella Althaus-Reid. Aldershot: Ashgate, 2006, 123–36.

Robinson Marsha S. *Writing the Reformation: Actes and Monuments and the Jacobean History Play*. Aldershot: Ashgate, 2002.

Roper, Lyndal. *Oedipus and the Devil: Witchcraft, Sexuality, and Religion in Early Modern Europe*. London: Routledge, 1994.

Rubin, Miri. *Mother of God: A History of the Virgin Mary*. New Haven: Yale University Press, 2009.

Emotion and Devotion: The Meaning of Mary in Medieval Religious Cultures. Budapest: Central European University Press, 2009.

"Mary." *History Workshop Journal* 58 (2004): 1–16.

Ruether, Rosemary. *Sexism and Godtalk*. Boston: Beacon Press, 1983.

"The Sexuality of Jesus." *Christianity and Crisis* 38 (May 29, 1978), 134–7.

Ryan, Denise. "Playing the Midwife's Part in the English Nativity Plays." *Review of English Studies* 54 (2003): 435–48.

Sabine, Maureen. *Feminine Engendered Faith: John Donne and Richard Crashaw*. Basingstoke: Macmillan, 1992.

"No Marriage in Heaven: John Donne, Anne Donne, and the Kingdom Come." In *John Donne's "Desir of More."* Ed. M. Thomas Hester. Newark, DE: University of Delaware Press, 1996, 228–55.

"Crashaw and Abjection: Reading the Unthinkable in his Devotional Verse," *American Imago* 63 (2007): 423–43.

"Richard Crashaw." The Poetry Foundation. www.poetryfoundation.org/archive/poet.html?id=1497. Accessed February 1, 2010.

Sanders, Wilbur. *The Winter's Tale*. Boston: Twayne, 1987.

Sawday, Jonathan. *The Body Emblazoned: Dissection and the Human Body in Renaissance Culture*. London: Routledge, 1995.

Sayers, Jane E. *The Making of the Medieval History of Evesham Abbey*. [Worcester]: Worcestershire Historical Society, 2004.

Schaberg, Jane. "Feminist Interpretations of the Infant Narrative of Matthew." In *Feminist Companion to Mariology*, ed. Levine and Robbins, 15–36.

Scherb, Victor I. *Staging Faith: East Anglian Drama in the Later Middle Ages*. Madison: Fairleigh Dickinson University Press, 1999.

Schwartz, Regina Mara. *Sacramental Poetics at the Dawn of Secularism: When God Left the World*. Stanford University Press, 2008.

Schwyzer, Philip. *Literature, Nationalism, and Memory in Early Modern England and Wales.* Cambridge University Press, 2004.
  Archaeologies of English Renaissance Literature. Oxford: Oxford University Press, 2007.
Scribner, Robert W. *For the Sake of Simple Folk: Popular Propaganda for the German Reformation.* Cambridge University Press, 1981.
Shagan, Ethan H. *Popular Politics and the English Reformation.* Cambridge University Press, 2003.
  "Confronting Compromise: The Schism and its Legacy in Mid-Tudor England." In *Catholics and the Protestant Nation.* Ed. Ethan Shagan. Manchester University Press, 2005, 49–68.
Shakespeare, William. *The Riverside Shakespeare.* Ed. G. Blakemore Evans et al. Boston: Houghton Mifflin, 1997.
  All's Well That Ends Well. Ed. G. K. Hunter. London: Methuen, 1959.
Shell, Alison. *Catholicism, Controversy, and the English Literary Imagination, 1558–1660.* Cambridge University Press, 1999.
  "St Winifred's Well and its Meaning in Post-Reformation British Catholic Literary Culture." In *Triumphs of the Defeated.* Ed. Peter Davison. Wiesbaden: Harrassowitz in Kommission, 2007, 271–80.
Sidney, Sir Philip. *The Poetry of Sir Philip Sidney.* Ed. William A. Ringler. Oxford University Press, 1962.
  Apology for Poetry (or the Defence of Poesy). Ed. Geoffrey Shepherd, rev. R. W. Maslen. Manchester University Press, 2002.
Sidney, Robert, Sir. *The Poems of Robert Sidney.* Ed. Peter Croft. Oxford: Clarendon Press, 1984
  Domestic Politics and Family Absence: The Correspondence (1588–1621) of Robert Sidney, First Earl of Leicester, and Barbara Gamage Sidney. Ed. Margaret P. Hannay, Noel J. Kinnamon, and Michael G. Brennan. Aldershot: Ashgate, 2005.
Simpson, James. *Reform and Cultural Revolution.* Oxford University Press, 2002.
  "The Rule of Medieval Imagination." In *Images, Idolatry, and Iconoclasm in Late Medieval England.* Ed. Jeremy Dimmock, James Simpson, and Nicolette Zeemen. Oxford University Press, 2002, 14–24.
Sissa, Giulia. "Maidenhood without Maidenhead: The Female Body in Ancient Greece." In *Before Sexuality: The Construction of Erotic Experience in the Ancient Greek World.* Ed. David M. Halperin, John J. Winkler and Froma I. Zeitlin. Princeton University Press, 1990, 339–64.
Smith, Lucy Toulmin, ed. *York Plays; The Plays Performed by the Crafts or Mysteries of York, on the Day of Corpus Christi in the 14th, 15th, and 16th Centuries.* New York: Russell & Russell, 1963.
Smith, Stanley. *The Madonna of Ipswich.* Ipswich: East Anglian Magazine Limited, 1980.
Southwell, Robert. *An Humble Supplication to Her Majestie.* Ed R. C. Bald. Cambridge University Press, 1953.
  Collected Poems. Ed. Peter Davison. Manchester: Fyfield Books, 2007.
Spenser, Edmund. *The Faerie Queene.* Ed. A. C. Hamilton. London: Longman, 1961.

Amoretti and Epithalamion: A Critical Edition. Ed. Kenneth J. Larsen. Tempe: Medieval & Renaissance Texts and Studies, 1997.

Spraggon, Julie. *Puritan Iconoclasm in the English Civil War*. Woodbridge, Suffolk: Boydell, 2003.

Spretnak, Charlene. *Missing Mary: The Queen of Heaven and her Re-emergence in the Modern Church*. New York: Palgrave Macmillan, 2004.

Spurr, Barry. *See the Virgin Blest: The Virgin Mary in English Poetry*. New York: Palgrave MacMillan, 2007.

Stafford, Anthony. *The Femall Glory, Or, the Life and Death of Our Blessed Lady the Holy Virgin Mary*. London, 1635. Ed. Orby Shipley. London: Longmans, Green, 1868.

The Femall Glory. Ed. Maureen Sabine. London: Scholars Facsimiles and Reprints, 1988.

Staley, Lynn. *The Book of Margery Kempe: A New Translation, Contexts, Criticism*. New York: W. W. Norton, 2000.

Stanbury, Sarah. *The Visual Object of Desire in Late Medieval England*. Philadelphia: University of Pennsylvania Press, 2007.

"The Virgin's Gaze: Spectacle and Transgression in Middle English Lyrics of the Passion." *PMLA* 106 (1991): 1083–93.

Stanton, Anne. "On the Lady Chapel of Ely Cathedral." Unpub. Diss., University of Texas, Austin, 1987.

Stapleton, Thomas. *A Fortresse of the Faith*. Antwerp, 1565.

Steinberg, Leo. *The Sexuality of Christ in Renaissance Art and Modern Oblivion*. New York: Pantheon Books. Rev. edn., 1996.

Stephenson, Colin. *Walsingham Way*. London: Darton, Longman, & Todd. 1970. Rev edn. Norwich: Canterbury Press, 2008.

Stevens, Martin. *Four Middle English Mystery Cycles: Textual, Contextual, and Critical Interpretations*. Princeton University Press, 1987.

Stewart, Agnes M. *The Life and Letters of Sir Thomas More*. London: Burns and Oates, 1876.

Stock, Lorraine Kochanske. "Lords of the Wildwood: The Wild Man, the Green Man, and Robin Hood." In *Robin Hood in Popular Culture: Violence, Transgression, and Justice*. Ed. Thomas G. Hahn. Cambridge: Brewer, 2000, 239–50.

Stokes, James. "Women and Performance: Evidences of Universal Cultural Suffrage in Medieval and Early Modern Lincolnshire." In *Women Players in England, 1500–1660: Beyond the All-Male Stage*. Ed. Pamela Allen Brown, and Peter Parolin. Aldershot: Ashgate, 2007, 25–44.

Stoller, Robert. *Perversion: The Erotic Form of Hatred*. London: Mansfield Library, 1975.

Observing the Erotic Imagination. New Haven: Yale University Press, 1985.

Stopford, Jennifer, ed. *Pilgrimage Explored*. Bury St. Edmunds: York Medieval Press, 1999.

Stow, John. *The Survey of London*. London: J. M. Dent, 1912.

Strickland, Agnes. *The Pilgrims of Walsingham or Tales of the Middle Ages. An Historical Romance*. London: Saunders and Otley, 1835; Philadelphia: Garrett & Co. 1854.

Strype, John. *Works*. Oxford: Clarendon Press, 1822.

Studlar, Gaylyn. *In the Realm of Pleasure: Von Sternberg, Dietrich, and the Masochistic Aesthetic*. New York: Columbia University Press, 1988.

Sugano, Douglas, ed. *The N-Town Plays*. Kalamazoo: Medieval Institute Publications, 2007.

Svendson, Eric D. "Is Mary Co-Redemptress of the World?" *Christian Research Journal* 31 (2008). www.equip.org. Accessed February 1, 2010.

Swanson, R. N., ed. *Promissory Notes on the Treasury of Merits: Indulgences in Late Medieval Europe*. Leiden: Brill, 2006.

Indulgences in Late Medieval England: Passports to Paradise? Cambridge University Press, 2007.

Sweeney, Anne R. *Robert Southwell: Snow in Arcadia: Redrawing the English Lyric Landscape, 1586–1595*. Manchester University Press, 2007.

Tassioulis, A. J. "Between Doctrine and Domesticity: The Portrayal of Mary in the N-Town Plays." In *Medieval Women in their Communities*. Ed. Diane Watt. University of Toronto Press, 1997, 222–45.

Theweleit, Klaus. *Male Fantasies*. Trans. Stephen Conway, Chris Turner, and Erica Carter. 2 vols. Minneapolis: University of Minnesota Press, 1987.

Thomas, Keith. *Religion and the Decline of Magic*. Harmondsworth: Penguin, 1971.

Thomas, William. *The Pilgrim: A Dialogue on the Life and Actions of King Henry the Eighth*. Ed. J. A. Froude. London, 1861.

Thompson, Ruby Reid. "Francis Tregian the Younger as Music Copyist: A Legend and an Alternative View," *Music & Letters* 82 (2001): 1–31.

Tiffany, Grace. *Love's Pilgrimage: The Holy Journey in English Renaissance Literature*. Newark: Delaware Press, 2006.

Tillyard, E. M. W. *Shakespeare's Last Plays*. London: Chatto and Windus, 1954.

Torsellino, Orazio. *The History of our B. Lady of Loreto*. [Saint-Omer], 1608.

Tottel's Miscellany (1557–1587). Ed. Hyder Edward Robbins. 2 vols. Cambridge, MA: Harvard University Press, 1966.

Trinkaus, C. E. *The Poet as Philosopher: Petrarch and the Formation of Renaissance Consciousness*. New Haven: Yale University Press, 1979.

Twycross, Meg. "Transvestism in the Mystery Plays." *English Medieval Theatre* 5 (1983): 123–80.

Tydeman, William. *The Theatre in the Middle Ages: Western European Stage Conditions, c. 800–1576*. Cambridge University Press, 1978.

Tyndale, William and John Frith. *The Works of the English Reformers*. London: Ebenezer Palmer, 1831.

Vail, Anne. *Shrines of Our Lady in England*. Leominster: Gracewing, 2004.

Valor Ecclesiasticus temp. Henr. VIII. Auctoritate Regia Institutus. Ed. John Caley, and Joseph Hunter. Vol. III. London: Great Britain Record Commission, 1810–34.

van der Horst, Pieter. "Sex, Birth, Purity and Asceticism in the Protevangelium Jacobi." In *Feminist Companion to Mariology*, ed. Levine, 56–66.

Vanita, Ruth. "Mariological Memory in *The Winter's Tale* and *Henry VIII*." *Studies in English Literature* 40 (2000): 311–37.

Vickers, Nancy J. "Diana Described: Scattered Woman and Scattered Rhyme." *Critical Inquiry* 8 (1981): 265–279.

Villegas, Alonso de. *The Lives of the Saints*. London: Scolar Press, 1977.

Vuola, Elena. "Seriously Harmful for your Health? Religion, Feminism and Sexuality in Latin America." In *Liberation Theology and Sexuality*. Ed. Marcella Althaus-Reid. Aldershot: Ashgate, 2006, 137–62.

Waller, Gary. *The Sidney Family Romance: Mary Wroth, William Herbert, and the Early Modern Construction of Gender*. Detroit: Wayne State University Press, 1993.

English Poetry of the Sixteenth Century. London: Longman, 2nd ed. 1994.

ed. *All's Well That Ends Well: New Critical Essays*. London: Routledge, 2007.

Walsingham and the English Imagination. Farnham: Ashgate, 2011.

"This Matching of Contraries: The Influence of Calvin and Bruno on the Sidney Circle." *Neophilologus* 56 (1972): 331–43.

"The Other Virgin: Walsingham and Robert Sidney's Sixth Song." *Sidney Journal* 25 (2007): 193–207.

"Shakespeare's Reformed Virgin." In *Renaissance Medievalisms*. Ed. Konrad Eisenbichler. Toronto: Centre for Reformation and Renaissance Studies, 2008, 107–19.

"From the Holy Family to the Sidney and Lee Warner Families: The Protestantization of Walsingham." In *Walsingham*, ed. Janes and Waller, 67–82.

"The Virgin's 'Pryvytes': Walsingham and the Late Medieval Sexualization of the Virgin." In *Walsingham*, ed. Janes and Waller, 113–30.

"Ralegh's 'As You Came from the Holy Land,' and the Rival Virgin Queens of Late Sixteenth-Century England." In *Literary Ralegh*. Ed. Christopher Armitage. Manchester University Press, forthcoming.

Walsham, Alexandra. *Church Papists: Catholicism, Conformity and Confessional Polemic in Early Modern England*. Woodbridge, Suffolk: Boydell and Brewer, 1993.

"Recording Superstition in Early Modern Britain: The Origins of Folklore." *Past & Present* 199 (2008): 178–206.

"The Reformation and 'The Disenchantment of the World'." *The Historical Journal* 51 (2008): 497–528.

"Reforming the Waters: Holy Wells and Healing Springs in Protestant England." In *Life and Thought in the Northern Church, c. 1100–1700*. Ed. Diane Wood. Woodbridge, Suffolk: Boydell and Brewer, 1999, 227–55.

Ward, Benedetta. *Miracles and the Medieval Mind: Theory, Record, and Event, 1000–1215*. Philadelphia: University of Pennsylvania Press, 1982.

Warner, Marina. *Alone of All Her Sex*. New York: Knopf, 1976.

Waterton, Edmund. *Pietas Mariana Brittanica*. 2 vols. London: St. Joseph's Catholic Library, 1879.

Webb, Diane. *Pilgrimage in Medieval England*. London: Continuum, 2000.

Weber, Max. *The Protestant Ethic and the Spirit of Capitalism*. Intro. Anthony Giddens. New York: Scribner, 1958.

Weir, Anthony and James Jerman. *Images of Lust: Sexual Carvings on Medieval Churches*. London: Batsford, 1986.

Wernham, R. B. *The Return of the Armadas*. Oxford: Clarendon Press, 1994.

Whatmore, Leonard E. *Highway to Walsingham*. Walsingham: The Pilgrim Bureau, 1973.

Whittington, Karl. "The Cruciform Womb: Process, Symbol and Salvation in Bodleian Library MS. Ashmole 399." *Different Visions: A Journal of New Perspectives on Medieval Art* 1 (2008): 1–24.

Wiener, Carol Z. "The Beleaguered Isle. A Study of Elizabethan and Early Jacobean Anti-Catholicism." *Past & Present* 51 (May, 1971): 27–62.

[Willesden, Our Lady of] www.stmarywillesden.org.uk/Virgin5-2.html. Accessed February 1, 2010.

Williams, C. H., ed. *English Historical Documents*. London: Eyre and Spottiswoode, 1967.

Williams, Charles. *The Figure of Beatrice: A Study in Dante*. Cambridge: Brewer, 1994.

Williams, David H. *The Welsh Cistercians*. Leominster: Gracewing, 2001.

Williams, Deanne. "Papa Don't Preach: The Power of Prolixity in *Pericles*." *University of Toronto Quarterly* 71 (2002): 179–213.

"Medievalism in English Renaissance Literature." In *A Companion to Tudor Literature*. Ed. Kent Cartwright. Oxford: Wiley-Blackwell, 2010, 213–28.

Williams, Garth. "Early Modern Blazons and the Rhetoric of Wonder: Turning Towards an Ethics of Sexual Difference." In *Irigaray and Premodern Culture*. Ed. Theresa Krier and Elizabeth D. Harvey. London: Routledge, 2005, 126–37.

Williams, Paul. "The English Reformers and the Blessed Virgin Mary." In *Mary*, ed. Boss, 238–55.

"The Virgin Mary in Anglican Tradition." In *Mary*, ed. Boss, 314–39.

Williams, Penry. *The Later Tudors: England, 1547–1603*. Oxford University Press, 1998.

Williams, Raymond. *Marxism and Literature*. Oxford University Press, 1977.

Keywords. Oxford University Press, 1983.

Williams, Rowan. "George Herbert and Henry Vaughan." www.archbishopofcanterbury. Accessed April 1, 2010.

Wilson, Richard. *Secret Shakespeare: Studies in Theatre, Religion and Resistance*. Manchester University Press, 2004.

Witt, Elizabeth A. *Contrary Marys in Medieval English and French Drama*. New York: Peter Lang, 1995.

Wizeman, William. *The Theology and Spirituality of Mary Tudor's Church*. Aldershot: Ashgate, 2006.

Wood, Charles T. "The Doctor's Dilemma: Sin, Salvation, and the Menstrual Cycle in Medieval Thought." *Speculum: A Journal Of Medieval Studies* 56 (1981): 710–27.

Woods, Susanne. "The Passionate Man's Pilgrimage: Ralegh is Still in the Running." *Modern Language Studies* 8.3 (Autumn, 1978): 12–19.

Wriothesley, Charles. *A Chronicle of England during the Reigns of the Tudors, from A.D. 1485 to 1559.* Ed. William Douglas Hamilton. London: Camden Society, 1877.

Wroth, Lady Mary. *The Poems of Lady Mary Wroth.* Ed. Josephine A. Roberts. Baton Rouge: Louisiana University Press, 1983.

Wyatt, Sir Thomas. *The Complete Poems.* Ed. R. A. Rebholz. New Haven: Yale University Press, 1981.

Zervos, George T. "Christmas with Salome." In *A Feminist Companion to Mariology,* ed. Levine, 77–98.

Index

Made in the USA
Middletown, DE
24 August 2018